IMAGES
of America

PURCELLVILLE

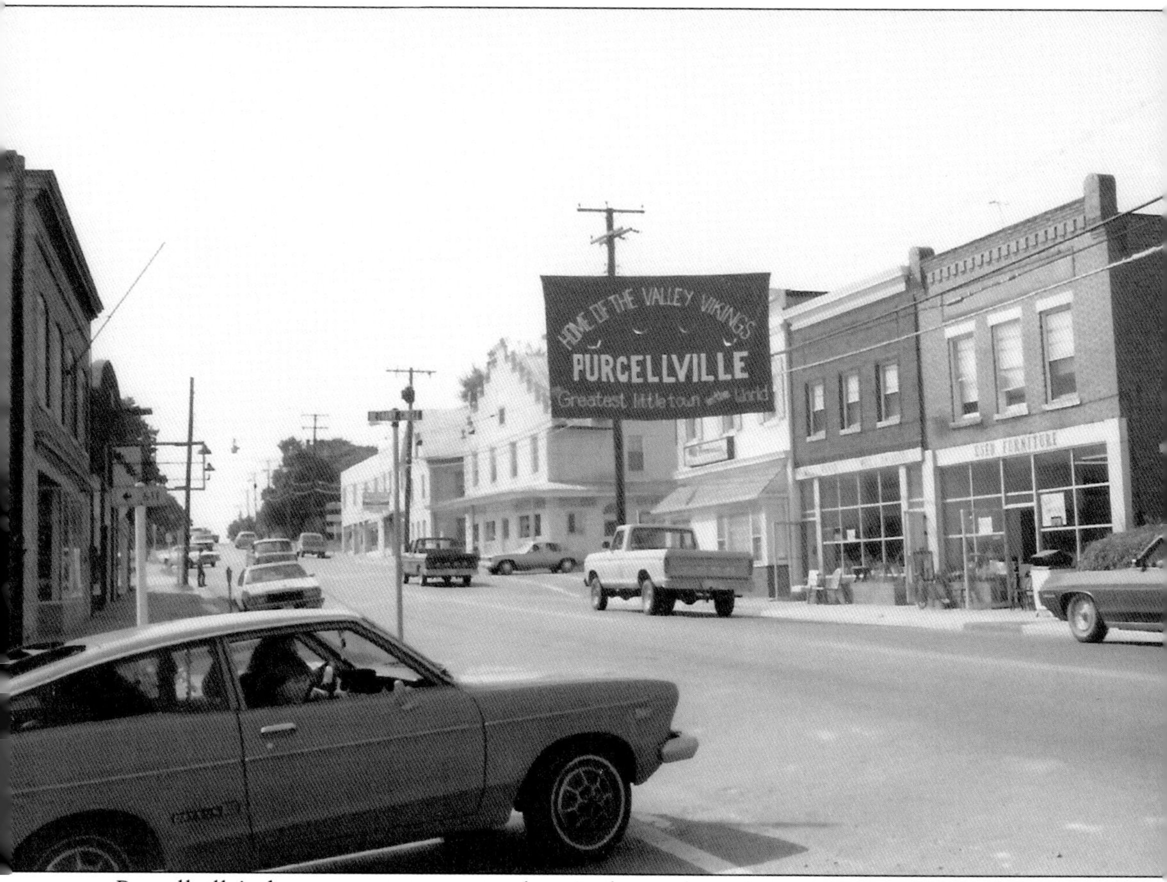

Purcellville's downtown intersection hasn't changed much in the last 100 years. As in any rural American town, the number of pickups, tractors, and farm trailers equaled the number of automobiles on Main Street through most of the 20th century. Things became quite different in the 21st century as the town's population doubled when it became a suburb of Washington, DC. Today, Purcellville's small-town pride is alive and well, just as it was in this 1972 photograph. The residents still boast that their small town is the "greatest little town in the world." (Courtesy of Jim and Betty Wiley.)

On the Cover: Taken in 1936, this Russell Gregg photograph captures Purcellville's downtown, which was located near the train station when the town thrived as a farming community. Back then, milk was king, and cows far outnumbered cars. (Courtesy of Purcellville Preservation Association.)

IMAGES
of America

PURCELLVILLE

Meredith Thomas and the
Purcellville Preservation Association
Foreword by Eugene Scheel

ARCADIA
PUBLISHING

ISBN 978-0-7385-8755-4

Published by Arcadia Publishing
Charleston, South Carolina

Printed in the United States of America

Library of Congress Control Number: 2010943017

For all general information, please contact Arcadia Publishing:
Telephone 843-853-2070
Fax 843-853-0044
E-mail sales@arcadiapublishing.com
For customer service and orders:
Toll-Free 1-888-313-2665

Visit us on the Internet at www.arcadiapublishing.com

Dedicated to Zora Mac Brownell who took me under her wing when we first hung our hat in Purcellville. She introduced me to the charm, beauty, and history of our hometown and its wonderful people and land. My friend's love of western Loudoun has influenced me greatly, and to her, I am eternally grateful to know such a place and call it home.

Contents

FOREWORD

With appropriate vintage photography, this book is both a visual and written commentary of Purcellville and its more than 250 years of history.

Purcellville is a small American town with subtle charm. There are no pretensions here. The banners and Christmas lights along Main Street, which have no brick sidewalks, are a common imagery in downtown. There are also the parades along the way and maybe a band or two, but you won't find Texas high schools stealing the show. Its small-town folks are not plain, but not one Purcellville resident would grace a *Great Gatsby* set. There are many eateries, but they're more of the local variety than fast-food chains. There is an old hardware store. Many businesses have locals behind their counters, but there is no Gap, J. Crew, or Tommy Hilfiger. The town has twelve churches and three public schools located in town, and three other schools on its outskirts. There is also a small college, and it was the first university to have a main campus in Loudoun. The town has many places where people can gather for meetings. All of Purcellville's attractions and buildings are used to serve its 7,000-plus residents and most of the Loudoun Valley as well.

Purcellville is the market town of western Loudoun and has held that position since 1901 when its first bank got things going. It is in this town where farmers buy their feed, supplies, and machinery, but also the place where they get their items repaired. However, the village still retains its small-town feel—residents know the people they see on the street, and a smile and verbal greeting are always in order.

And there are many firsts in Loudoun County like the Robey Foundation, which was established in 1958 to benefit religious, charitable, scientific, literary, and educational purposes. Its founder, who was an initial woman's suffragette, led an expedition to the US capital to further the cause of women's rights. Also, the first woman in the county to vote was a Purcellville resident. The town also holds the first public library in the county as well.

Purcellville embodies the small American town. Just look at the downtown in 1915, with its brick and block: out of context, you might think you're in the middle of Wyoming. And look at the neighborhoods and how each one represents a different style, period of architecture, and urban planning. It is small-town America to the core.

—Eugene Scheel

Acknowledgments

I give my heartfelt thanks to the many historians whose research and printed works provided much of the information for this project. I also thank the following people for their support in deciphering Purcellville's history and for their collection of photographs.

I thank Elizabeth Bray, from Arcadia Publishing, for her guidance, patience, and most especially for believing in this book before it ever even began.

My treasured brain trust—Rich Gillespie, Deborah Lee, Paul McCray, Tom Priscilla, and Eugene Scheel—was invaluable. They were the early readers who provided well-needed advice and kept my edges sharp along the way.

The townspeople (and my new best friends) were crucial, and I cannot thank them enough for sharing their photograph collections and helping me fill in many blanks.

I am indebted to the members of the Purcellville Preservation Association for their support and resounding cheers, which have helped me tell this never-ending story of our Purcellville.

I would also like to thank my husband, Fred, for allowing me to indulge in a town way too far away from his job and a good movie theater.

And finally, I want to thank my children Oscar and Vera. They have let me live the promise of a perfect childhood that I have always hoped for them—living in a small town in the country where all is safe and sound.

Introduction

Founded in 1985, the Purcellville Preservation Association's volunteers and friends have worked hard to ensure that the town's history is kept alive. Purcellville's history gives us a sense of identity, belonging, and purpose.

Historians have suggested that Purcellville should be a national park because all the old homes and buildings that still stand appear as they did in a bygone era. You can still see how this town has worked since the late 18th century. From 1740, when Lord Fairfax issued the first land grant, Purcellville's different phases of historical downtown areas have remained intact, providing a visual link of how life has evolved in this small town. Learning about Purcellville's history evokes the past, which makes it comes to life.

As might be expected, it would take a road to make a town. The early ox-cart track, which wound westward from Alexandria and was known later as the "Great Road," served that purpose by putting Purcellville on the map. The first recorded business along the road was an ordinary (a combined store and inn) that was established in 1799, followed by a second ordinary in 1804. Soon after, Valentine Purcell established Purcell's Store and the post office; subsequently, the town was named after him.

Purcellville was the perfect halfway point for travelers making their way west from Alexandria to Winchester. Many stopped for a rest along the Great Road in the beautiful valley at the foothills of the Blue Ridge, hitching their horses at the livery stable and hanging their hats at the Hampton Hotel. Many of those travelers stayed, and opened up the hardware stores, blacksmith shops, markets, and other necessary businesses that make a village into a town. Although its location in the Loudoun Valley served it well for a long time, Purcellville was within range of a growing urban center that contributed to a drastic change in the town's character.

With current and vintage photographs, we tell the story of how Purcellville formed along the Great Road. Today, we can see how it happened all around town. We see how the townspeople of yesterday lived, where they went to work, where they went to school, where they worshipped, where they shopped, and where they played. From the days of the ox cart, we have come to understand that the various phases of Purcellville were largely based on the evolution of transportation.

Every attempt has been made to portray a broad section of interesting photographs and historical information. However, we acknowledge that there will always be more stories to tell.

One

Days of Settlement

Loudoun's history begins with geographical factors that created the fertile soils to support early Native American farming societies. There is evidence of Algonquian groups fighting each other over hunting areas even before Columbus landed in America in 1492. By the early 1600s, there were as many as 65,000 Native Americans living in Virginia. This was around the same time Capt. John Smith and his group struggled to survive at Jamestown. It is believed that white man's diseases, such as smallpox, measles, and viral hepatitis, may have killed as much as 95 percent of the native population. By 1720, Governor Spotswood negotiated the Treaty of Albany with the weakened Iroquois, who pledged not to cross the Potomac River or the Blue Ridge without permission. With this pledge removing the possible threat of the Native Americans, the county was open to settlement by European colonists. Early 19th-century inhabitants were German, English, and Scots-Irish farmers, as well as enslaved Africans, who made up a quarter of the population. Its rich soils, ample water supplies, and labor force made Loudoun an early leader in Virginia's farming industry. The 1700s were a time of westward expansion across most of the country. Speculators set their sights on Western Loudoun because of its fertile, rich soil, and ideal location between the Catoctin Mountain and the Blue Ridge.

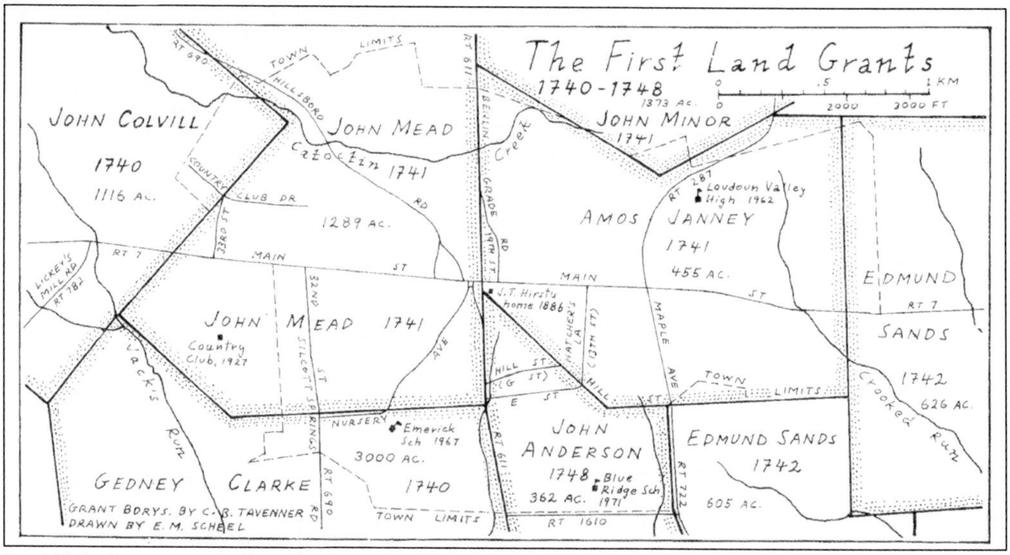

By 1725, three years after the Treaty of Albany, the flood of settlers had begun in Loudoun County. Purcellville's first speculators bought up large tracts of land, which they later divided up into farms. The first settlers were armed with the ax and musket as they cleared the land and hunted wildlife for food. They used timber for building and heating. Around each dwelling was a patchwork of small fields. (Courtesy of Eugene Scheel.)

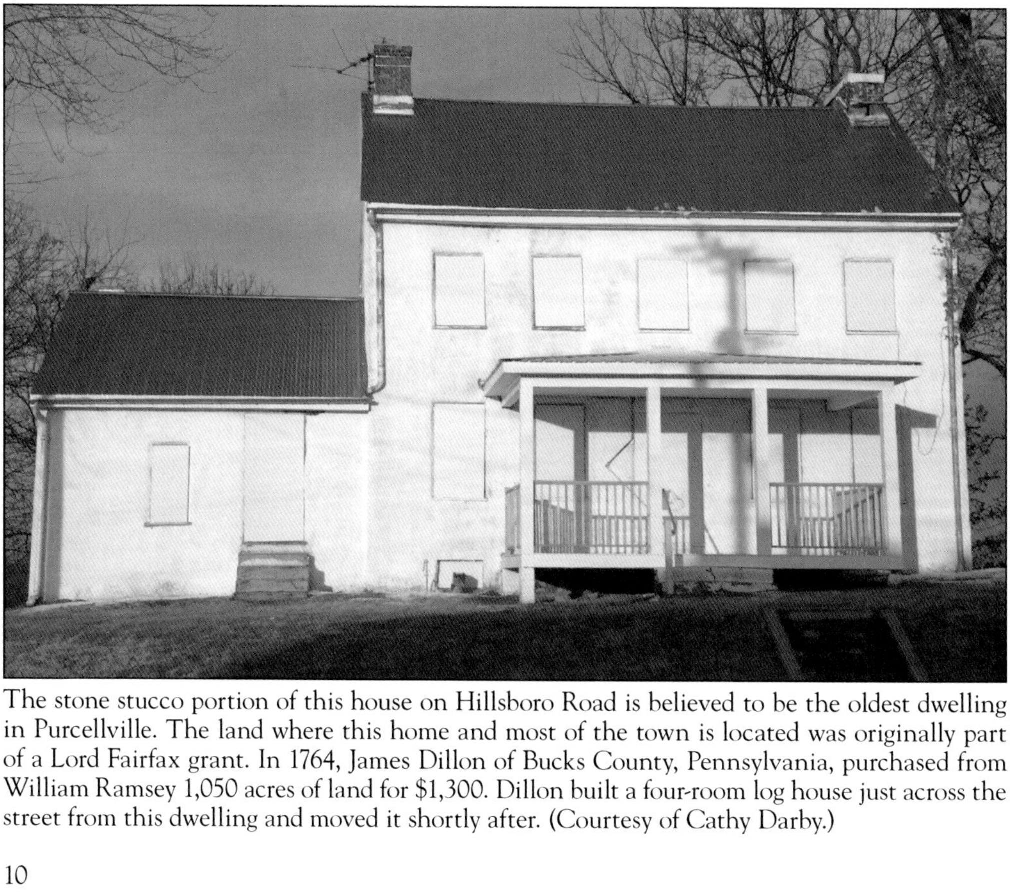

The stone stucco portion of this house on Hillsboro Road is believed to be the oldest dwelling in Purcellville. The land where this home and most of the town is located was originally part of a Lord Fairfax grant. In 1764, James Dillon of Bucks County, Pennsylvania, purchased from William Ramsey 1,050 acres of land for $1,300. Dillon built a four-room log house just across the street from this dwelling and moved it shortly after. (Courtesy of Cathy Darby.)

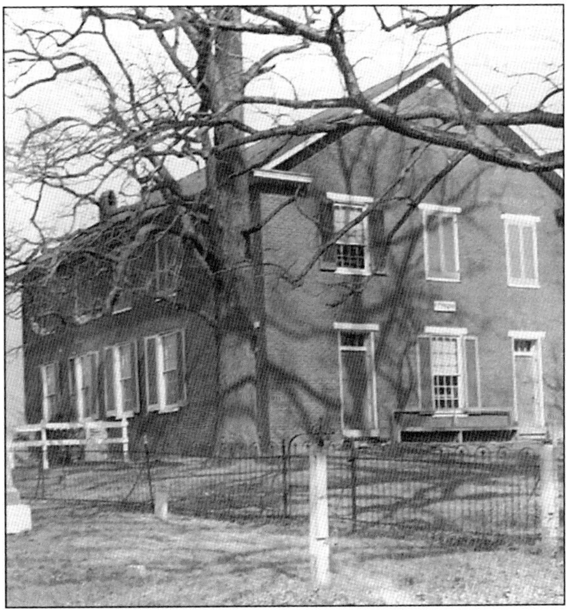

Ketoctin Baptist Church off Allder School Road is one of Loudoun's earliest churches. It was constituted in 1751, before the French and Indian War, beginning with seven members and Rev. John Marks. While Reverend Marks actively preached in favor of the Revolution, it was his son Isaiah (buried at Ketoctin) who fought in the war. Since the church is known to have accepted African Americans, it is possible that the building's side door was used by slaves, who presumably sat separate from white members of the congregation. There is at least one grave of a former slave inside the walls of the cemetery: Gemima Pearson, who died in 1868, three years after emancipation. A historical marker is located on the front of the church building. (Courtesy of Thomas Balch Library.)

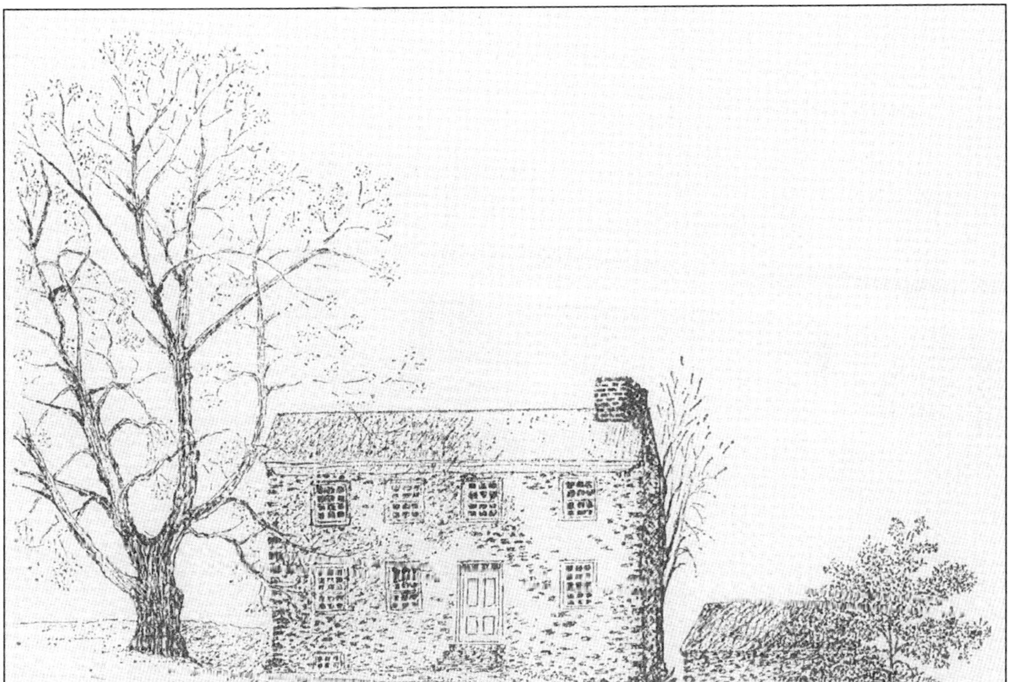

Purcellville was surrounded by a primeval forest in 1764, and James Dillon set to work clearing a portion of it almost immediately. He built a brick factory, a grain mill, a sawmill, a blacksmith shop, and a carpenter shop on his plantation. The Dillon House shown in this sketch is almost in the center of Purcellville in the Loudoun Valley. (Courtesy of Evelyn Taylor Adams.)

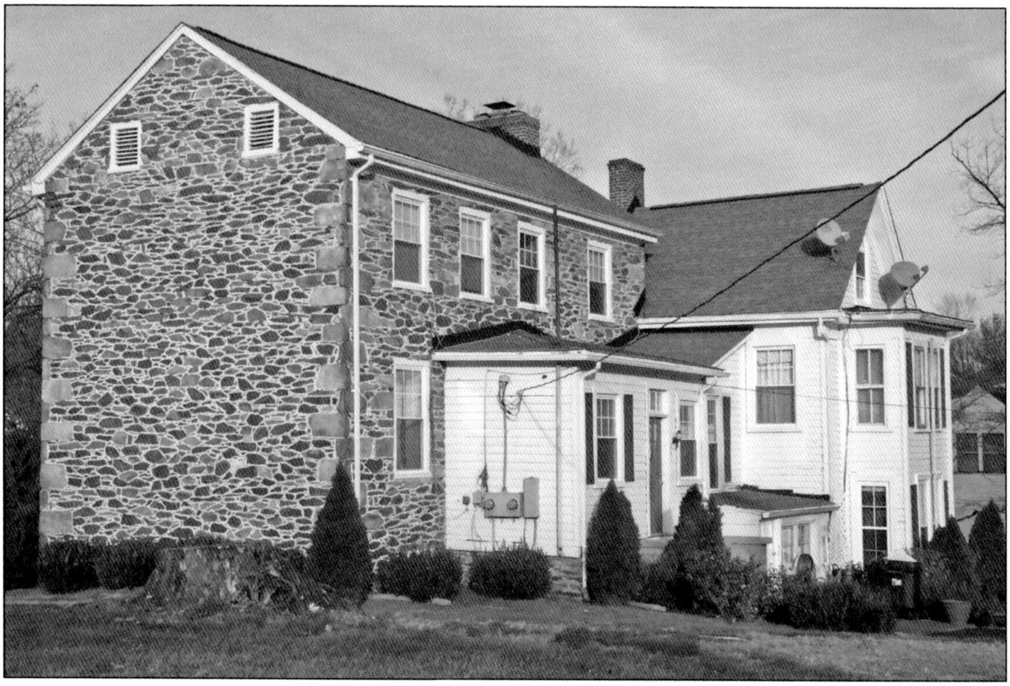

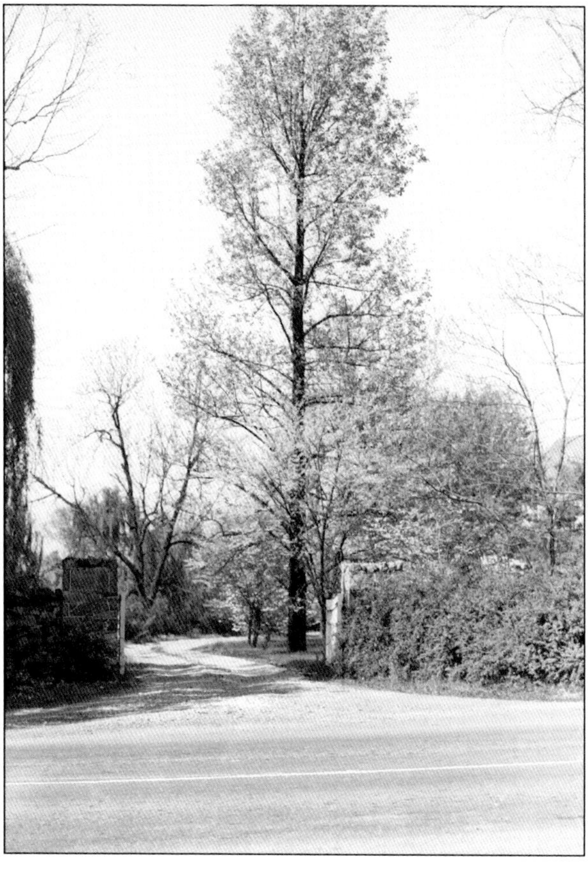

About two-thirds of the town is located on the southeast part of Dillon's purchase, including one of Purcellville's oldest dwellings on J Street, the stone portion being the Dillon House. When Dillon died in 1804, his youngest son, Abdon, inherited what was left of the estate because the eldest son, Moses, had already been given his share. (Courtesy of Purcellville Preservation Association.)

In 1801, Dr. James Heaton built one of Purcellville's grandest and earliest homes on Main Street, which was commonly called the Great Road in the early days. Heaton named the building Exedra, which means "gathering place" in Greek, because the citizens of Loudoun Valley needed a big place to meet. Unfortunately, Exedra was demolished in the 1950s to make way for the Loudoun Valley Shopping Center on the east side of town. (Courtesy of Thomas Balch Library.)

Dr. James Heaton was buried at the Ketoctin Baptist Church cemetery. He was active in promoting the interests of the American Colonization Society, which was organized in 1816 and whose purpose was to "free all African slaves and their descendants held in the United States." Among the Heaton family records were a number of letters from two former slaves who had emigrated to Liberia. (Courtesy of Purcellville Preservation Association.)

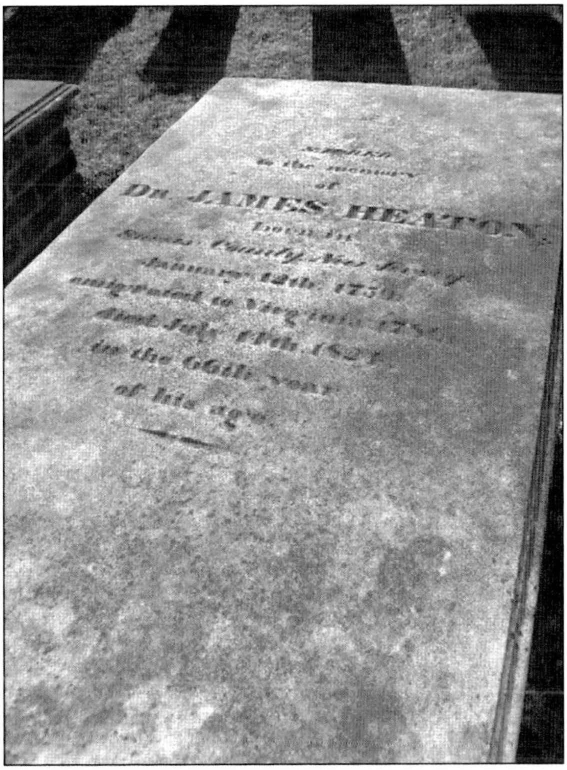

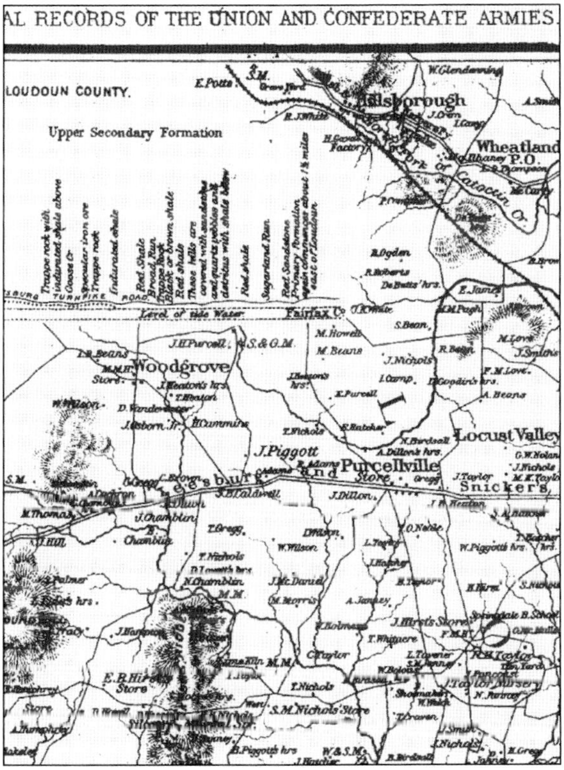

Purcellville saw little action in the Civil War, though armies of both sides passed through the village. In 1862, a New York correspondent traveling with Maj. Gen. George Brinton McClellan's army described the scene: "For the first few miles after leaving Berlin, the people are staunch Unionists, but on penetrating the county, the people were found to be tainted with the secession epidemic until reaching this vicinity, where, with the exception of Quakers, they are fairly rampant. . . . 'Purcellsville' cannot be dignified with the title of 'village,' consisting merely of a few straggling houses. . . . The cavalry regiments are encamped in some delightful groves extending along the road." (Courtesy of Rich Gillespie.)

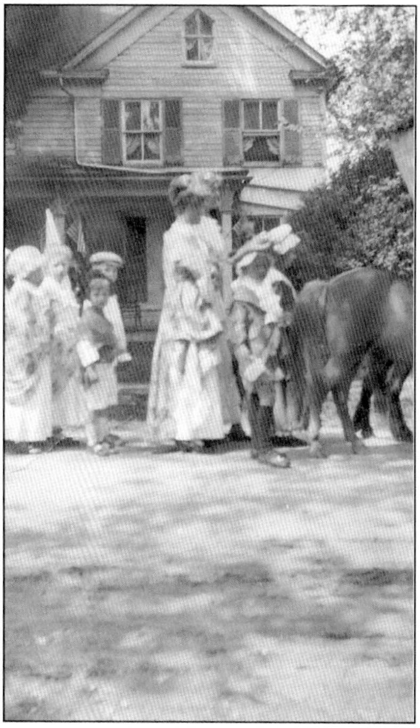

General McClellan stayed in the house pictured here in 1862. The photograph was taken during a children's school parade in 1910. The home was located on the Great Road and housed the postmaster as well. Dating to 1822, it is known to be the only building to house a shop, post office, and home still standing in Virginia today. The first known stagecoach came through town in 1841 on the line from Washington to Winchester via Leesburg, Hamilton's Store, and Purcell's Store. The one-way trip cost four dollars, leaving at 4:00 a.m. and arriving at Winchester at 6:00 p.m. The building is still standing, divided into several businesses. (Courtesy of Jane Hirst Bogle.)

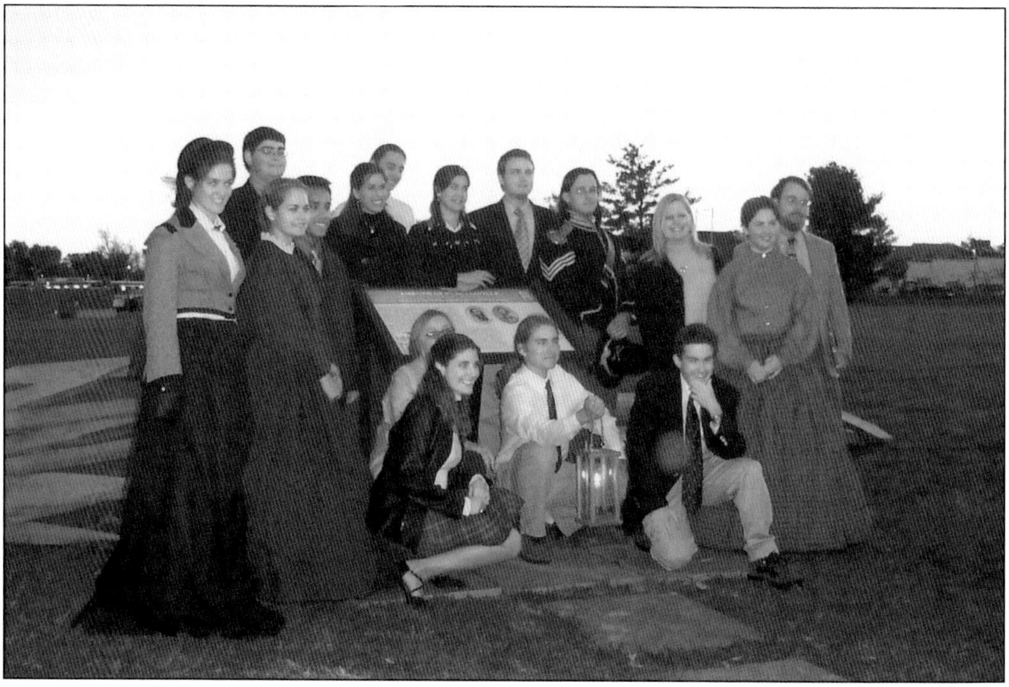

In this 2003 photograph, the Loudoun Valley History Club shows off Purcellville's Virginia Civil War Trails sign on dedication day. The club's board members are, from left to right, (kneeling) Jane Claterbos, Julie Beggs, Charlie Haack, and Keegan Donovan; (standing) Katie Allen, Mandy Juraschek, Andrew Thompson, Miguel Pelton, Kathleen Keenan, Matt Werling, Emily Frost, Olive Mathis, Jim Cross, Susan Stevens, Kristen Kelley, and Rich Gillespie. (Courtesy of Rich Gillespie.)

This photo is of Col. William Tibbetts of the 21st New York Cavalry, who led the detachment that ambushed Gen. Jubal Early's army as it retired west to the Shenandoah Valley after their Washington raid. This was a Union ambush by Tibbetts's force on Early's retreating army. Seeing the last of Early's forces pass through, curious Purcellville citizens flocked to see the damage after the ambush at Heaton's Crossroads, located at the intersection of Ninth and Main Streets, where Rite Aid is today. (Courtesy of Rich Gillespie.)

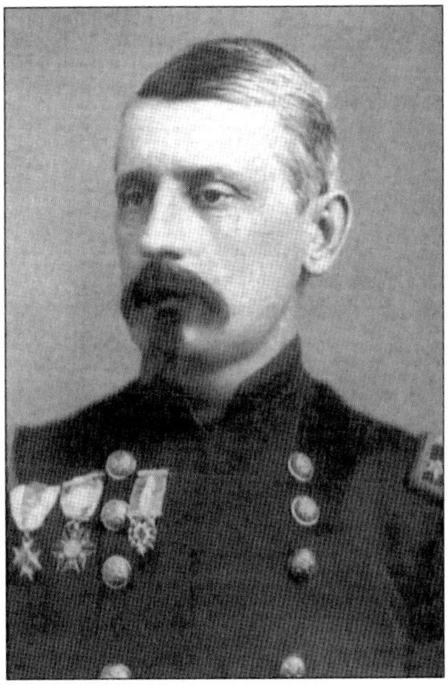

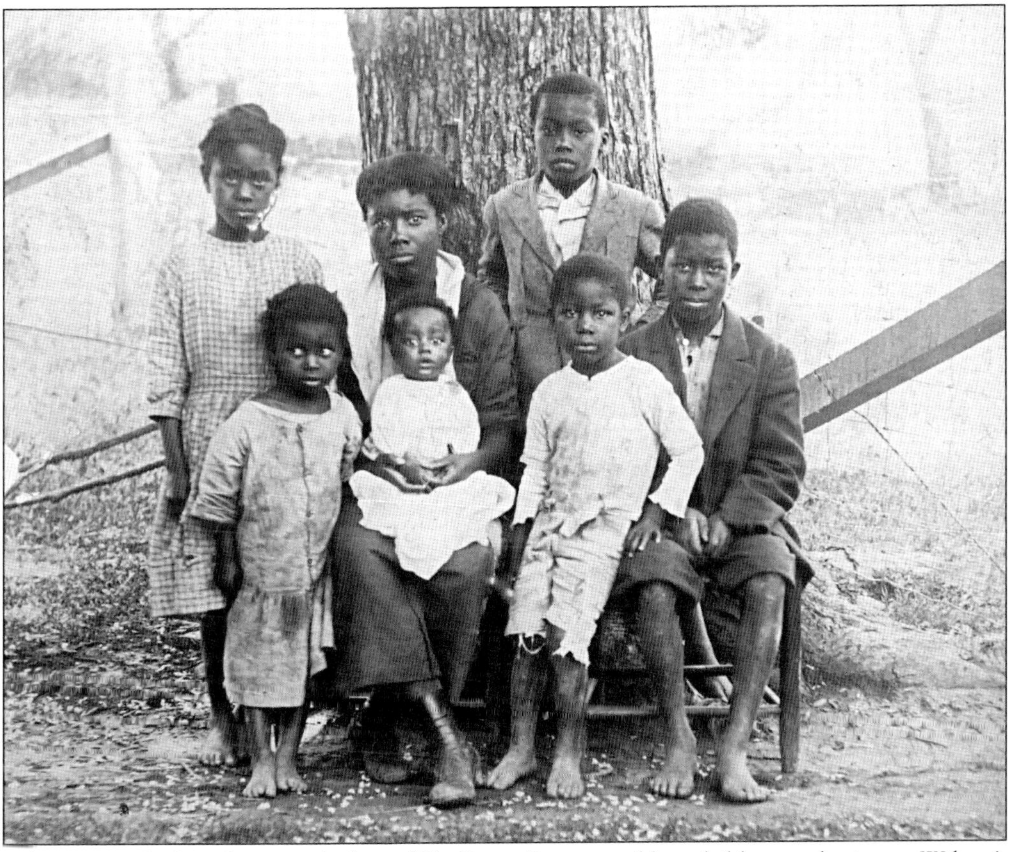

Taken in 1890, this photograph shows Ella Brent Simms and her children gathering at Wilson's Farm, which was located south of town. In 1824, the Quakers formed the Loudoun Manumission and Emigration Society, stressing the exposure of the "evils of African slavery." In 1865, the Freedmen's Bureau of Loudoun County was established to educate and protect freed African Americans, helping them adjust to a free society. (Courtesy of Reginald Simms.)

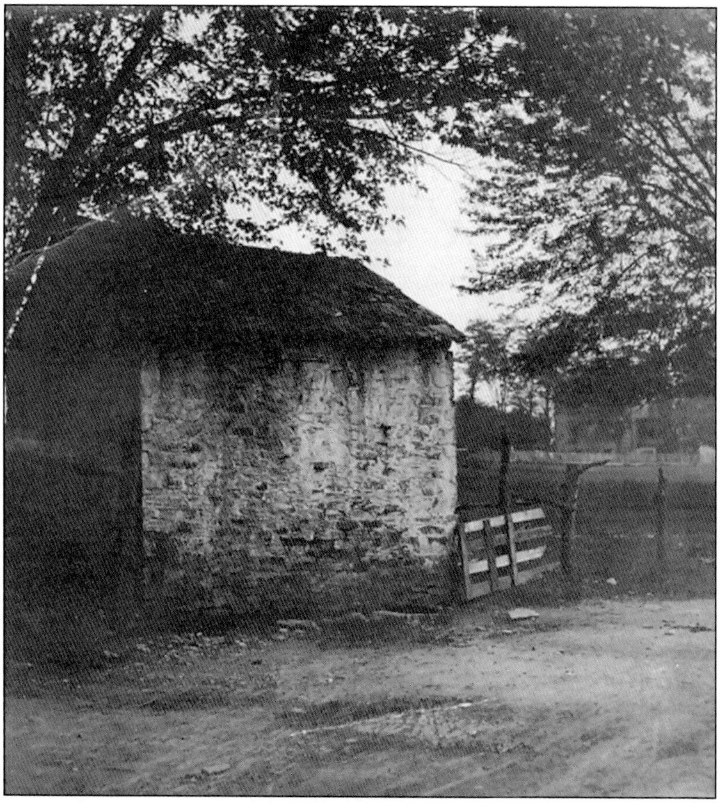

In 1795, Mahlon Taylor built a springhouse that was part of an estate near the east end of town on Main Street. Taylor was appointed the overseer of the Great Road. Since 1875, the springhouse has been a Purcellville landmark. However, the structure was disassembled and rebuilt a few yards east of its original location by the Purcellville Preservation Association in 1998. (Courtesy of Jane Hirst Bogle.)

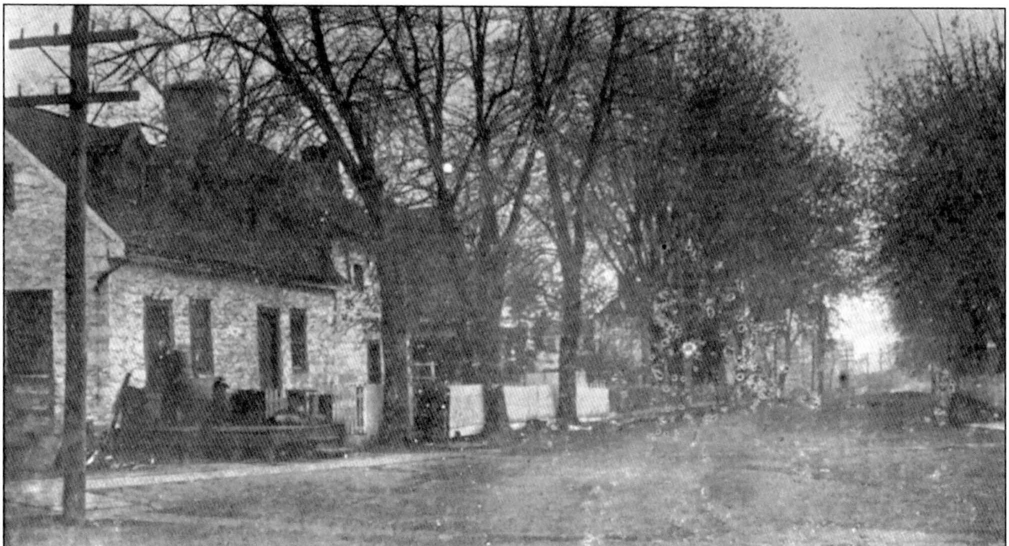

In addition to running the two earliest farms in Purcellville, Moses Dillon branched out into operating an ordinary along the Great Road from 1796 to 1808. Subsequently, Dillon sold out to Valentine Purcell in 1809. Taken in 1908, this photograph shows the first recorded business in town, which was the ordinary located on the left. The word "ordinary" derived from the French word *ordinaire*, which was an inn where meals and accommodations were provided at a fixed price. (Courtesy of Jane Hirst Bogle.)

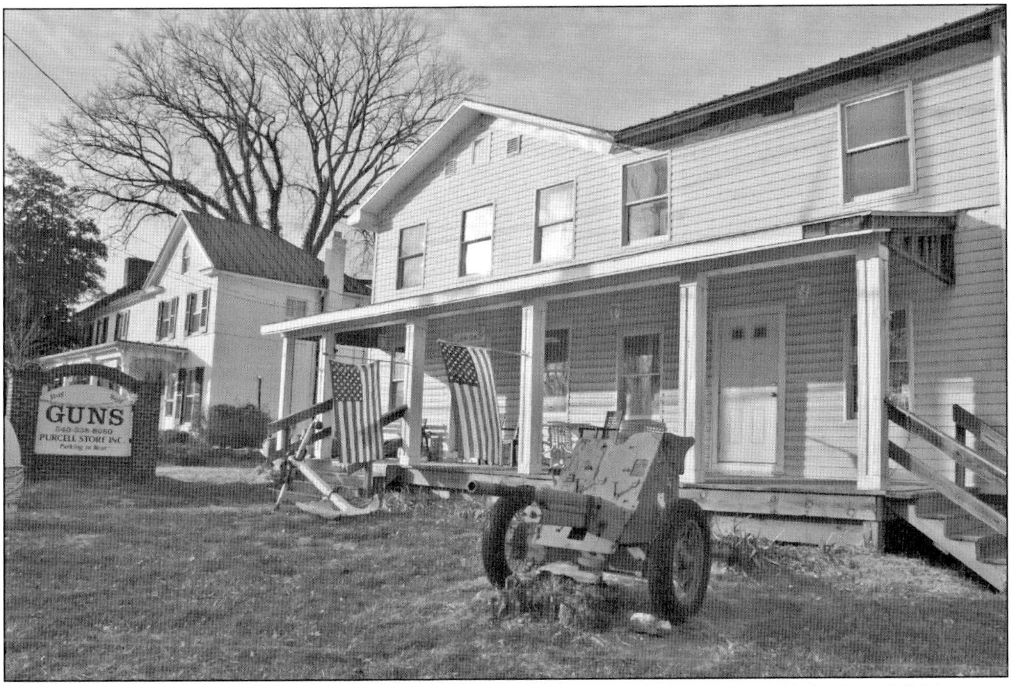

In 1822, this store and post office, which is now Purcell's Gun Shop, was established with Valentine Purcell as its head postmaster. The village was officially named "Purcell's Store" in 1822, changing its name to Purcellville in 1852. (Courtesy of Purcellville Preservation Association.)

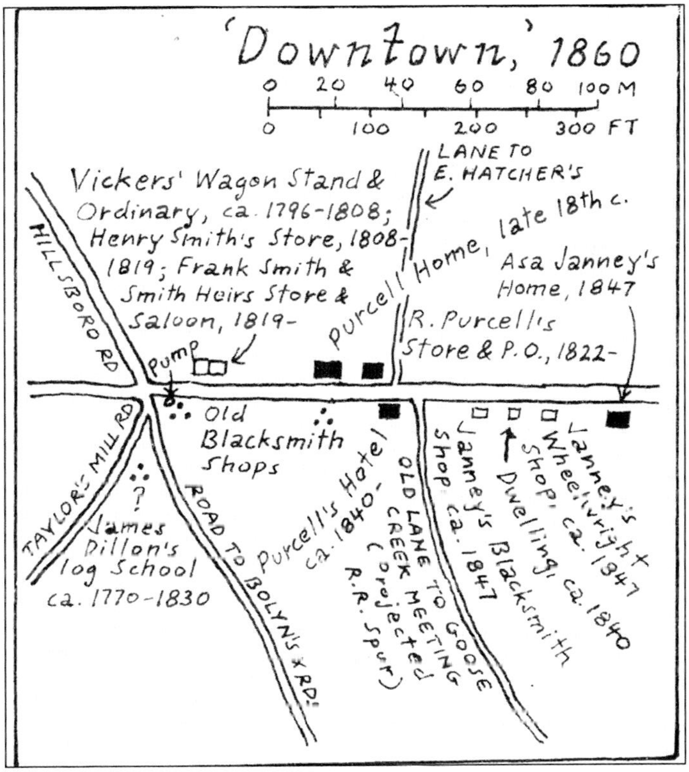

Leesburg Pike, also called Virginia State Route 7, became an authorized turnpike in 1785 and extended westward from Alexandria, Snickers Gap, and beyond to Winchester. The Leesburg Turnpike Company started the construction and improvements on the road in 1832, and travel through Purcellville began to increase. (Courtesy of Eugene Scheel.)

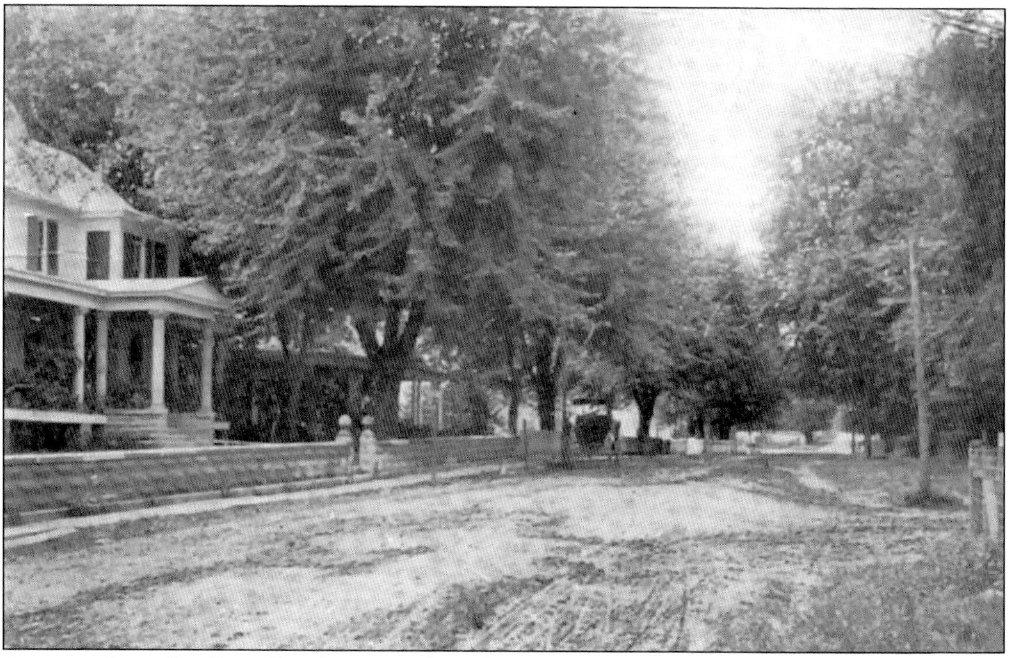

Activity along the Great Road increased, and in 1838, Samuel Purcell had a small hotel built. As one of the only hotels in Purcellville, Hampton Hotel was a key stop for stagecoaches. This photograph was taken around 1900. (Courtesy of Thomas Balch Library.)

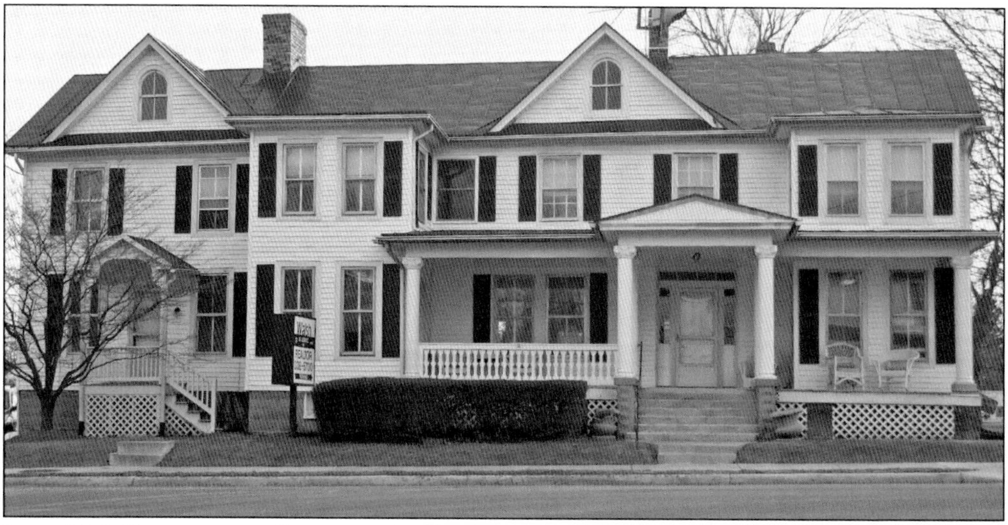

Later, Nick Hampton would manage the Hampton Hotel, and advertised that guests would enjoy what the railroad promoted, which was a "region of inspiring scenery, pure bracing air, and healthful climate . . . calculated to favorably respond to the desire for rest, pleasure, health, and recreation." The hotel closed in 1924, although the building is still standing. (Courtesy of Jack Darby.)

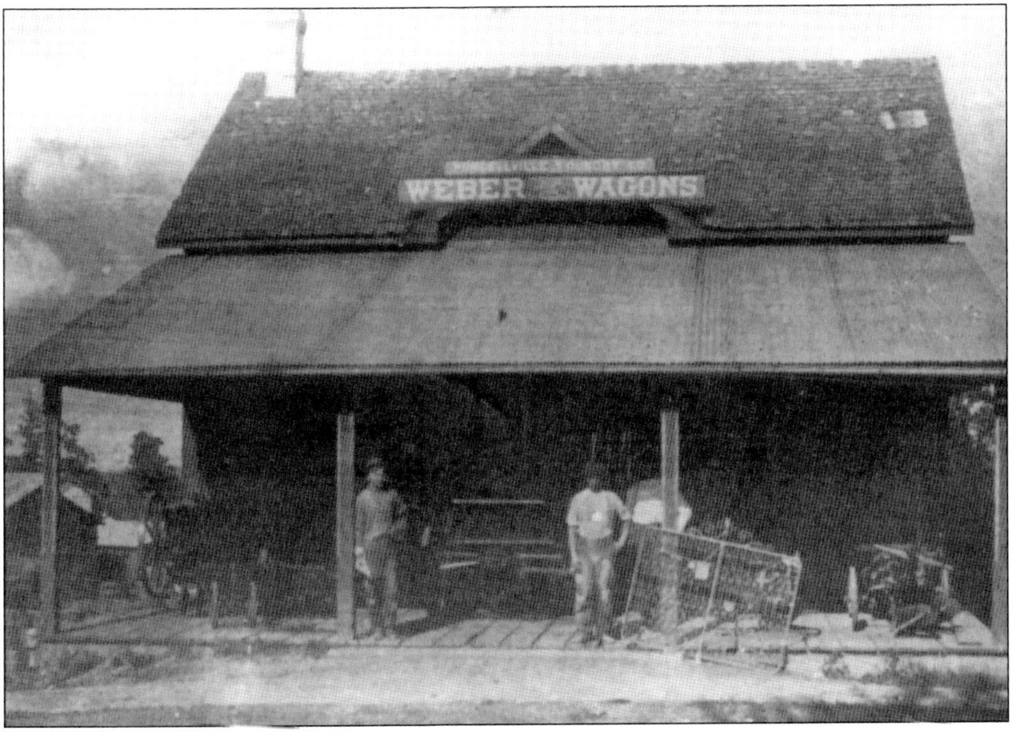

From 1874 to 1914, Weber Wagons were a popular and upscale mode of conveyance. They were assembled and sold along the railway line. (Courtesy of Thomas Balch Library.)

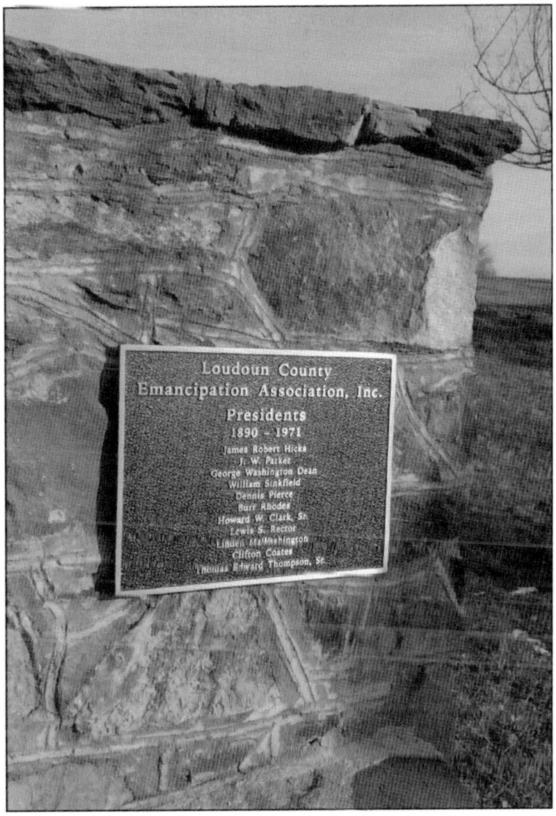

In 1910, the Loudoun County Emancipation Association bought 10 acres of land for its Lincoln Park, which is known as "the Emancipation Grounds." A plaque at the entrance marks the founding directors of the association: James Hicks, J.W. Parker, George Dean, William Sinkfield, Dennis Pierce, Burr Rhodes, Howard Clark Sr., Lewis Rector, Linden McWashington, Clifton Coates, and Thomas Thompson Sr. (Courtesy of Cathy Darby.)

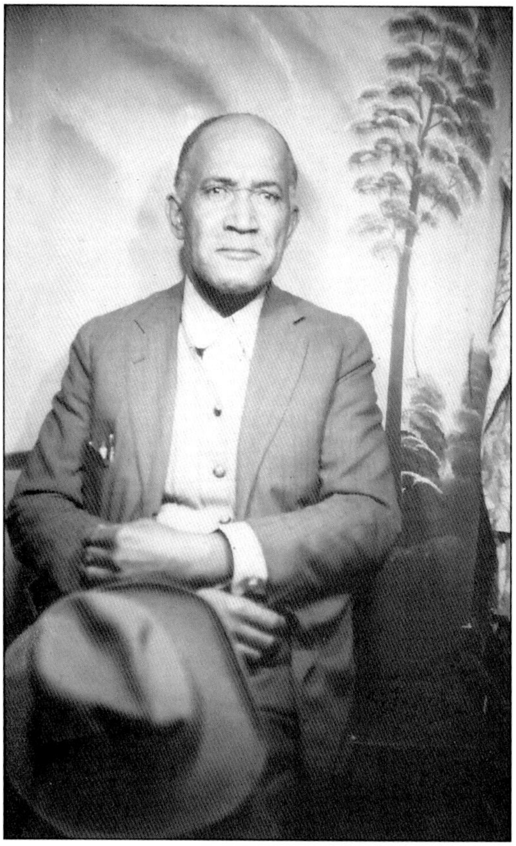

One of the early directors of the Emancipation Association of Loudoun, John Furr was in charge of the grounds and rentals committees. A stonemason by profession, he helped construct the still-standing stone posts at the entrance to the Emancipation Grounds. His parents, Gregg and Mary Ellen Furr, had been allowed to marry while enslaved in Aldie, where they petitioned in the court for their rights. Gregg Furr was a delegate at a Colored Mass Meeting in 1883. (Courtesy of Reginald Simms.)

This historical marker at the entrance of the grounds is where thousands used to gather to celebrate the Emancipation Proclamation. Visitors dressed in high style, traveling on special excursion trains to Purcellville. In 2008, Elaine Thompson, descendent of former officers of the Emancipation Association, reunited with friends and family on the grounds: "We return in honor of our forefathers and our mission . . . where the celebration of the anniversary of the Emancipation Proclamation took place and will always be in our hearts." (Courtesy of Cathy Darby.)

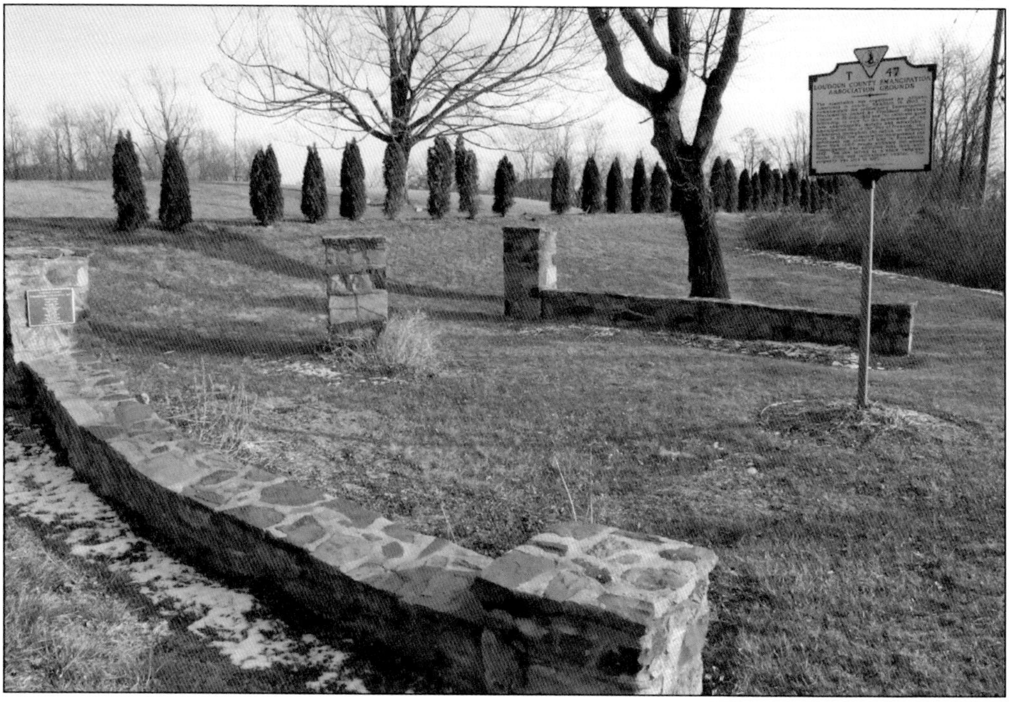

Two

At School

In 1823, a local paper reported of Purcellville: "Strange to say, this village has neither a school, nor a church, or a meeting house of any religious denomination." While Virginia allowed public schools by local option in 1846, only four counties had them. In order to reenter the Union after its defeat in the Civil War, Virginia had to offer public schools in all counties. Loudoun began its public school system in 1871. It took over several schools that were built for African Americans by the Freedmen's Bureau of the US government. When Loudoun public schools opened in the fall of 1871, there were 46 schools, and by 1883, the number was at 75. Overcrowding continues to plague Loudoun, even though there are new schools under construction each year. In 2011, Purcellville is home to three elementary schools (Emerick, Mountain View, and Kenneth W. Culbert), two middle schools (Blue Ridge and Harmony), and two high schools (Loudoun Valley and Woodgrove). Patrick Henry College, a private Christian institution, is also located in Purcellville.

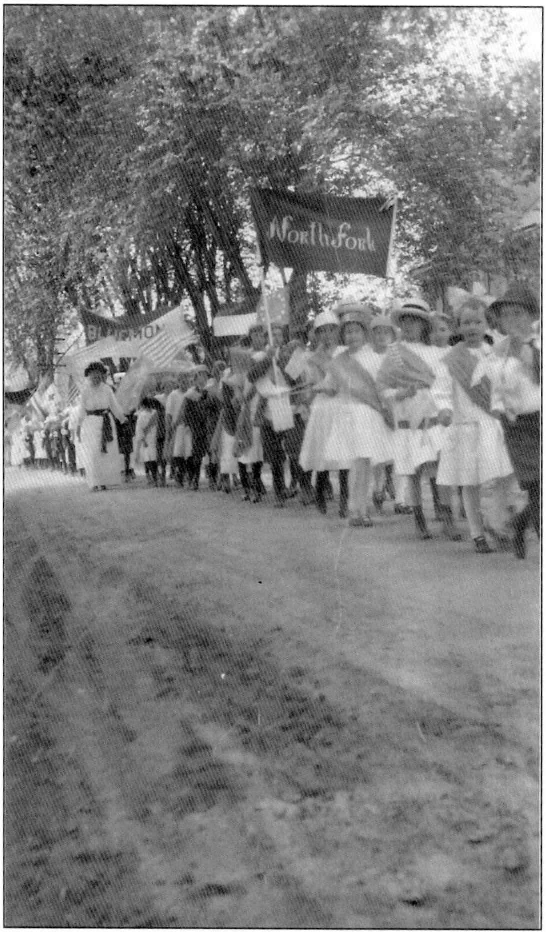

In 1910, beautiful poplar trees lined Purcellville's Main Street. Within a few years, the town council voted to widen the roadway and build sidewalks. By 1920, these trees were uprooted and the shaded canopy was lost forever. (Courtesy of Jane Hirst Bogle.)

From 1898 to 1922, the Purcellville Graded School was the town's public school for white children. This building still stands; however, it has been divided into several apartments. Before this school house was built, the town's first school, as part of the county's public school system that was established in 1871, was located closer to the Great Road from 1885 to 1898. (Courtesy of Thomas Balch Library.)

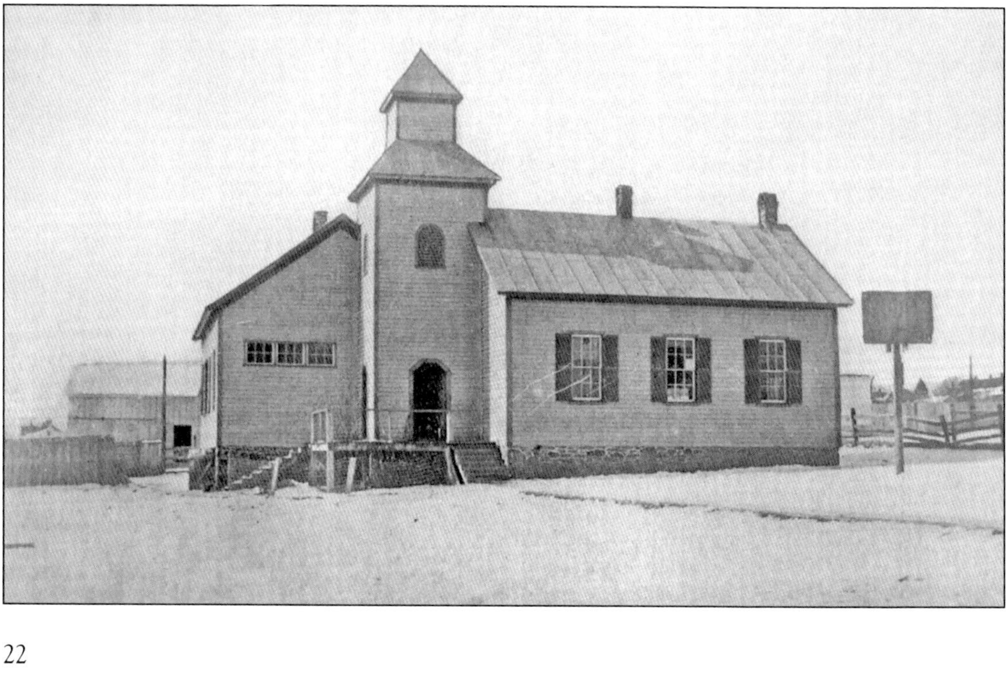

The schools for white children annually celebrated with a day devoted to competition, which emphasized arts, crafts, and games. In the western counties, there was the school parade with banners, floats, costumes, vehicles, and marching bands from neighboring towns that would march down Purcellville's Main Street. (Courtesy of Jane Hirst Bogle.)

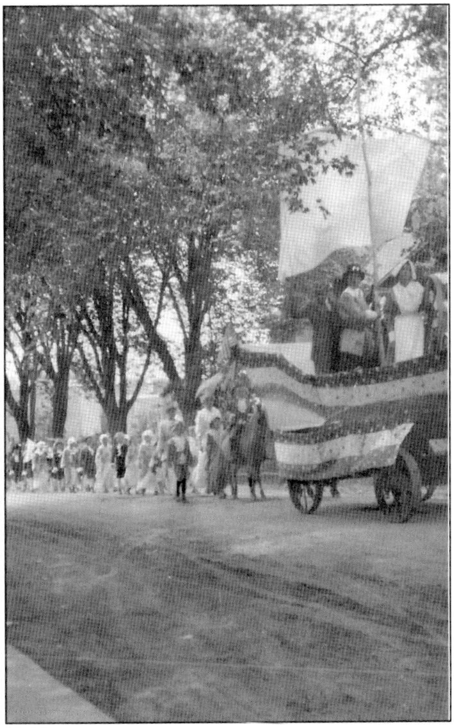

In this 1914 photograph, the Purcellville Graded School celebrates the holiday season with a Christmas tree adorned with the students' handmade ornaments. (Courtesy of Jane Hirst Bogle.)

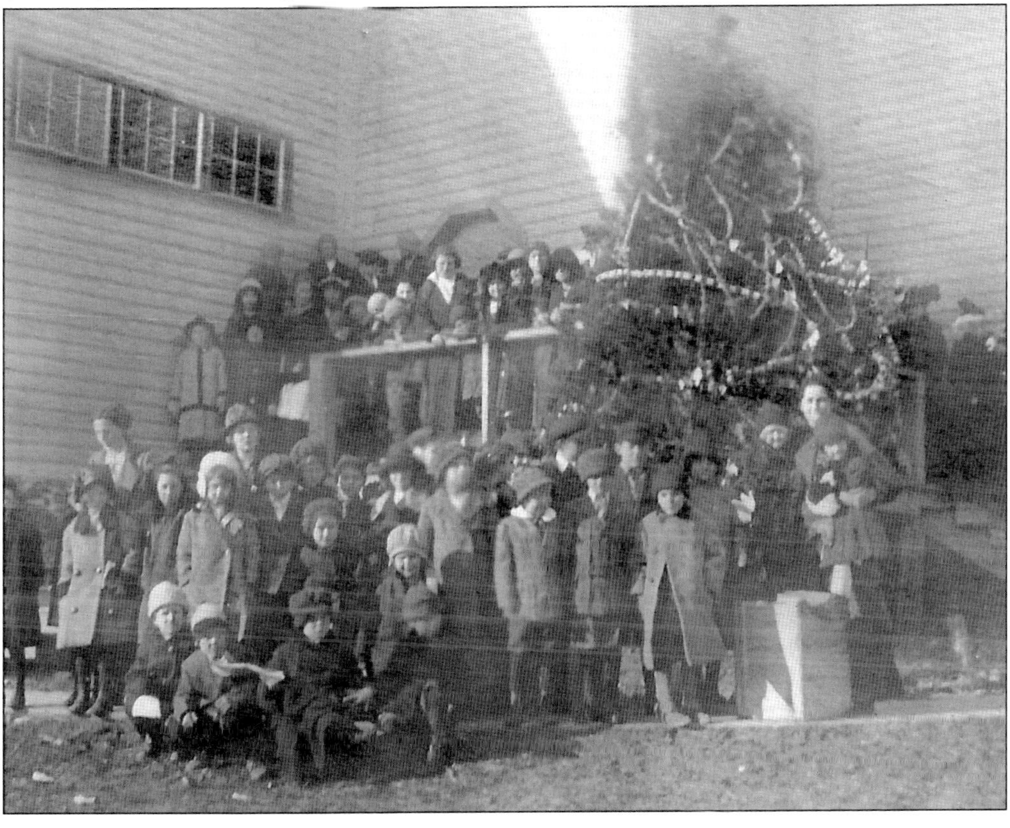

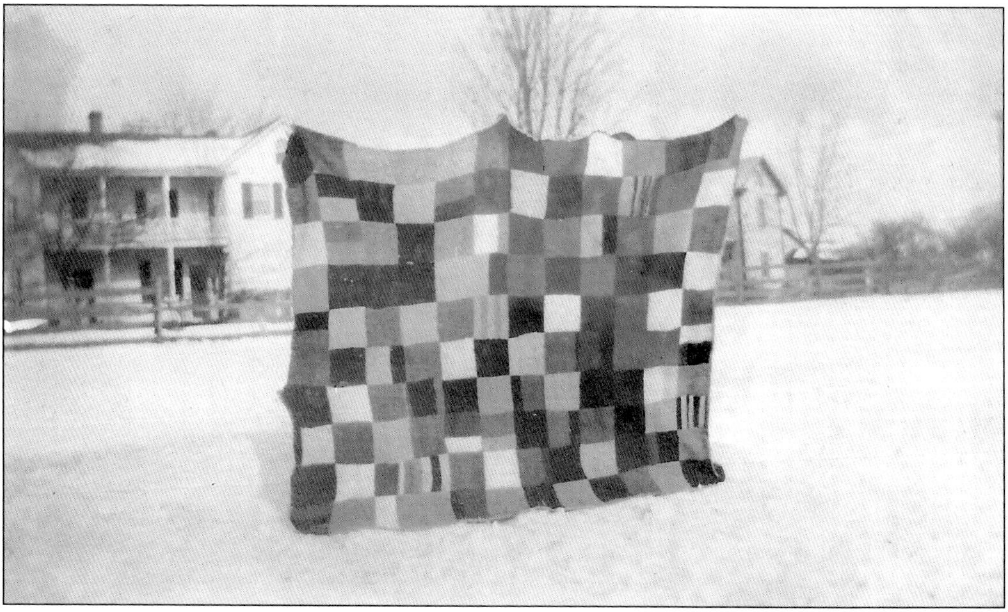

There were 4,094 men from Loudoun County registered in the draft for World War I. During this time, it was unusual to meet a woman on the street who did not have a knitting bag on her arm, because many formed knitting and sewing circles in support of the troops. In this 1917 photograph, a student from the Purcellville Graded School presents a handmade quilt for the soldiers in front of the Hampton Hotel on Main Street. (Courtesy of Jane Hirst Bogle.)

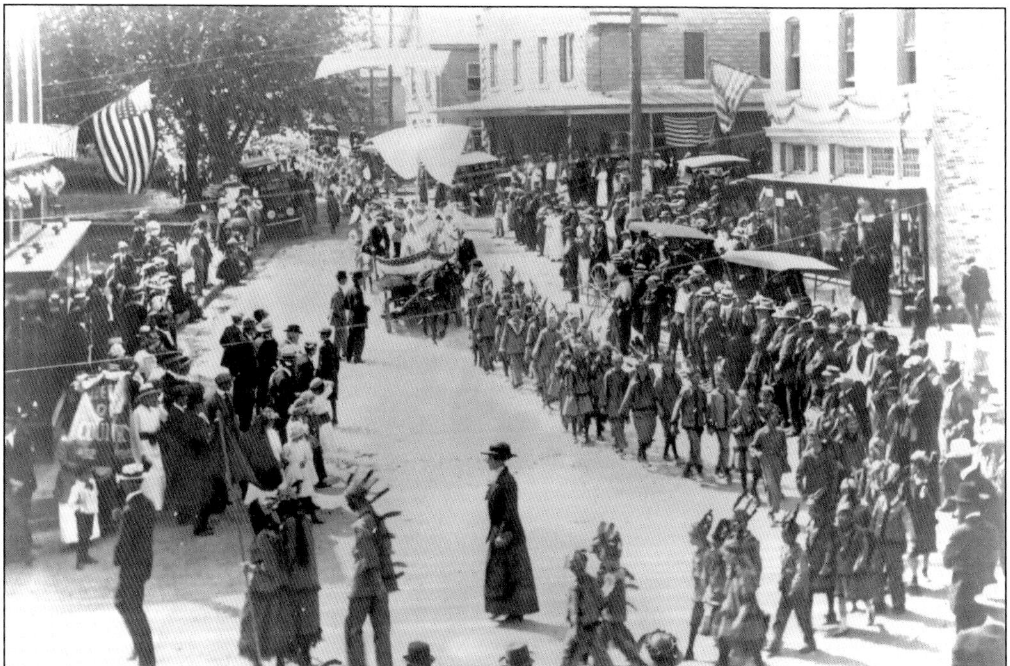

This 1916 photograph shows the parade of Loudoun school districts that was part of the countywide school fair, with annual competitions in athletics and scholastic debates. (Courtesy of Thomas Balch Library.)

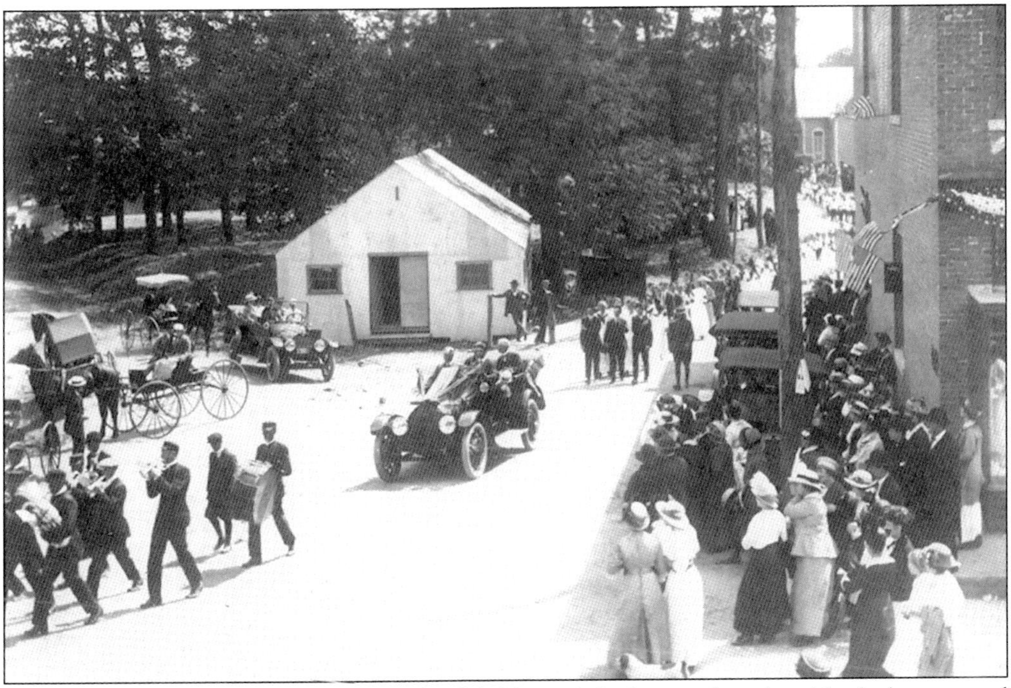

Family, friends, and teachers cheer the schoolchildren while the marching band leads them toward Main Street. Purcellville's first public school for white children was near this intersection from 1885 to 1898. (Courtesy of Jane Hirst Bogle.)

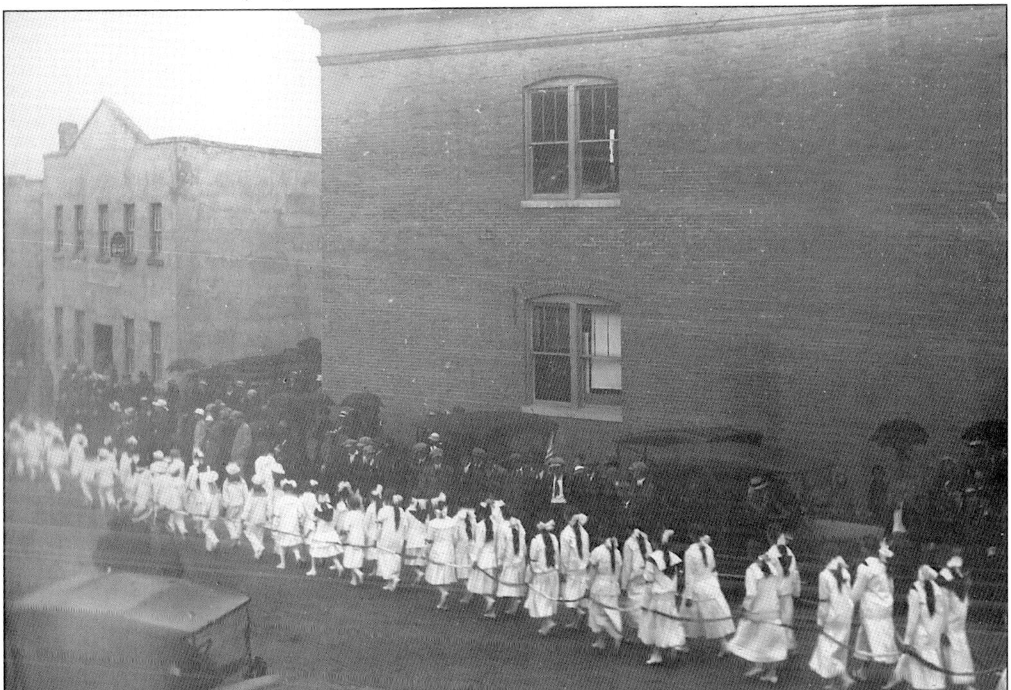

In this 1917 photograph, students make their way back to the Purcellville Graded School after their annual parade on Main Street. (Courtesy of Jane Hirst Bogle.)

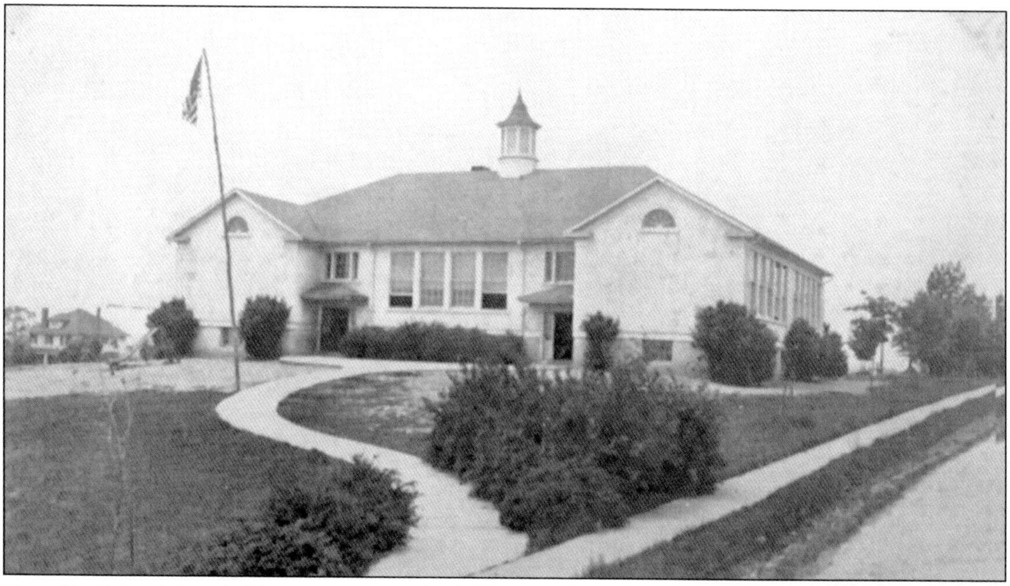

Purcellville's white children moved to Arch Simpson's new seven-classroom building in 1923, complete with a gymnasium, cafeteria, and auditorium. This school was one of the first in the county to be built with bank loans. It received a $5,000 loan from Purcellville National Bank and a $3,000 loan from Farmers & Merchants in Hamilton. Neither bank exists today. (Courtesy of Thomas Balch Library.)

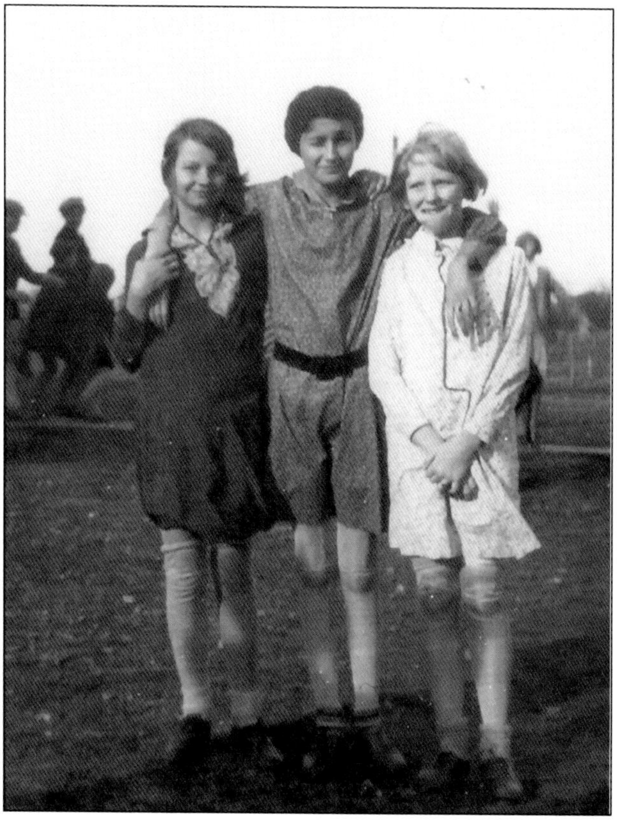

Classmates take a break on the playground during recess in this 1925 photograph, taken soon after their new seven-room school house was built on Nursery Avenue. During its first year, the teachers at Purcellville Graded School were Louise Tillet, Lydia Barton, Evelyn Adams, Rebecca Lloyd, and Bertha Gruver. (Courtesy of Robert Lyon.)

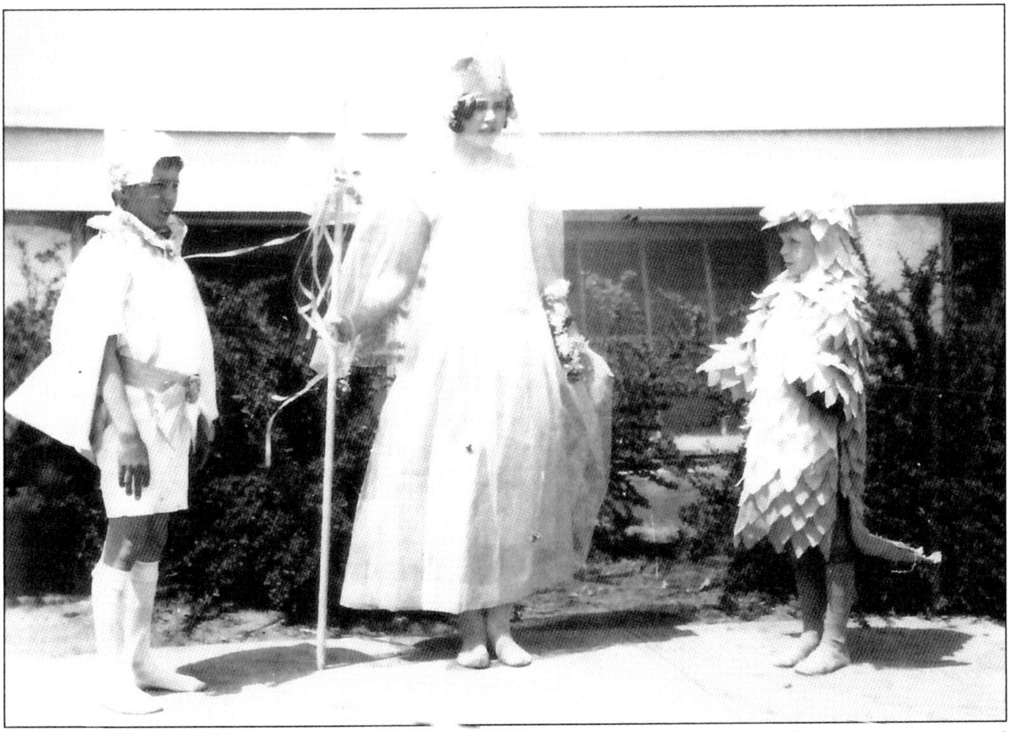

Taken in 1928, this photograph shows schoolchildren practicing their lines for the spring annual play, *A Spring Glow*. Pictured from left to right are Moncure Lyon Jr. as Jack Frost, Elizabeth Nichols as the princess, and Julian Hirst as the bluebird. (Courtesy of Robert Lyon.)

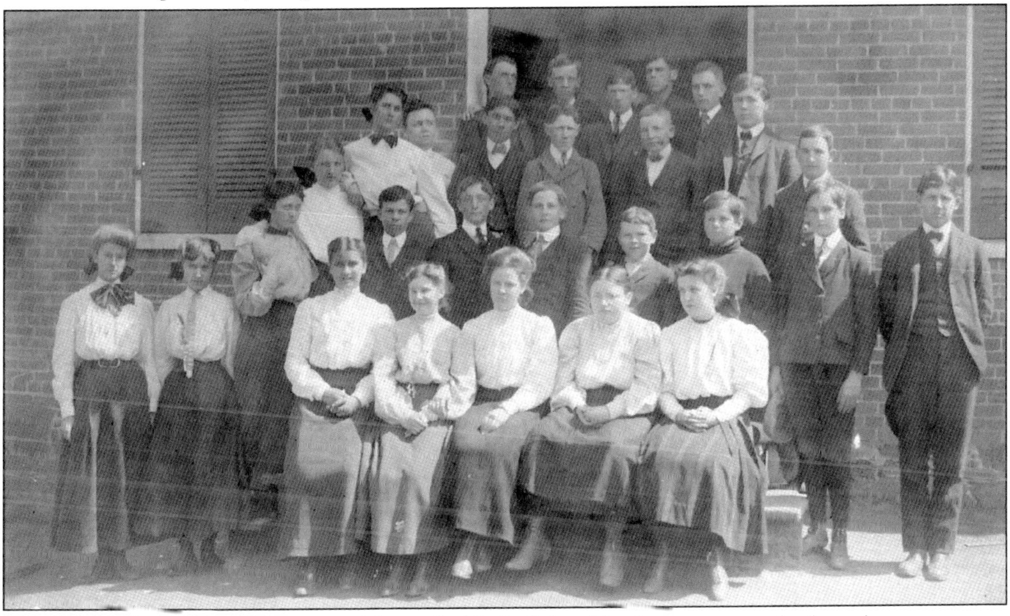

In 1906, students from the original Lincoln High School had to wear sturdy shoes because many walked to the school. Others remember catching the horse-drawn school carriage at the bank building on Main Street, but they still spent a good portion of the morning walking from their farms. (Courtesy of Jane Hirst Bogle.)

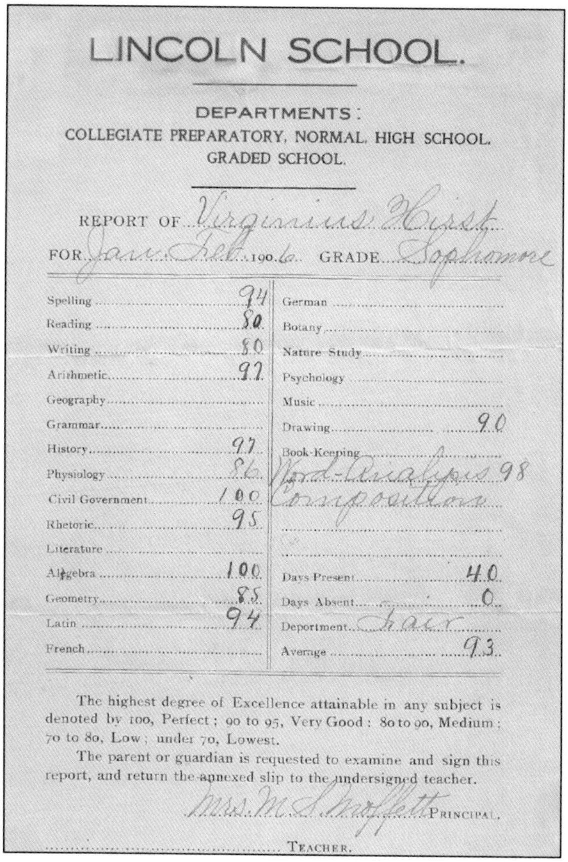

LINCOLN SCHOOL.

DEPARTMENTS:
COLLEGIATE PREPARATORY, NORMAL HIGH SCHOOL.
GRADED SCHOOL.

REPORT OF Virginius Hirst
FOR Jan. Feb. 1906 GRADE Sophomore

Spelling	94	German	
Reading	80	Botany	
Writing	80	Nature Study	
Arithmetic	92	Psychology	
Geography		Music	
Grammar		Drawing	90
History	92	Book-Keeping	
Physiology	86	Word-Analysis	98
Civil Government	100	Composition	
Rhetoric	95		
Literature			
Algebra	100	Days Present	40
Geometry	85	Days Absent	0
Latin	94	Deportment	Fair
French		Average	93

The highest degree of Excellence attainable in any subject is denoted by 100, Perfect; 90 to 95, Very Good: 80 to 90, Medium; 70 to 80, Low; under 70, Lowest.

The parent or guardian is requested to examine and sign this report, and return the annexed slip to the undersigned teacher.

Mrs. M. S. Moffett PRINCIPAL.

.... TEACHER.

This was sophomore Virginius Hirst's report card from Lincoln High School for January and February 1906. With these high marks, Virginius would go on to graduate from Virginia Military Academy and receive his medical degree from the University of Virginia. (Courtesy of Jane Hirst Bogle.)

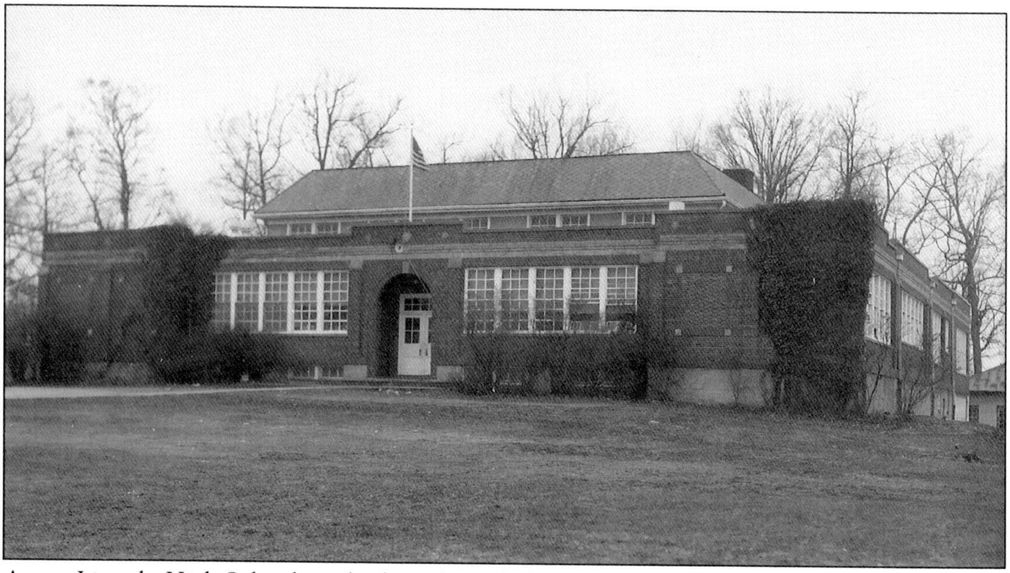

A new Lincoln High School was built exclusively for white children, and was dedicated in 1927. In 1954, when Loudoun County High School opened its doors, other small-town high schools throughout Loudoun, such as this one, were closed. It is now Lincoln Elementary School. (Courtesy of Brad Kilgour.)

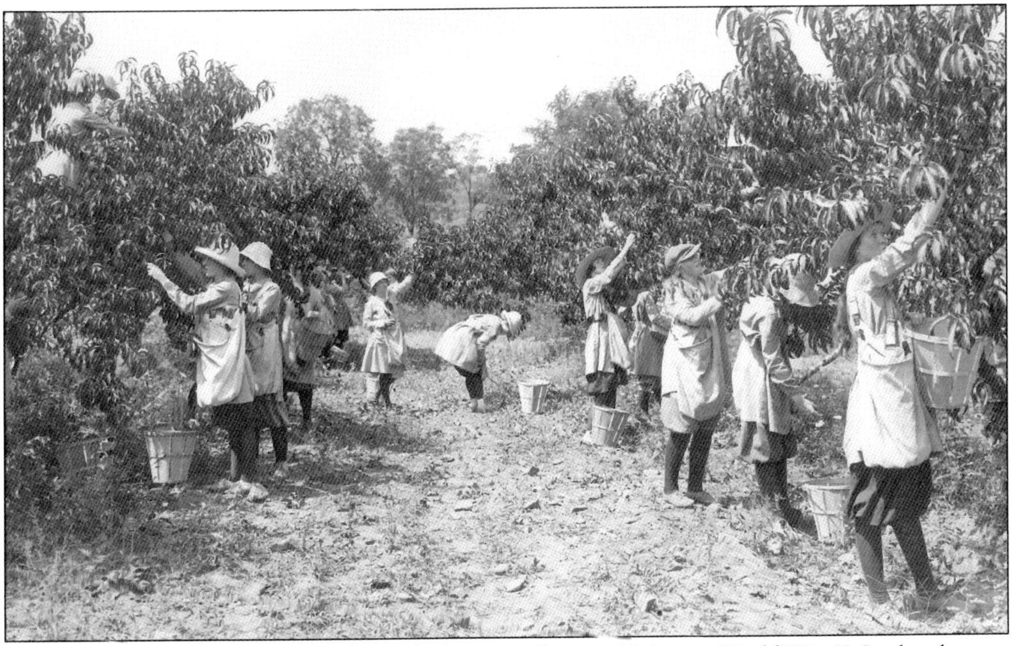

Purcellville's women and children helped whenever they could during World War II. In the absence of men, women moved outside their traditional roles and took jobs usually reserved for men, like working in the fields. This 1940 photograph shows young women picking the fruit at harvest in an orchard. Children in town organized scrap drives at their schools where rubber tires, metal, and newspapers were collected and recycled for the war effort. (Courtesy of Thomas Balch Library.)

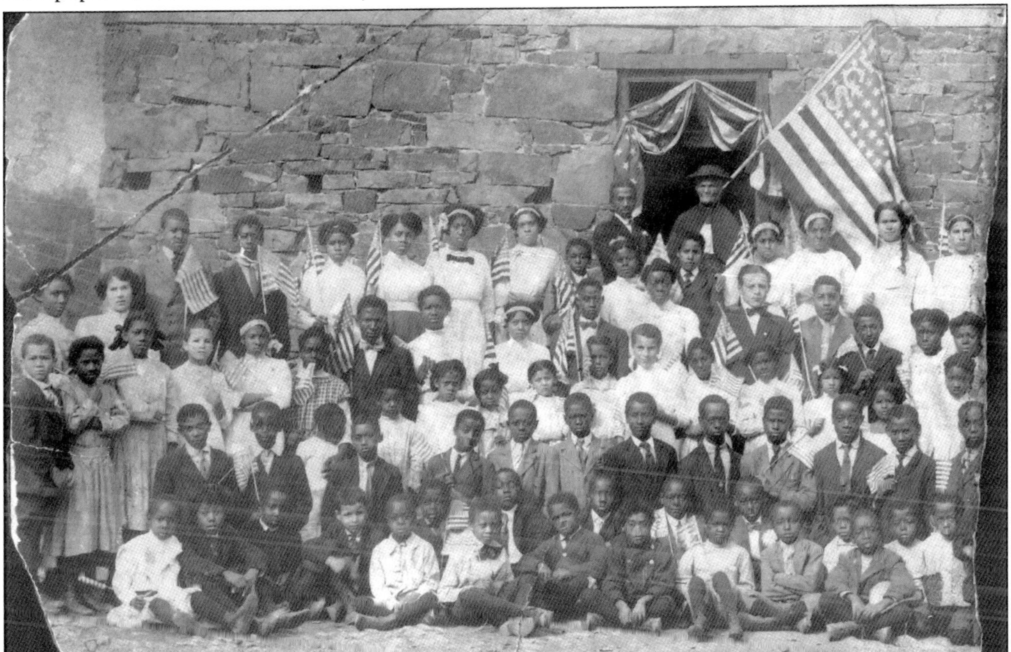

African American children from Purcellville, shown in this 1910 photograph, had to walk two miles to Lincoln to attend Goose Creek School. It was commonly referred as the "schoolhouse under the hill." It was built and founded by the Freemen's Bureau in 1866. (Courtesy of Reginald Simms.)

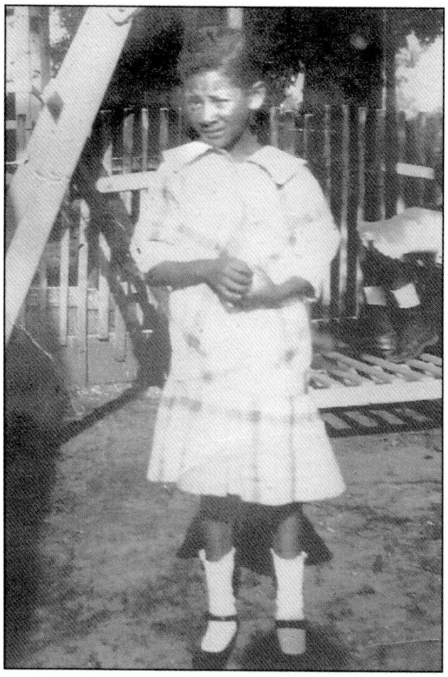

Joseph Cook's young daughter Maxine, shown in this 1914 photograph, had been ill with scarlet fever and could not endure the long walk to Lincoln. Joseph Cook, a carpenter, and other members of the Willing Workers Club built Purcellville's first school for African Americans in 1919 so that his daughter could attend the school in the fall. (Courtesy of Sheila Pinkney Kelly.)

Lena Stewart Cook (middle) and Joseph Cook (far right) were the benefactors of Purcellville's first two-room school for African Americans. Organized in 1917, the Willing Workers Club was incorporated in 1919 "to assist in providing proper educational facilities for the colored children in Purcellville and to provide further religion training of such children and to . . . equip and maintain a Library and Reading room for such children." (Courtesy of Sheila Pinkney Kelly.)

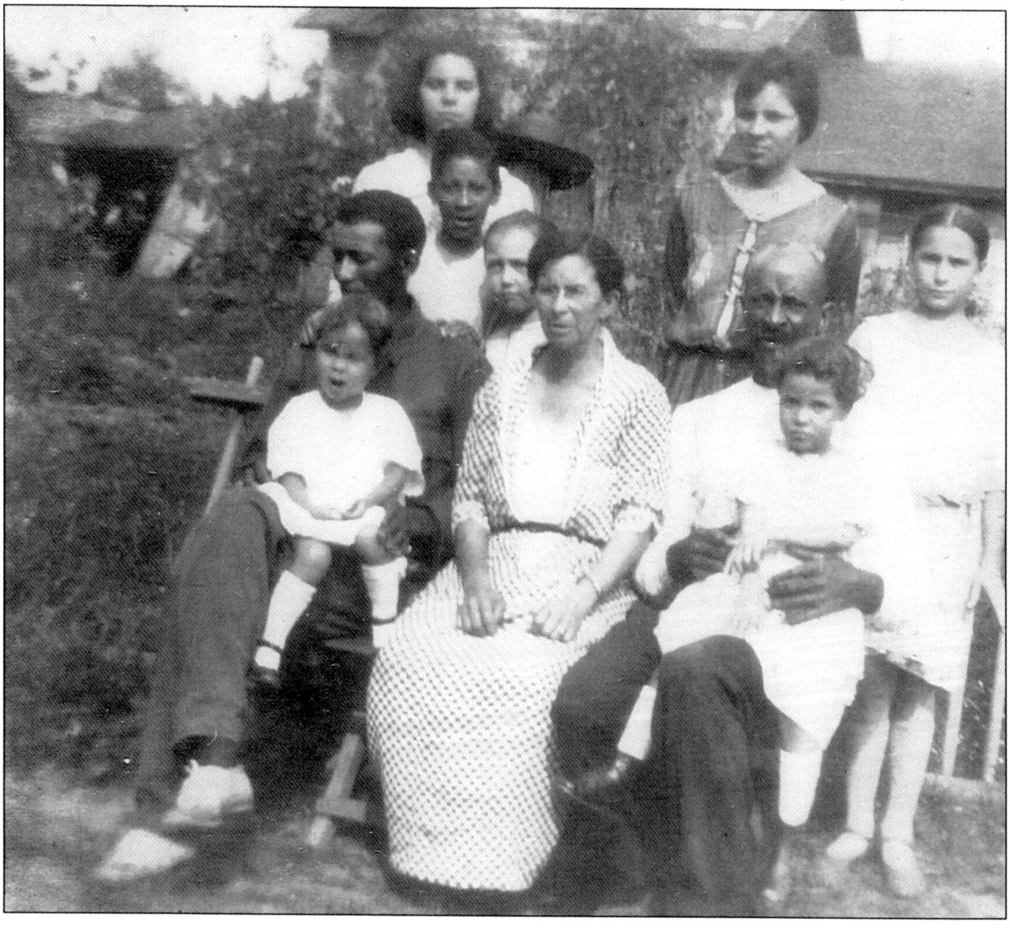

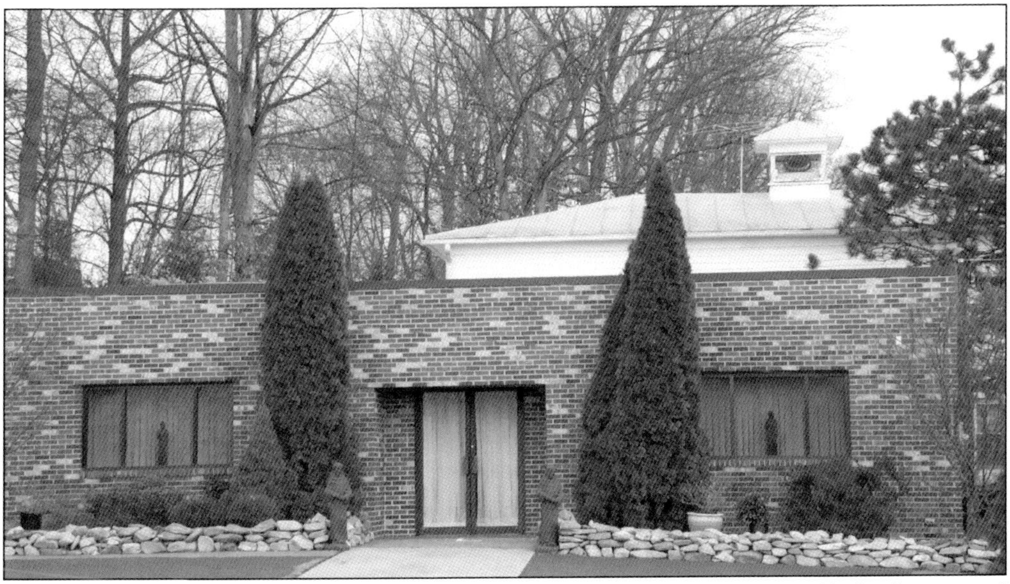

Joseph Cook built the two-room school for African American children in Purcellville that opened in 1920. The school building also housed a library for African American patrons because they were banned from the public library on Main Street. In 1957, African American residents Samuel Cordoza Murray and his wife, Josie Cook Murray, pursued legal action and brought official desegregation to public libraries in Loudoun County. The school's bell tower and schoolhouse structure can still be seen as part of Lyles Funeral Home on Twentieth Street (Courtesy of Cathy Darby.)

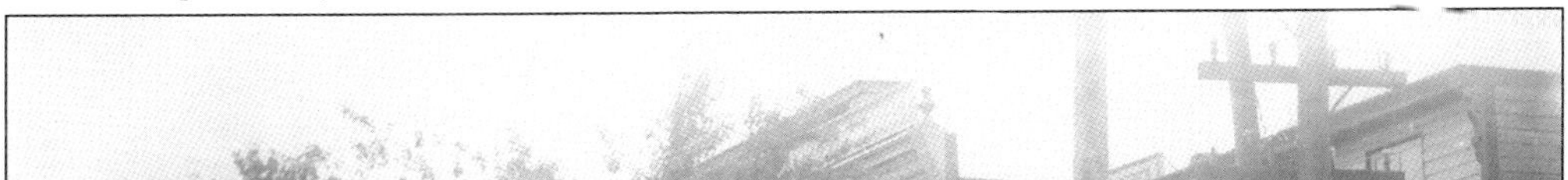

Joseph Janney, who was also the town's jeweler, managed Purcellville's first official library for white residents. Janney had four shelves of books on loan in his shop, which was located on the second floor of the building on the far right (where the lady is standing). In 1885, patrons could borrow all they wanted for 25¢ a year; otherwise it was 5¢ a book with a heavy penalty for overtime (Courtesy of Thomas Balch Library.)

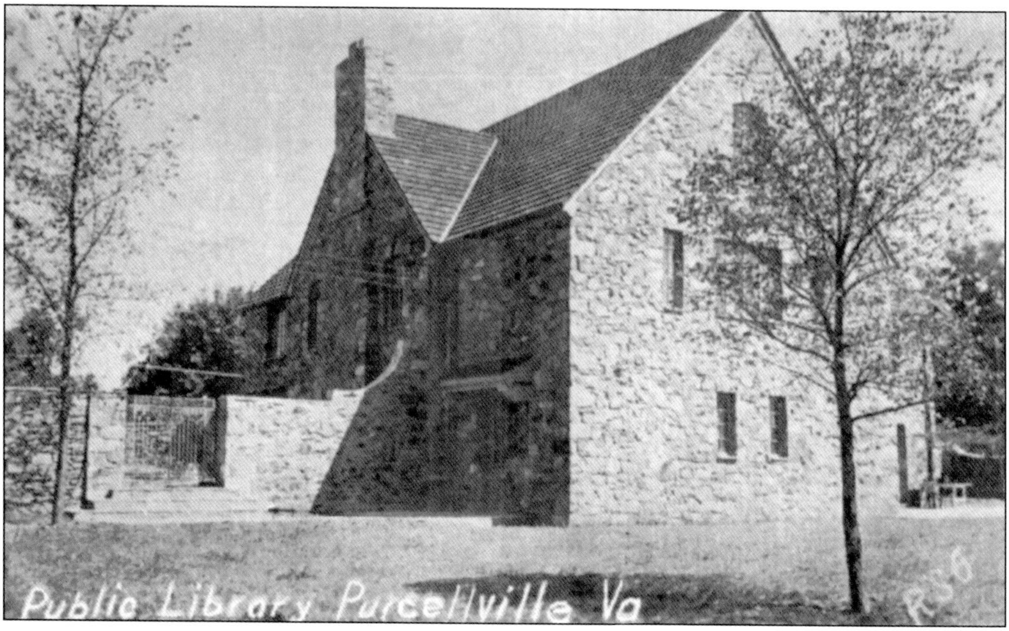

In 1936, Laura A. Cornwell, Edna Ray, and Eva Wimer gave land for a new library. The Public Works Administration made a considerable donation as well, which was largely because of Gertrude Robey's persistence. Her husband, Clarence Robey, was the president of Purcellville National Bank. The library was designed by Delos H. Smith and built by L.J. Keller & Sons in 1937. (Courtesy of Thomas Balch Library.)

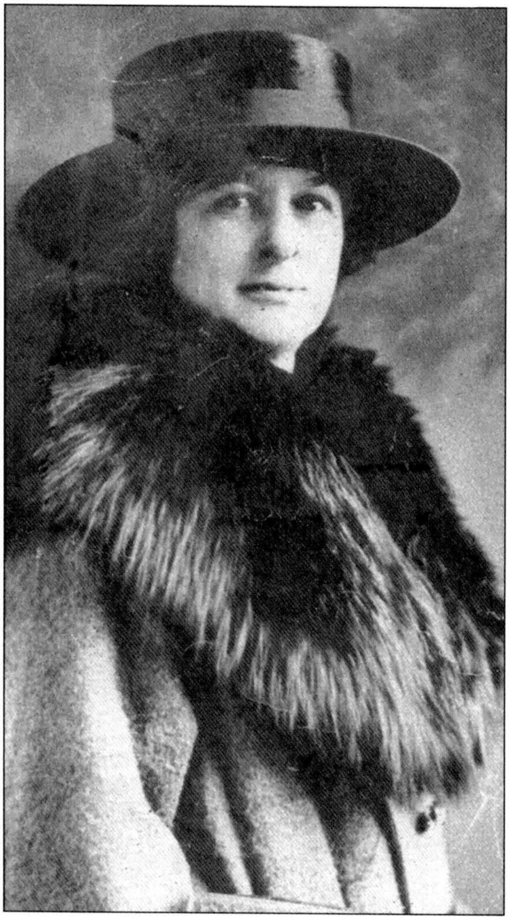

The town's library owes its existence to the energy and public spirit of Gertrude Robey. She not only helped fund the first public library in Loudoun but also was diligent in seeing to its completion. On one particular inspection of the construction, Robey climbed the scaffolding, only to fall and break her leg. (Courtesy of Reginald Simms.)

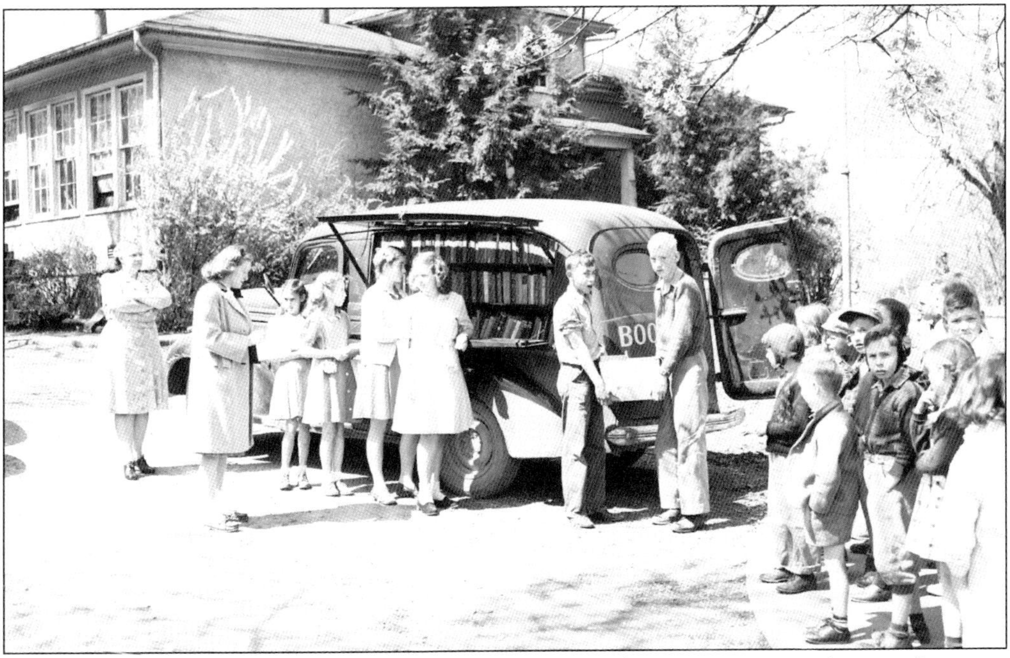

In 1937, the library's bookmobile started its service. According to town council notes, there was a drive to desegregate the library in the 1950s. Town council member Ed Nichols said, "We had a very forward-looking librarian, Jean Caulkins Carruthers, who had already started desegregation with the bookmobile, stopping quietly on her own to people's homes so they could have books." (Courtesy of Thomas Balch Library.)

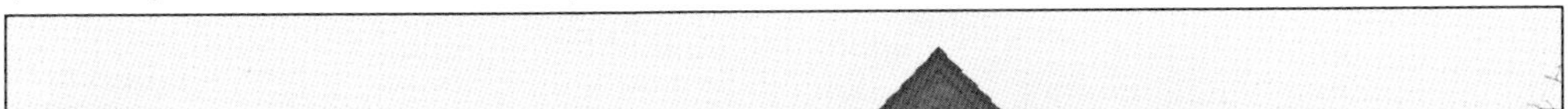

Private organizations, the state, and town council once supported Purcellville's library, which is now part of the Loudoun County Public Library. While on the town council in the 1950s, Ed Nichols remembered how he made the motion that the council should omit the town's appropriation for the library if they didn't officially desegregate. He recalls, "You could hear a pin drop. Dead silence. In the next election, I didn't get reelected." (Courtesy of Cathy Darby.)

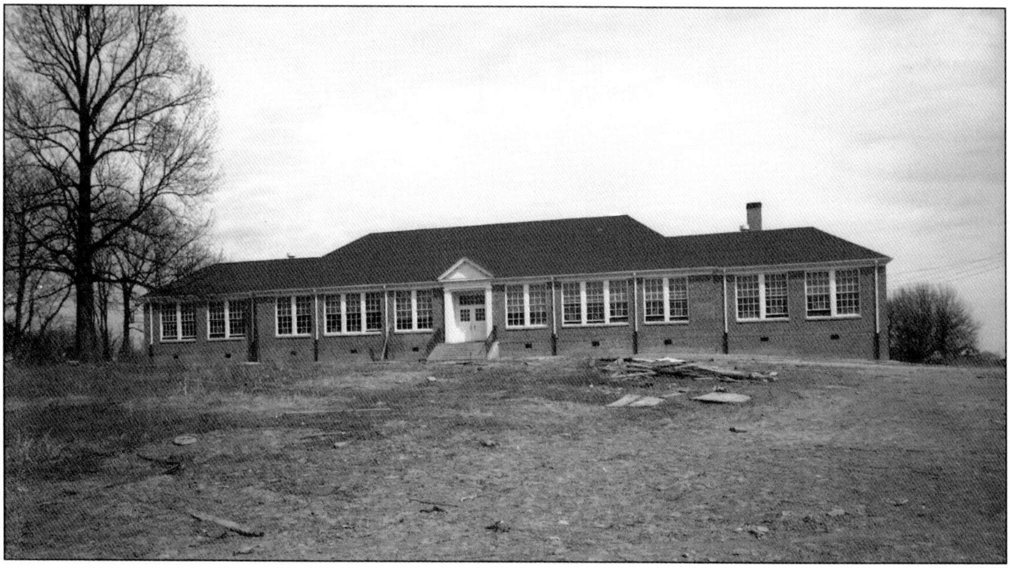

School Board minutes of 1927 note: "colored people were heard concerning the erection of a new colored school at Purcellville. Action was postponed." It turned out to be a twenty-year postponement, as the eight-room George Washington Carver School wasn't built until 1947, on seven acres bought for $2,000 from Joe Cook's heirs in 1945 on Twentieth Street near the Emancipation Grounds. The school was a source of great pride and strength for the community until it closed for integration in 1968. (Courtesy of Thomas Balch Library.)

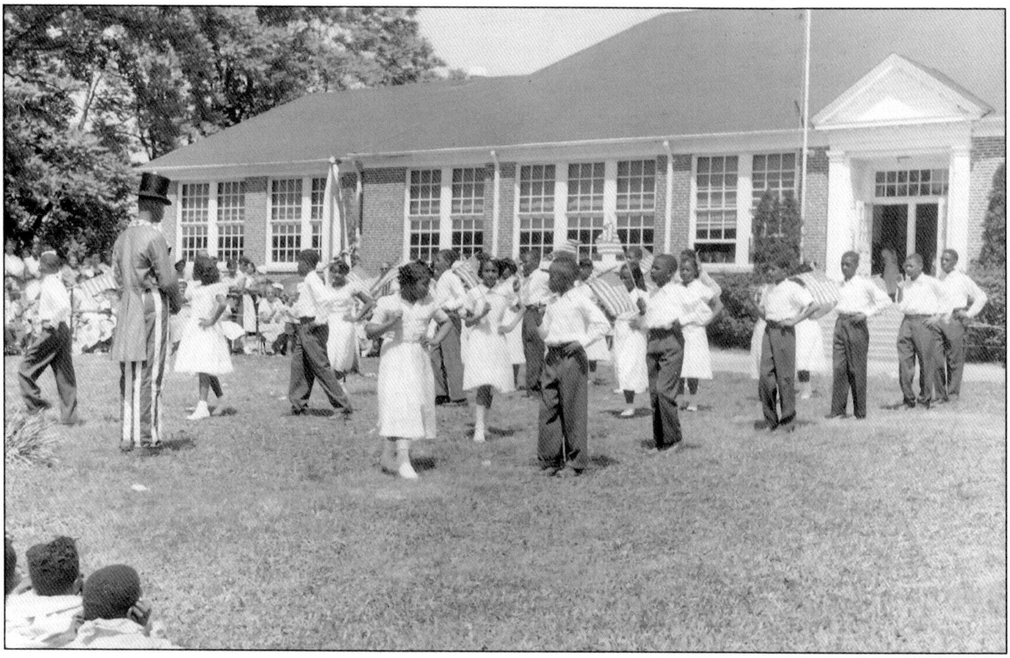

Proud schoolchildren present their patriotic skit at the annual May Day celebration in the 1950s. The George Washington Carver School's alumni remember how the school pulsed with energy and gave a sense of place and stability to many children, especially those who worked hard in the fields to support their families. Alumni also remember the excellent teachers, even if they did administer the "occasional rap on the knuckles." (Courtesy of Reginald Simms.)

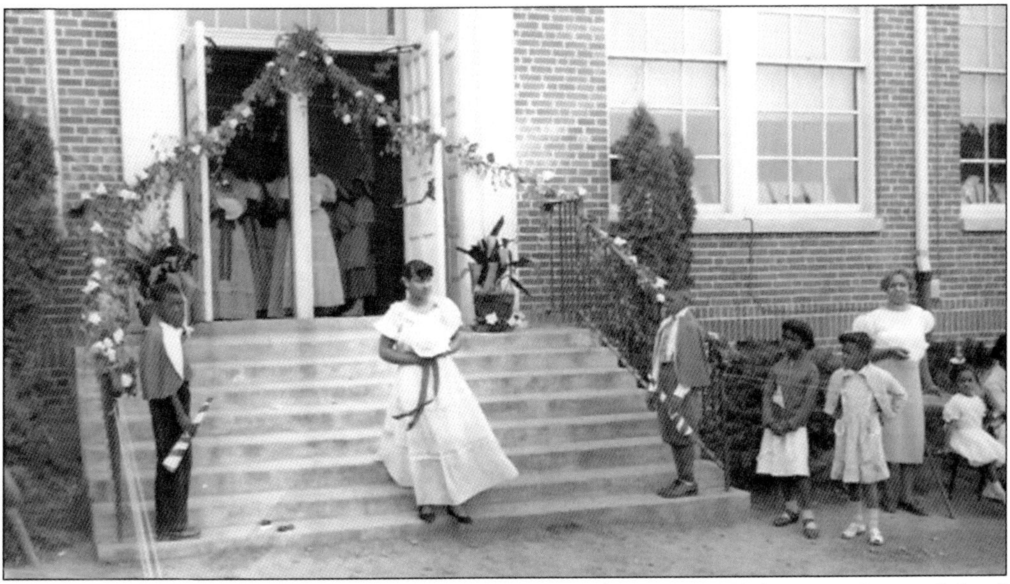

One of the biggest highlights of the year for students at the George Washington Carver School was the annual May Day. Sheila Pinkney Kelly remembers how her teacher Helen Lee Gross, with the help of her grandmother Myrtle Cook Henderson, would hand-sew the costumes each year. Shown in this photograph is one of the queens of the May Day Court. The crown would be awarded to the student who raised the most money for the school's art and music programs. (Courtesy of Purcellville Preservation Association.)

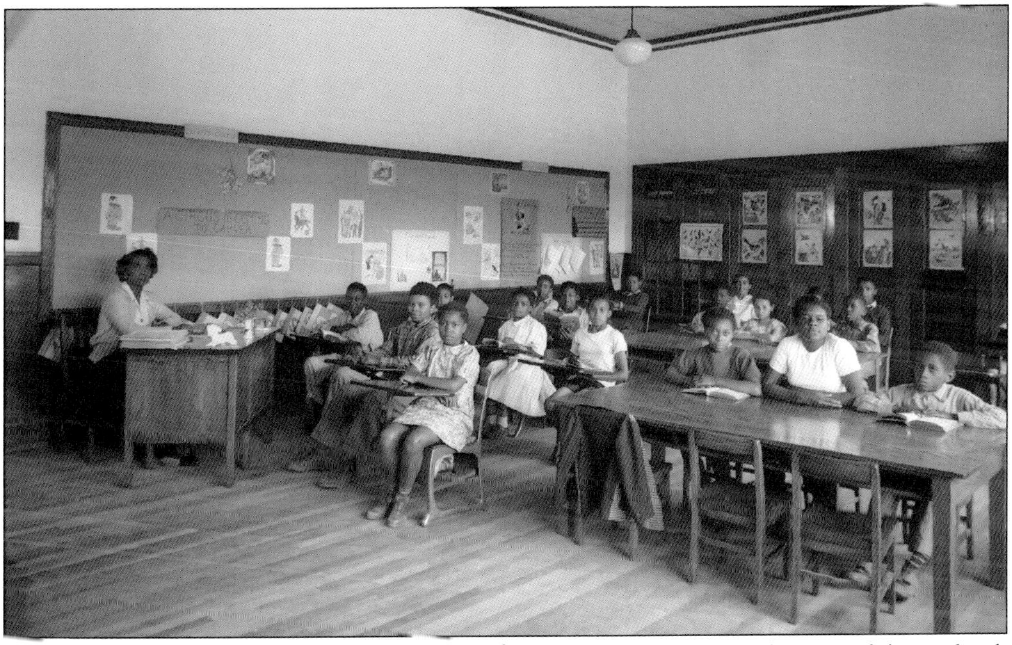

Students at the George Washington Carver School took great pride in the care of their school. After integration, the school was abandoned for several decades. Wanting to bring the beautiful building back to life, community activists Martha Barnhart, Mae Brownell, and Mattie Lassiter spearheaded the project. In 2007, the Carver Center opened its doors for senior citizens and other community activities. (Courtesy of Alumni of Carver.)

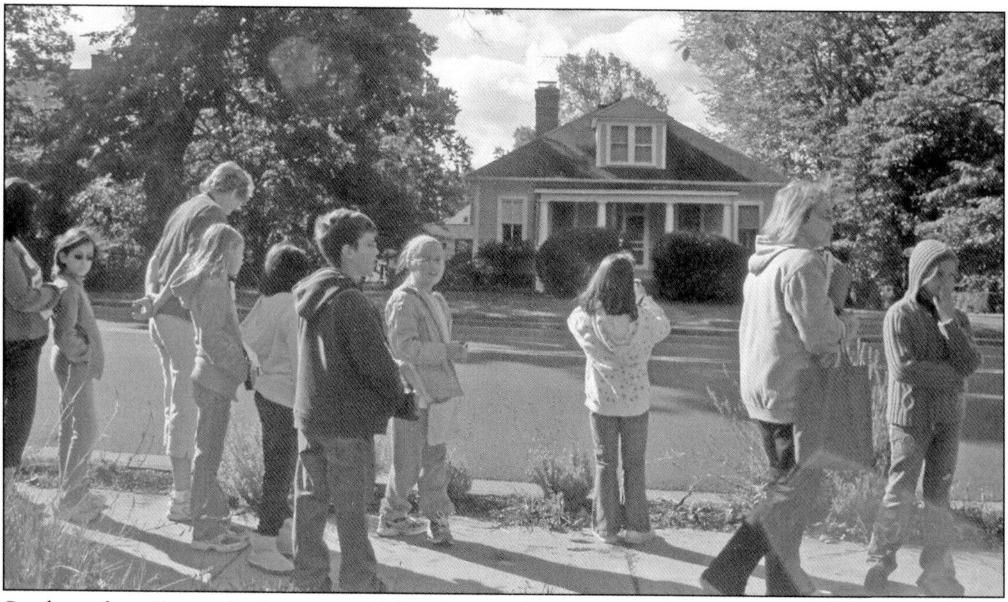

Students from Emerick Elementary School take a field trip on a walking tour where the house of Loudoun County's first superintendent Oscar Emerick is pointed out on Main Street. Oscar's wife, Carrie, is famous for being the first woman in Loudoun County to pay her poll tax and qualify to vote with the passage of the Women's Suffrage Amendment in 1920. (Courtesy of Purcellville Preservation Association.)

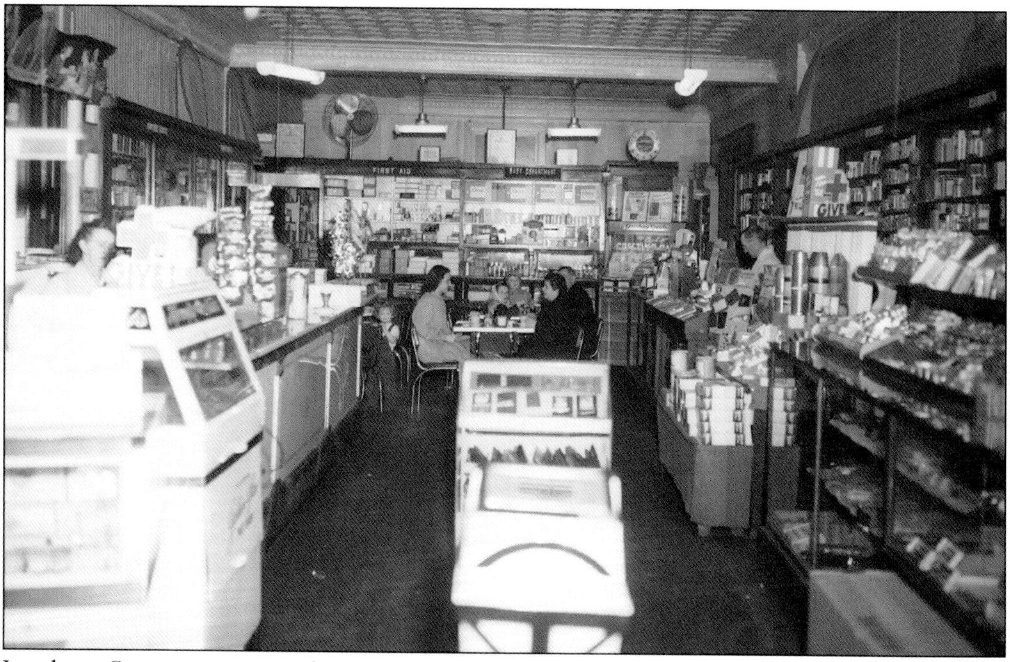

Loudoun County superintendent Oscar Emerick's first office was in his home until the school board rented an office for him above N.G. Miller's Purcellville Pharmacy on Twenty-First Street. Shown in this 1935 photograph are a few townspeople having lunch in the rear of the pharmacy. The Loudoun County School Board's offices remained above the pharmacy until they moved to Leesburg in 1935. (Courtesy of Thomas Balch Library.)

With the closing of the Purcellville Graded School in 1967, Emerick Elementary School was built across the street. Former students remember gathering their textbooks from their old desks and taking the walk across Nursery Avenue to their new desks inside the newly constructed school. This 1970 photograph shows schoolgirls at one of the school's first graduation ceremonies. (Courtesy of Jim and Betty Wiley.)

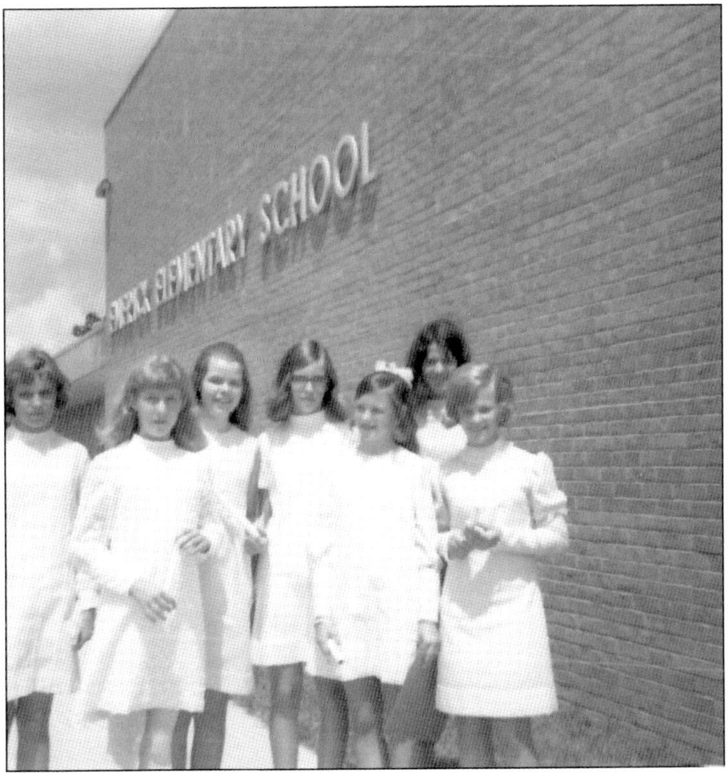

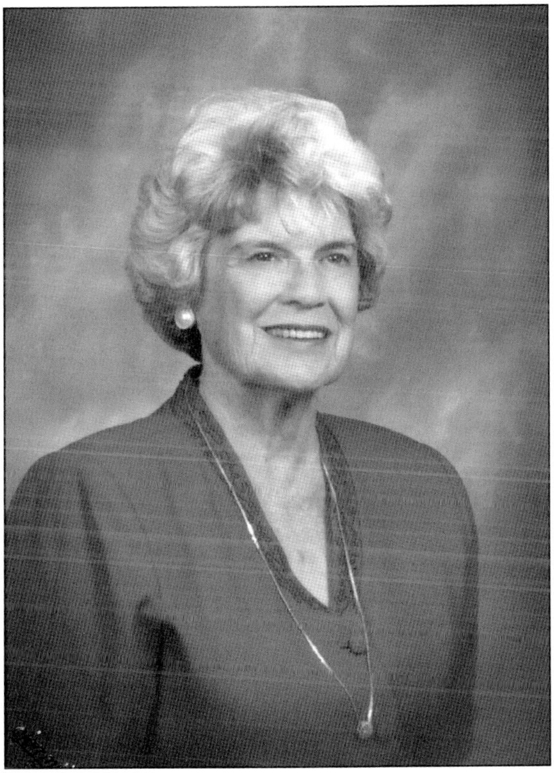

After Emerick Elementary School opened, the Purcellville Graded School across the street collected cobwebs. Mother and activist Betty Wiley saw a void that needed to be filled and set out, with the help of friends and the county, to turn the abandoned schoolhouse into a community center for the children and their families in Purcellville. (Courtesy of Betty Wiley.)

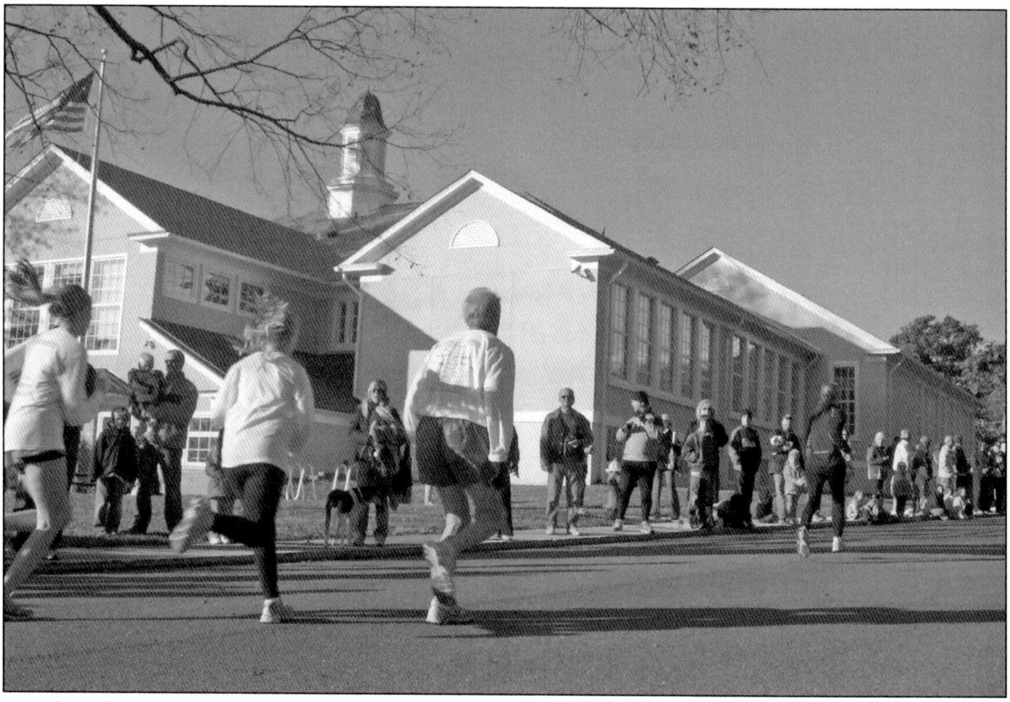

In a bond referendum in 2004, Loudoun County voters agreed to fund the renovation of the Loudoun Valley Community Center with more than $4 million in upgrades. The annual Turkey Trot 5K and Fun Run attracts hundreds of runners. It is the advisory board's largest fundraiser that benefits the children's programs at the center. (Courtesy of the Turkey Trot Committee.)

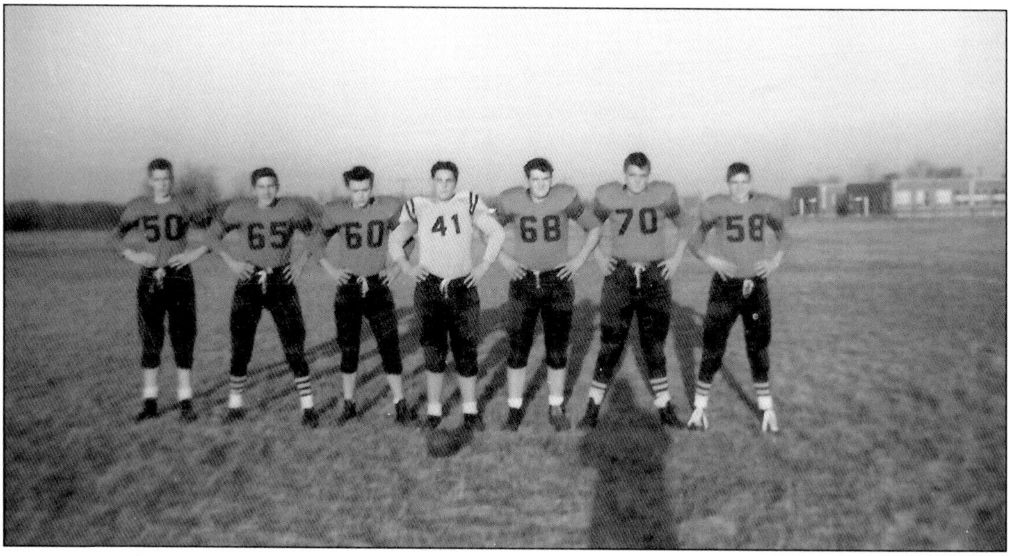

In 1954, Loudoun County High School was built in Leesburg as the only all-white high school for the county. This 1958 photograph shows some of the school's varsity football squad. The consolidation of the county's many white high schools into one was very controversial. The termination of the small town high schools was seen as a threat to local education and community spirit, despite the state-wide project's goal for better facilities, more course offerings, and better recreational facilities. (Courtesy of Beverly Bowman Chiasson.)

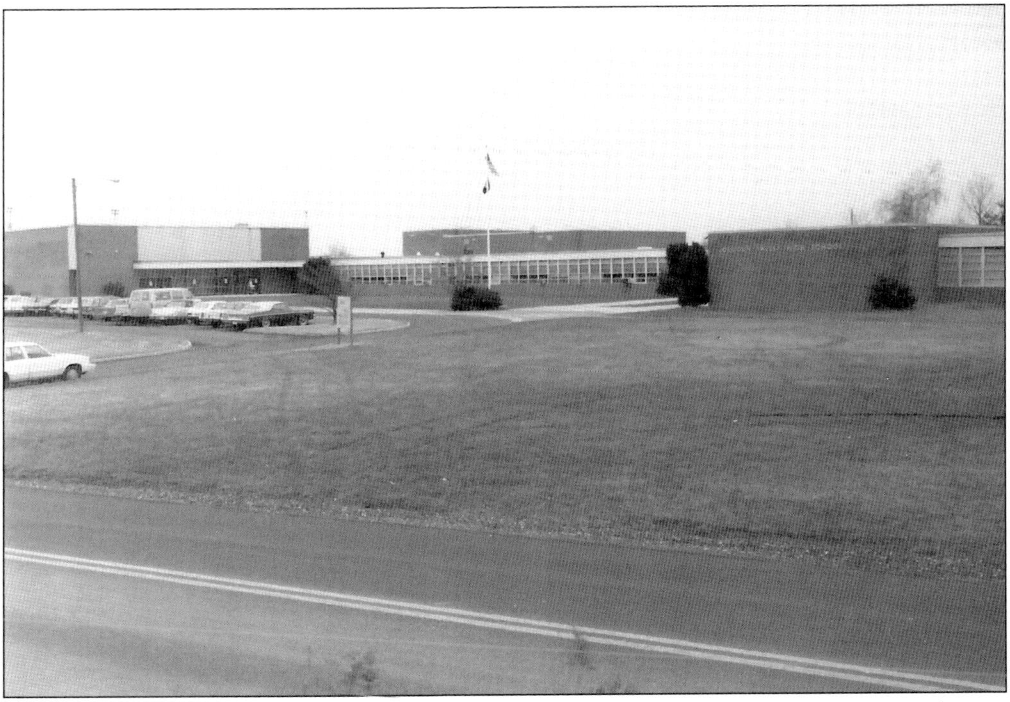

Within a decade, the one-school plan was unable to support the county's surging population. In 1962, Loudoun Valley High School opened to students living in Western Loudoun. For the past 15 years, an average of three new schools were built to support the growth in the county. This 1984 photograph shows Loudoun Valley High School before its extensive additions in 1995. (Courtesy of Thomas Balch Library.)

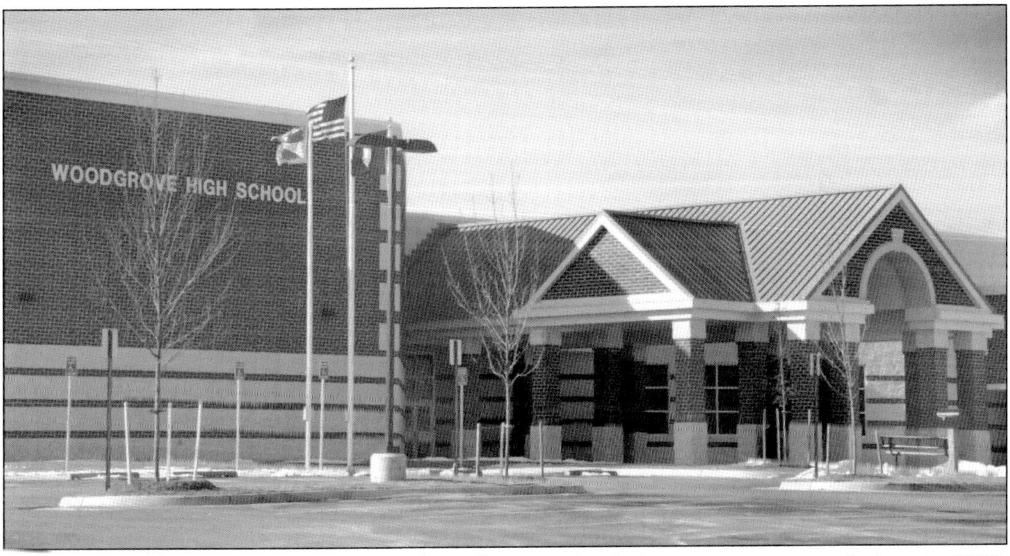

It was inevitable that Purcellville would need more schools for its growing population. In 2009, Loudoun County was the fourth-fastest growing county in the nation. Eventually, Purcellville would get its second high school, Woodgrove, which was opened in 2010 north of town. In 1810, some of the land was deeded to build a one-room school in Western Loudoun; coincidentally, it was to be called Woodgrove School. (Courtesy of Jack Darby.)

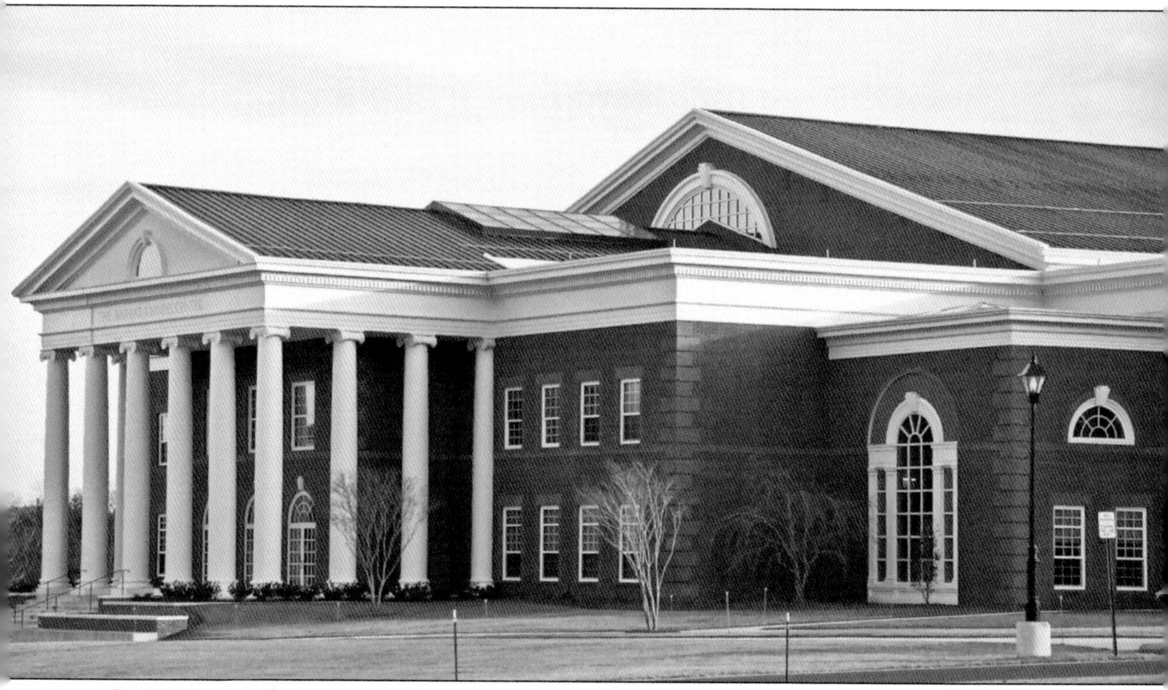

In 2000, Patrick Henry College opened its doors on the east end of town on Berlin Turnpike. Its high academic credentials have already led to a book called *God's Harvard*, and its students once defeated England's Oxford University debating teams. (Courtesy of the Purcellville Preservation Association.)

Three

When the Trains Came to Town

The image of the village changed radically when the Washington & Ohio Railroad (W&O) officially reached Purcellville at noon on March 31, 1874. The *Times Mirror* reported that the "running of the trains has set the little village aglow with activity . . . reminding us of accounts we have read of towns and cities springing up as it were, in a night." Purcellville grew up after that first train rolled through, which put the town on the map. Later, it would be the automobile that would change the nature of Purcellville. Once the railroad arrived out west, Purcellville's boomtown atmosphere would stay with the village through the next several decades because of its location. It was in the dead center of the rich agricultural heartland in the Loudoun Valley, making it a place where farmers want to be. The increased mobility and roads allowed Purcellville's residents to work in other places and shop in bigger shops, adding more variety to their daily lives. Ultimately, this change would alter the social setup of the small rural town. By the 1980s, Purcellville had become a suburb of Washington, DC, where many of its residents commuted to.

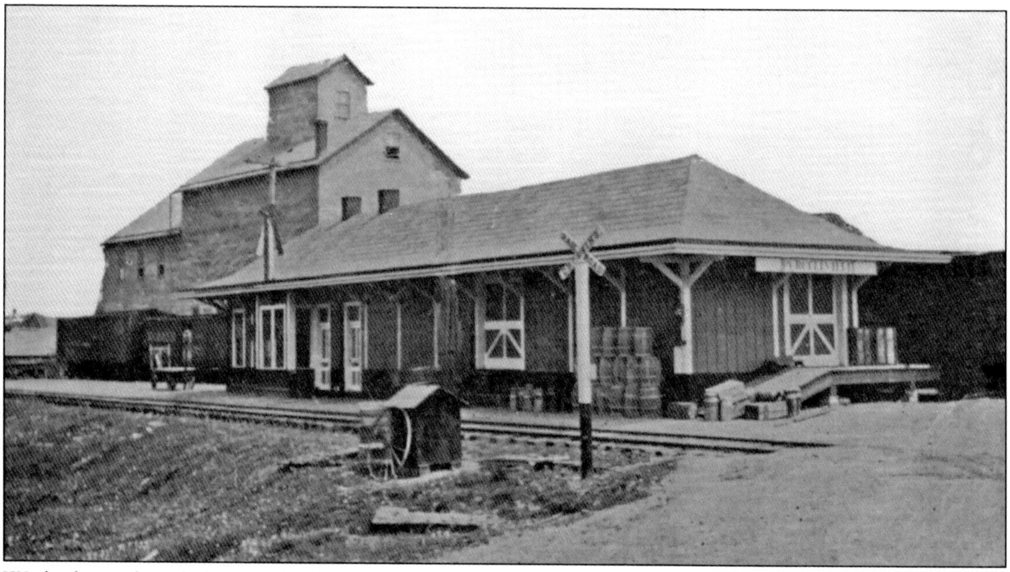

With the railroad, farmers had an easy and quick way to get their products to the city. Imported goods from the port of Alexandria were taken west, making business very profitable. Taken in 1910, this photograph shows the Purcellville Train Station when farmers brought their milk cans to the station for shipment eastbound. (Courtesy of Northern Virginia Regional Park Authority.)

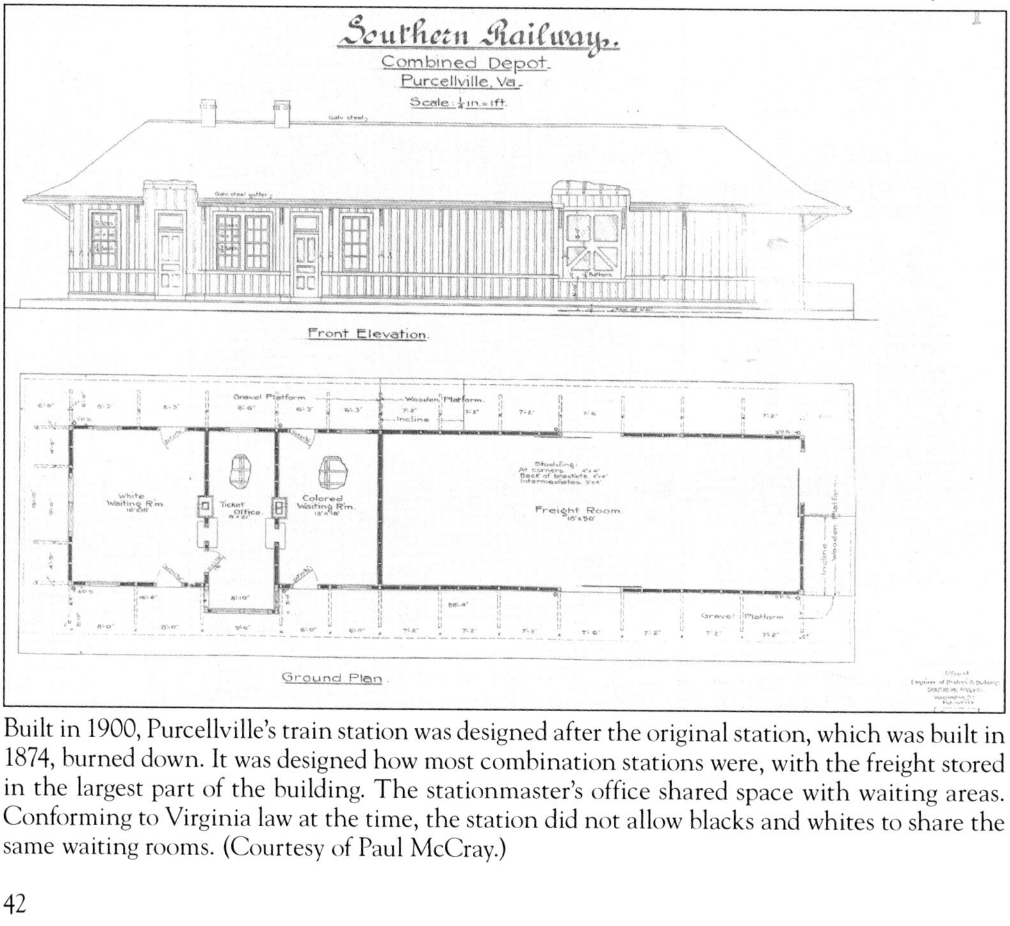

Built in 1900, Purcellville's train station was designed after the original station, which was built in 1874, burned down. It was designed how most combination stations were, with the freight stored in the largest part of the building. The stationmaster's office shared space with waiting areas. Conforming to Virginia law at the time, the station did not allow blacks and whites to share the same waiting rooms. (Courtesy of Paul McCray.)

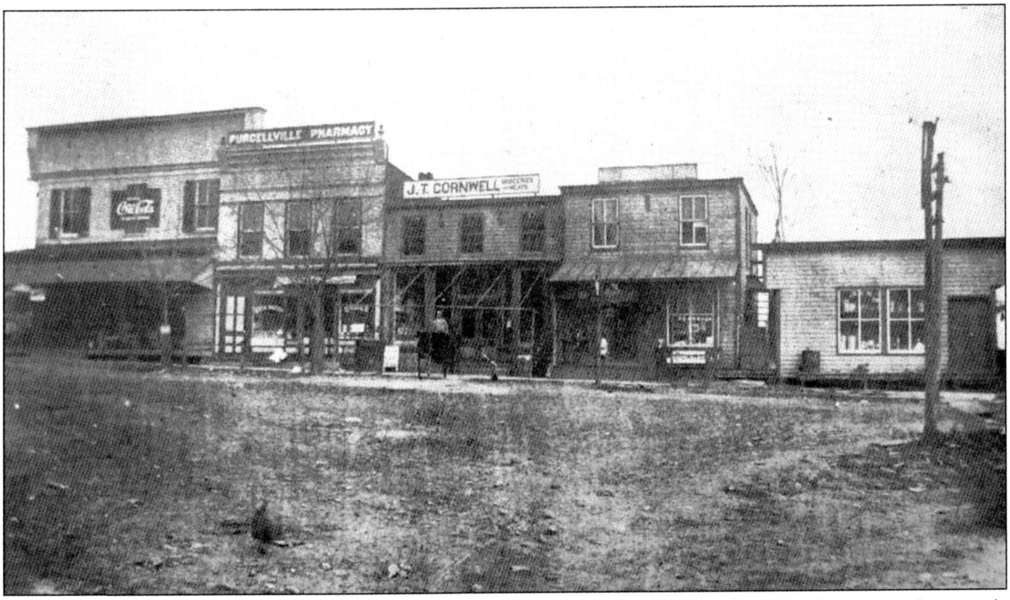

By 1908, Purcellville had around 30 businesses on its downtown blocks, which were a few yards from Purcellville Train Station. Just down from the station, the buildings were within 600 feet of six unpaved roads, where animal and vehicle traffic converged. (Courtesy of Thomas Balch Library.)

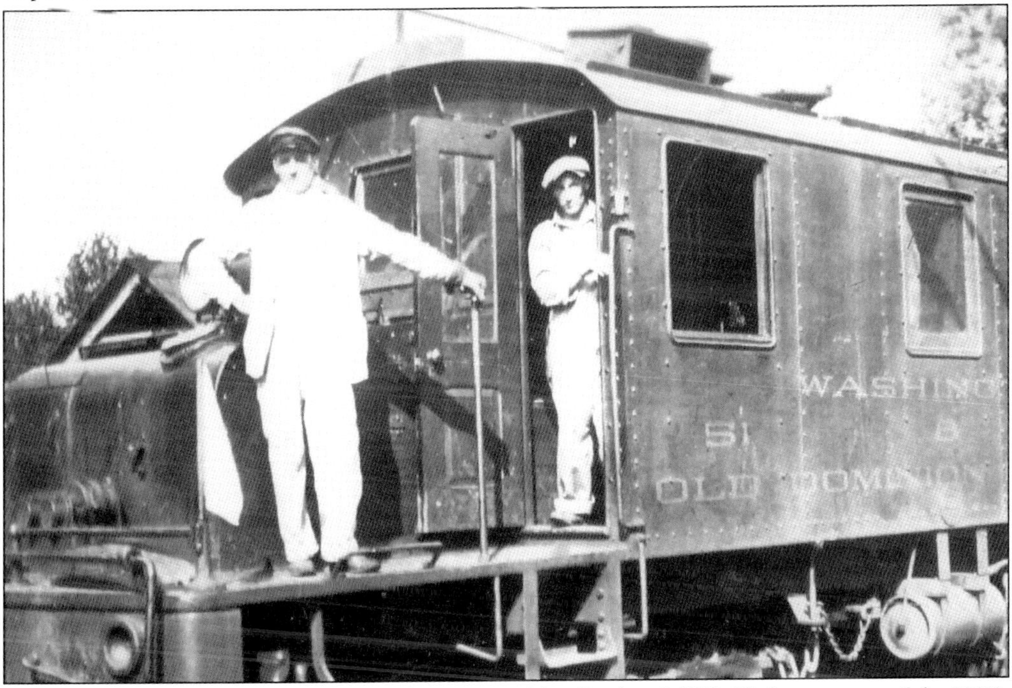

Walter Beatty (left) worked for the Washington & Ohio Railroad (W&O) during most of the 1920s before joining the booming dairy farming industry. His family was rooted in Bluemont where his father, James Clayton Beatty (the postmaster for Bluemont), founded the private Willowbrook Academy for Boys on Clayton Hall Road. In 1919, when Washingtonians were starting to come out to the cool climate at the foot of the Blue Ridge for a vacation in the summer on the train, the school was closed and re-opened as a "tourist home" called The Loudoun. (Courtesy of Donnie and Lindsay Hope.)

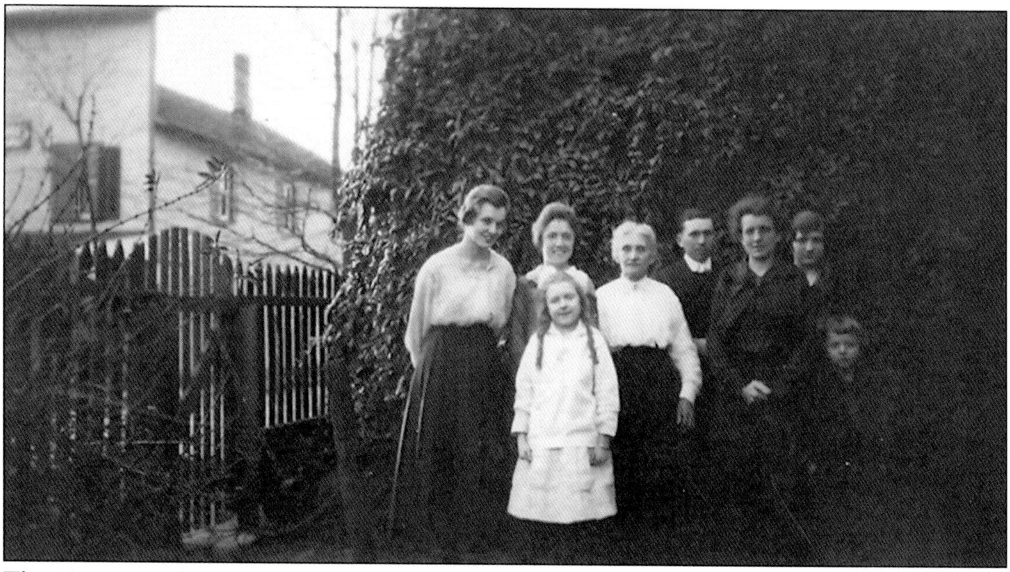

This 1914 image shows people gathered near the train station's yard, where most of the townspeople's social life took place. Before technology brought telephones, radio, and cars to every home, the train station in Purcellville was the center of activity for residents. Behind the group is the still-standing livery stable on Twenty-First Street. (Courtesy of Jane Hirst Bogle.)

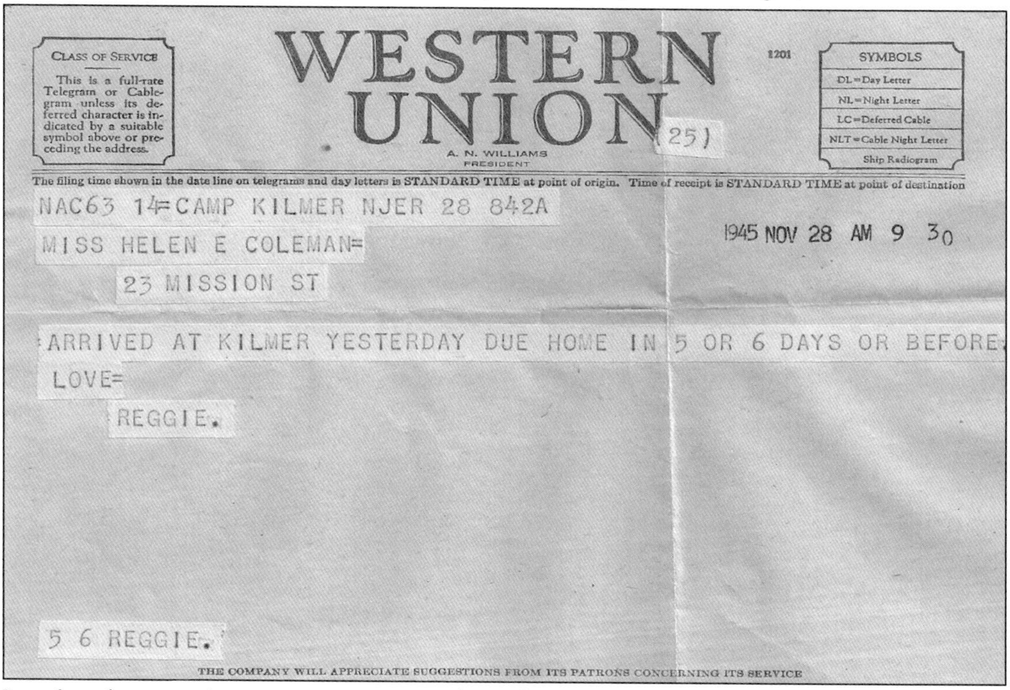

CLASS OF SERVICE
This is a full-rate Telegram or Cablegram unless its deferred character is indicated by a suitable symbol above or preceding the address.

WESTERN UNION (25)
A. N. WILLIAMS PRESIDENT

1201

SYMBOLS
DL=Day Letter
NL=Night Letter
LC=Deferred Cable
NLT=Cable Night Letter
Ship Radiogram

The filing time shown in the date line on telegrams and day letters is STANDARD TIME at point of origin. Time of receipt is STANDARD TIME at point of destination

NAC63 14=CAMP KILMER NJER 28 842A

1945 NOV 28 AM 9 30

MISS HELEN E COLEMAN=

23 MISSION ST

ARRIVED AT KILMER YESTERDAY DUE HOME IN 5 OR 6 DAYS OR BEFORE

LOVE=

REGGIE.

5 6 REGGIE.

THE COMPANY WILL APPRECIATE SUGGESTIONS FROM ITS PATRONS CONCERNING ITS SERVICE

Local and national news came to town through the telegraph, which was manned by the stationmaster. This made the station a popular social spot. Local boys would hang out at the depot hoping to earn a dime by delivering a telegram. This telegram was from Reggie Stewart in November 1945. For 75 years, all mail came through the railroad station in Purcellville. For much of that time, packages were delivered at the station through a railway freight service. (Courtesy of Reginald Simms.)

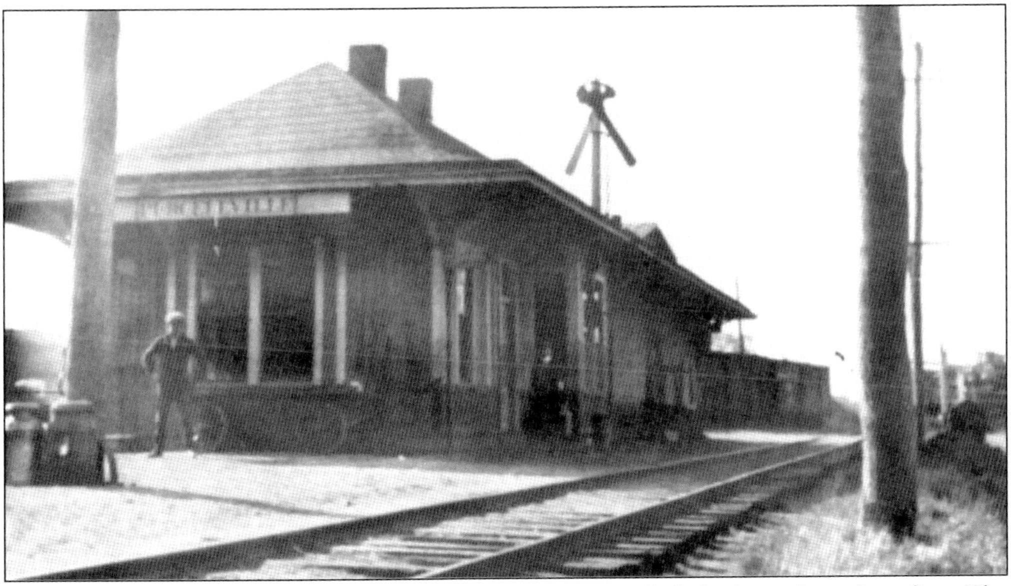

By the turn of the century, Purcellville was a major mercantile hub along the railway line. The center of business shifted from Purcell's Store, which was on Main Street, to the railroad station. On any given morning, the station would be crowded with farm wagons awaiting the milk train, as shown in this 1923 postcard. (Courtesy of Paul McCray.)

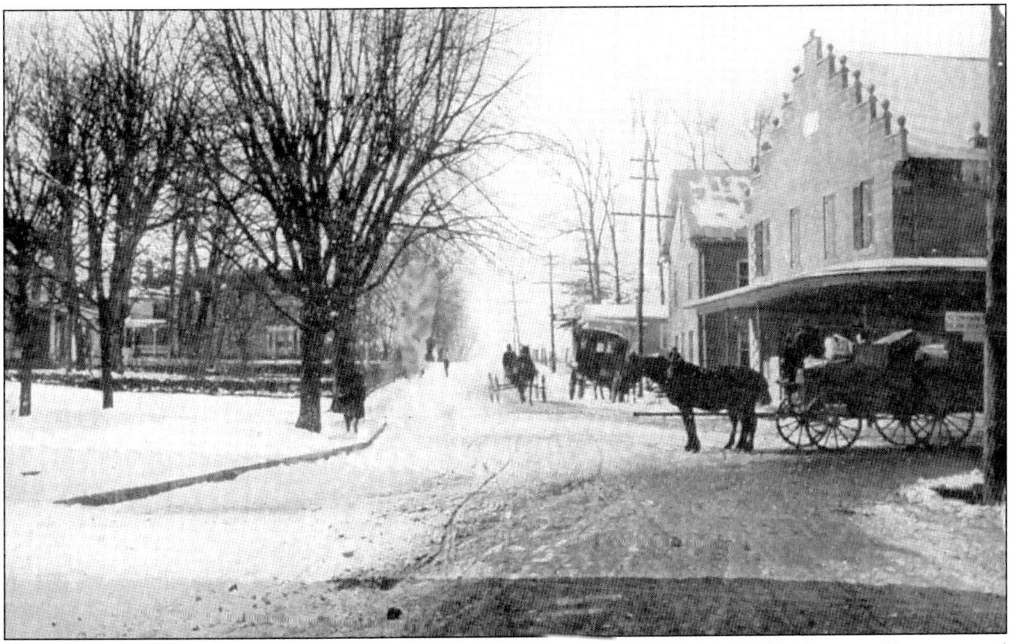

Even though most townspeople chose the train service, there were still plenty of horses and buggies throughout the area in the early 1900s. In this 1915 photograph, a horse leaves the train station area where presumably goods from the city were picked up. The trip by train was several hours from Purcellville to Rosslyn. (Courtesy of Thomas Priscilla.)

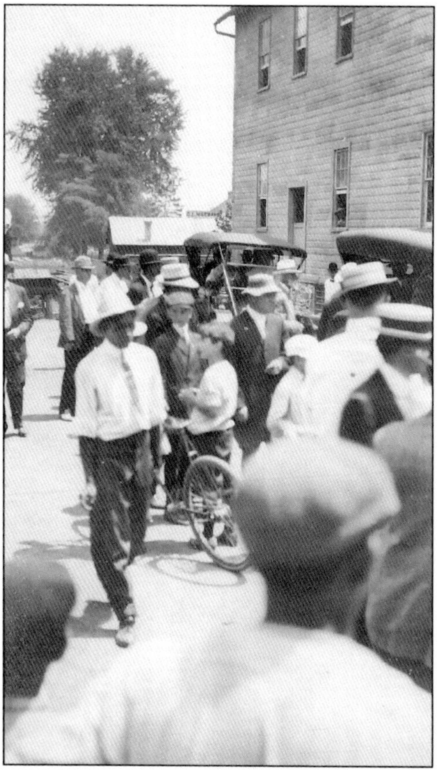

The train station was a hotbed of activity during most of the 19th and 20th centuries. Many of Purcellville's first businesses couldn't have existed without the railroad. The train transported their products and raw materials, including items for sale at Nichols Hardware, materials for the nearby cinder-block plant, and lumber for the local lumberyard. Farmers shipped livestock and produce, and Cornwell's slaughterhouse, which was just across the tracks from the station, transported processed meats. (Courtesy of Jane Hirst Bogle.)

Round Oak Farm and many other dairy farms surrounding Purcellville were in full operation. Farmers were bringing their products to the depot, and their produce would be sent to Alexandria. Farming diversified when corn replaced wheat as the main crop. The dairy and beef industries gained importance as well. Round Oak Farm is now a fox-hunting reserve. (Courtesy of Donnie and Lindsay Hope.)

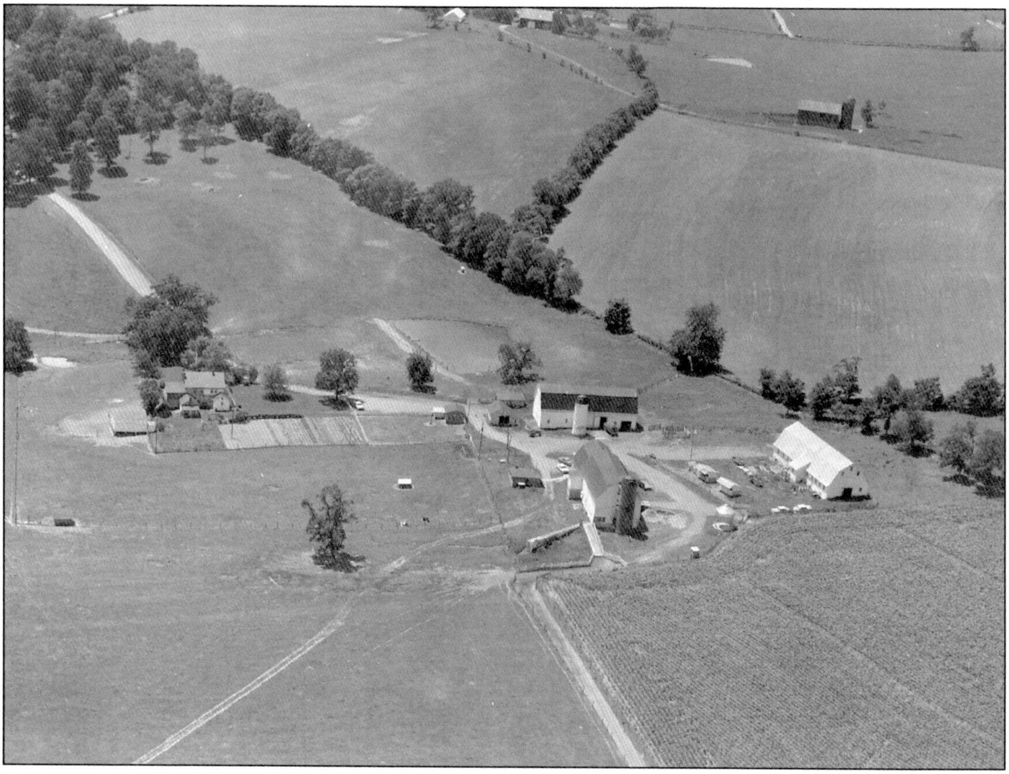

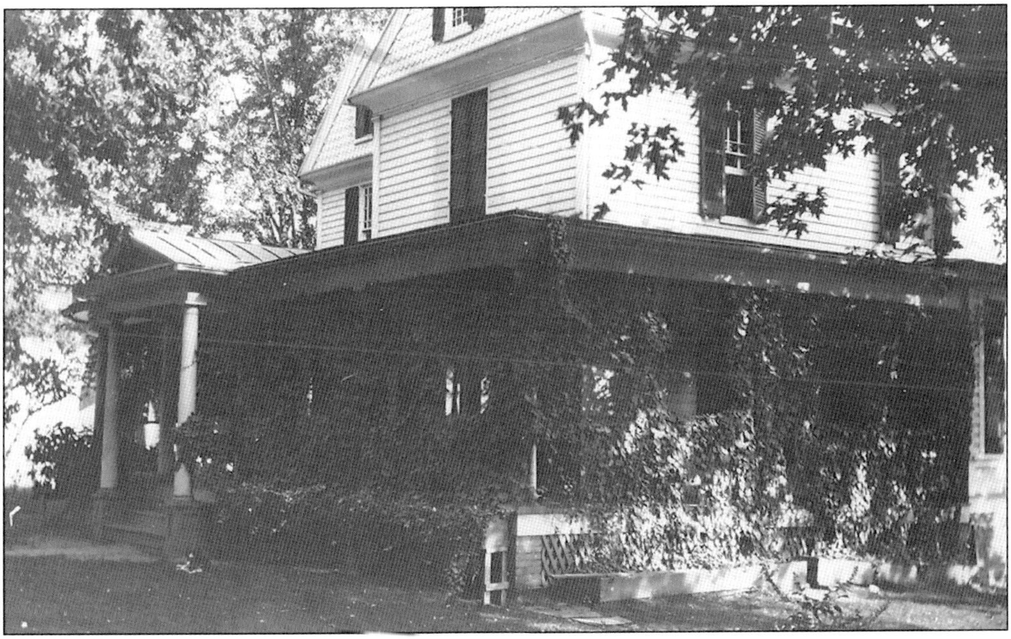

J.T. Hirst built his home during the boomtown era on Main Street, when the trains were first coming to town, bringing Purcellville great prosperity. Most of the town's stately residential section along the Great Road was built during this time. The trains brought many kinds of goods to Purcellville, including new types of food, materials for clothes, and furniture. (Courtesy of Jane Hirst Bogle.)

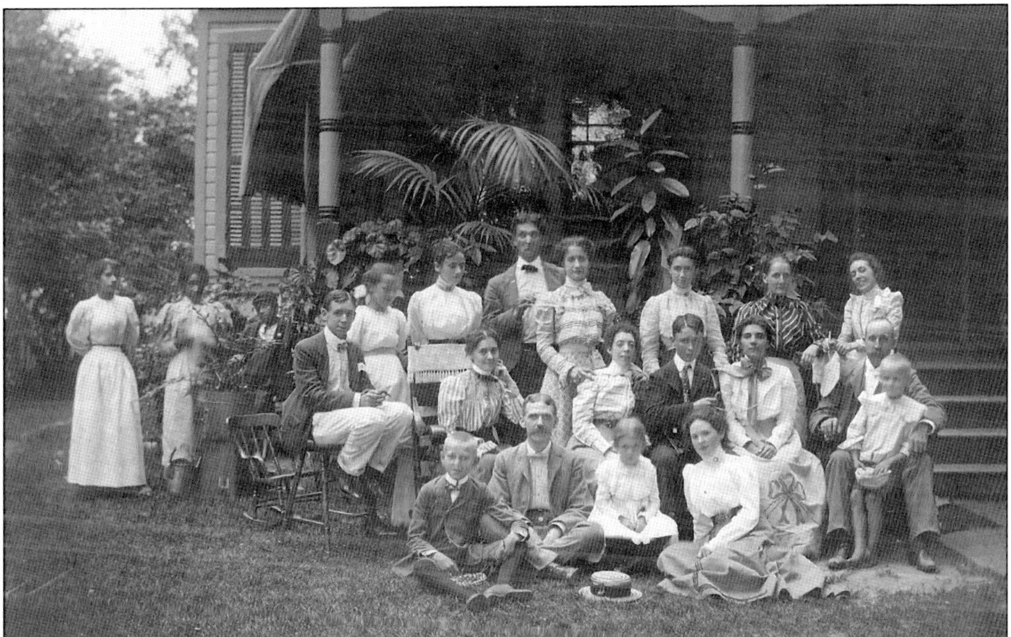

Building materials for the new Victorian homes arrived by the freight trains. Specialty foods also came by the train, such as seafood. Oysters became a local favorite. Discarded oyster shells were so plentiful that they were used as gravel around town. (Courtesy of Jane Hirst Bogle.)

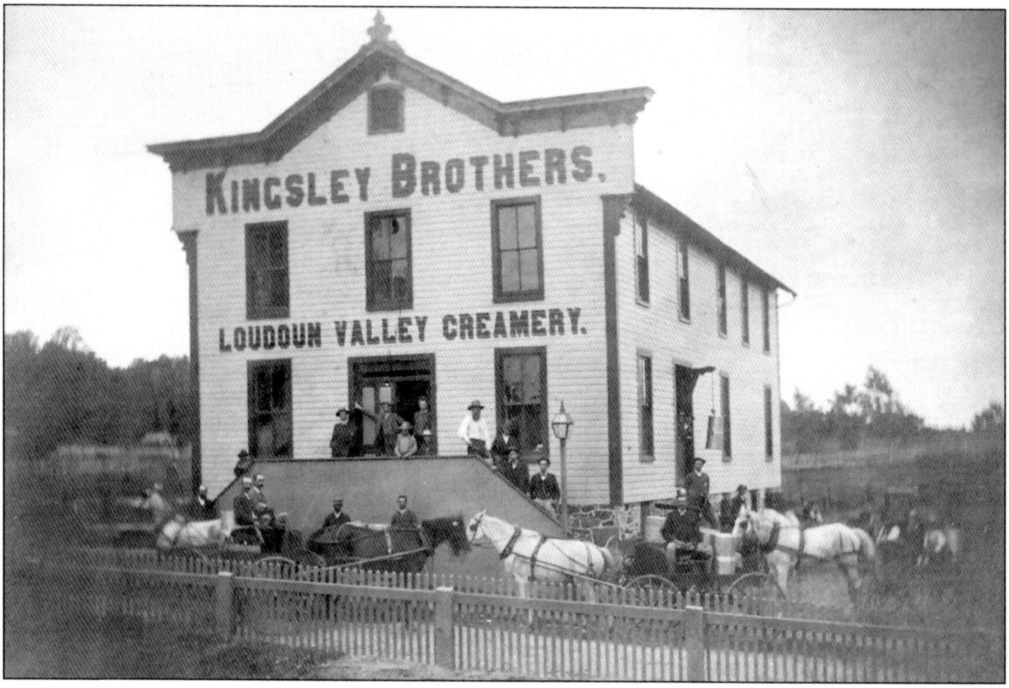

This 1890 photograph shows the Kingsley Brothers Creamery in Hamilton. It mostly produced butter, although sweet cream and milk could be supplied on order. In the 1880s, the Loudoun Valley Creamery expanded with other branches in nearby towns. (Courtesy of Thomas Balch Library.)

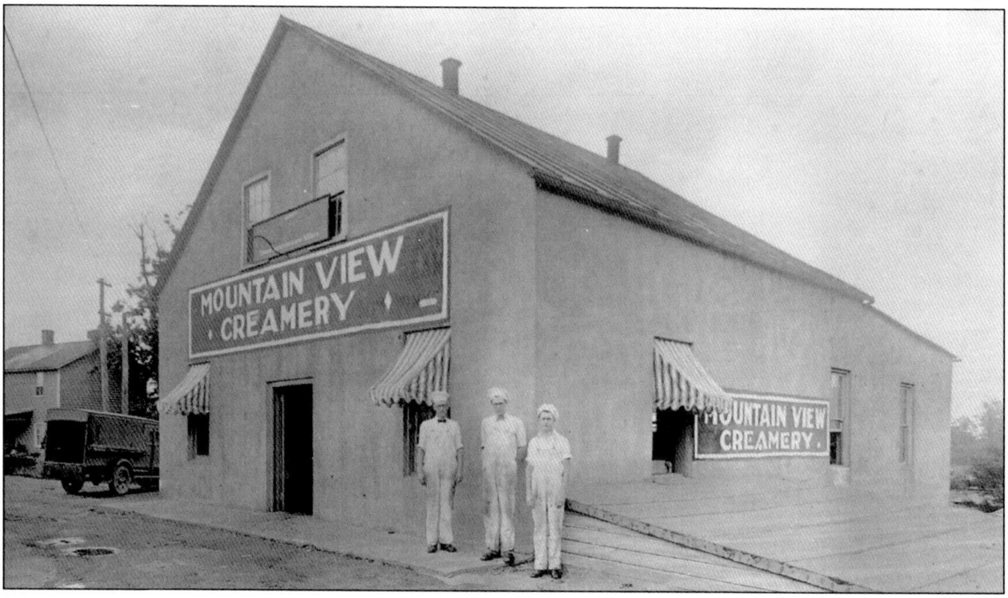

Mountain View Creamery was conveniently located near the Washington & Old Dominion (W&OD) railway line. Rail service helped the growth of dairy farms that were located near the railroad. As cities passed ordinances against keeping milk cows within city limits, the demand for outside milk gave rise to the Loudoun dairy industry. In this 1932 photograph, creamery employees Linden McDaniel, Milton McDaniel, and Johnnie Hall come out for a breath of fresh air. (Courtesy of Thomas Balch Library.)

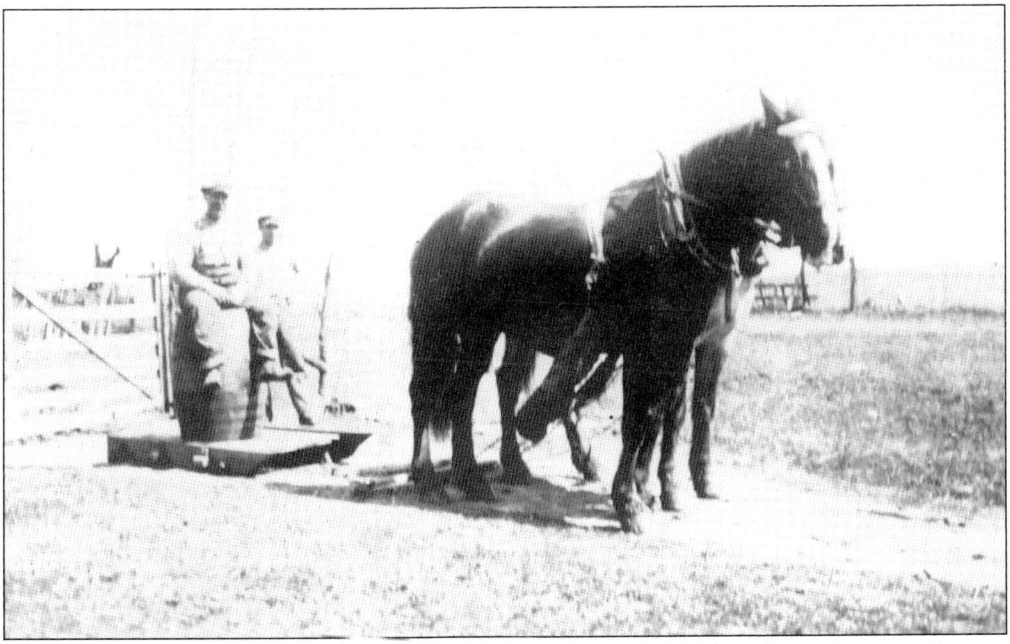

For farmers, the railroad was a fulfilled promise. While continuing to rely on horse-drawn machinery, they now had trains to ship their products to the market east of Purcellville. Perishable products, such as milk, were shipped in just a few hours. (Courtesy of Thomas Balch Library.)

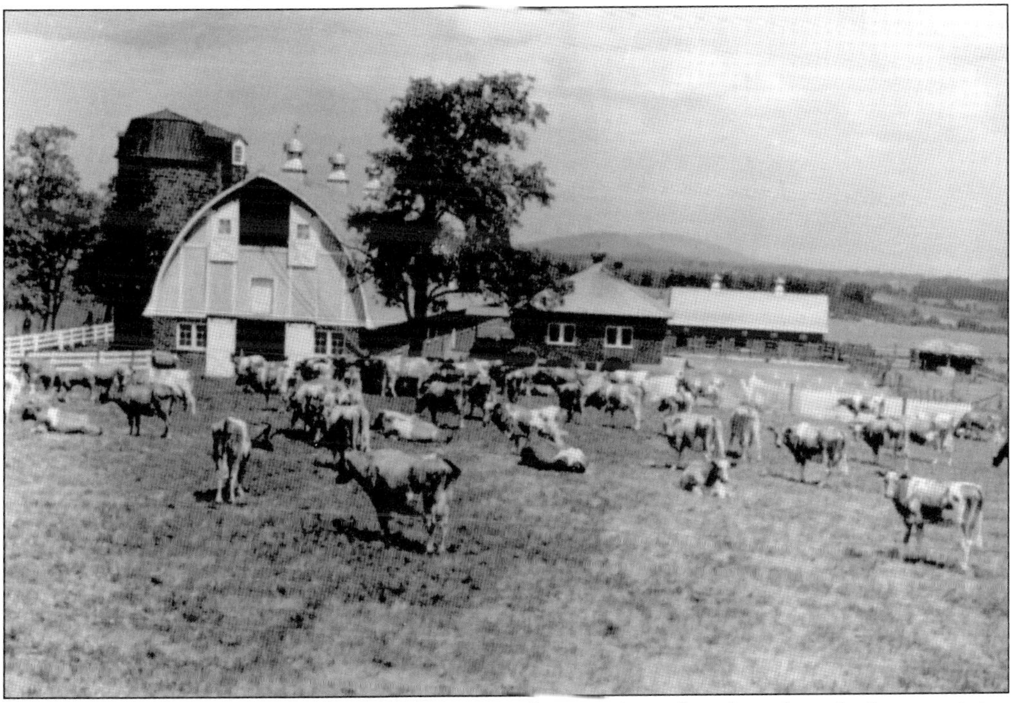

Farmers relied heavily on the trains for exporting their products, but they also relied on receiving products from elsewhere, such as grain for cattle or lime, fertilizer, and seeds. It made sense that the mills were built right next to the tracks. This 1930 photograph shows Black Oak Farm, which was southwest of town and one of Purcellville's many dairy farms. (Courtesy of Robert Lyon.)

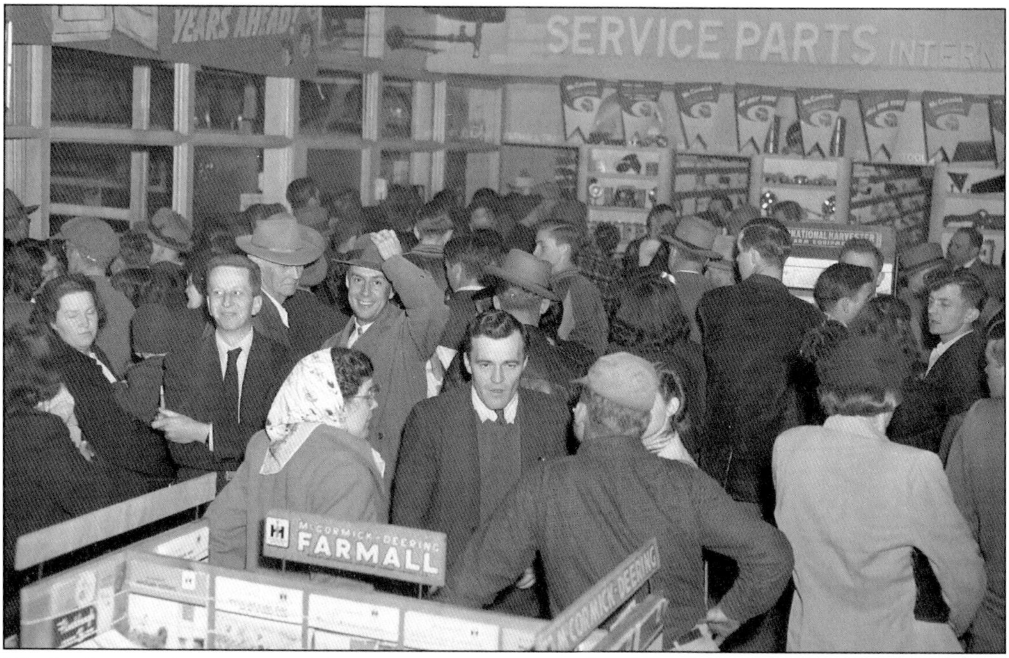

The businesses that supported farming grew exponentially as the farming industry became more profitable. Throughout the 20th century, Whitmore and Arnold prospered greatly as a farm machinery dealership. This photograph shows a group of customers at the shop's showroom counter in 1951. (Courtesy of Mary Whitmore.)

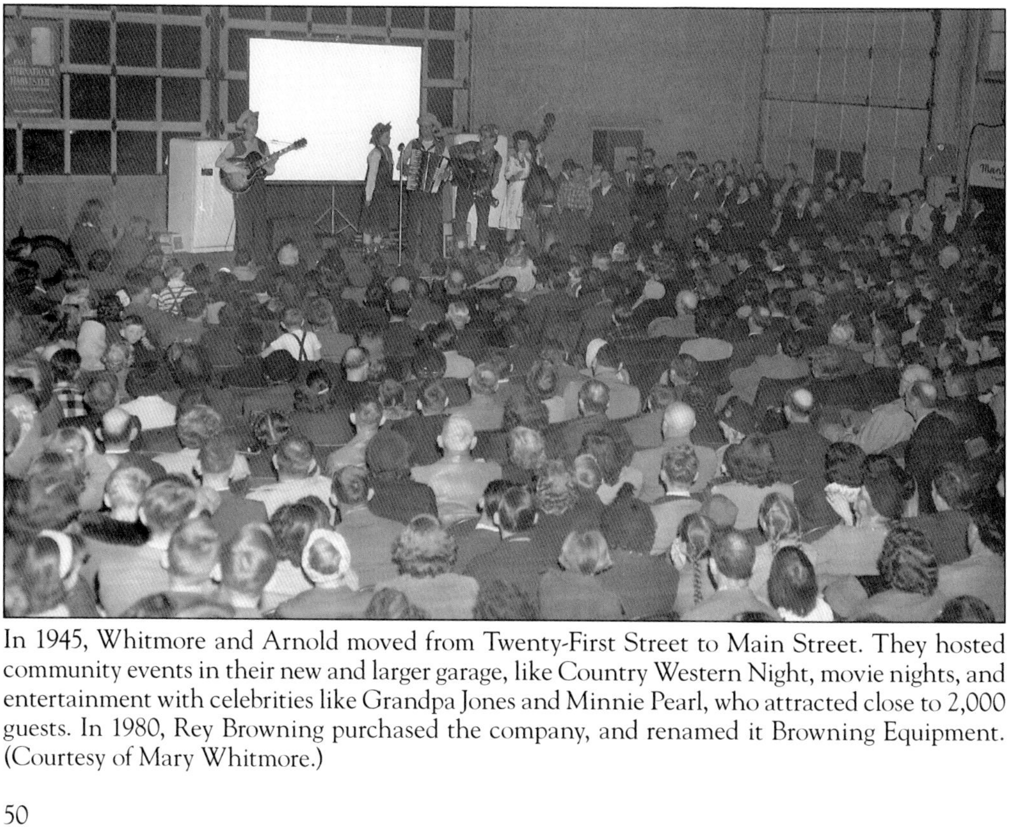

In 1945, Whitmore and Arnold moved from Twenty-First Street to Main Street. They hosted community events in their new and larger garage, like Country Western Night, movie nights, and entertainment with celebrities like Grandpa Jones and Minnie Pearl, who attracted close to 2,000 guests. In 1980, Rey Browning purchased the company, and renamed it Browning Equipment. (Courtesy of Mary Whitmore.)

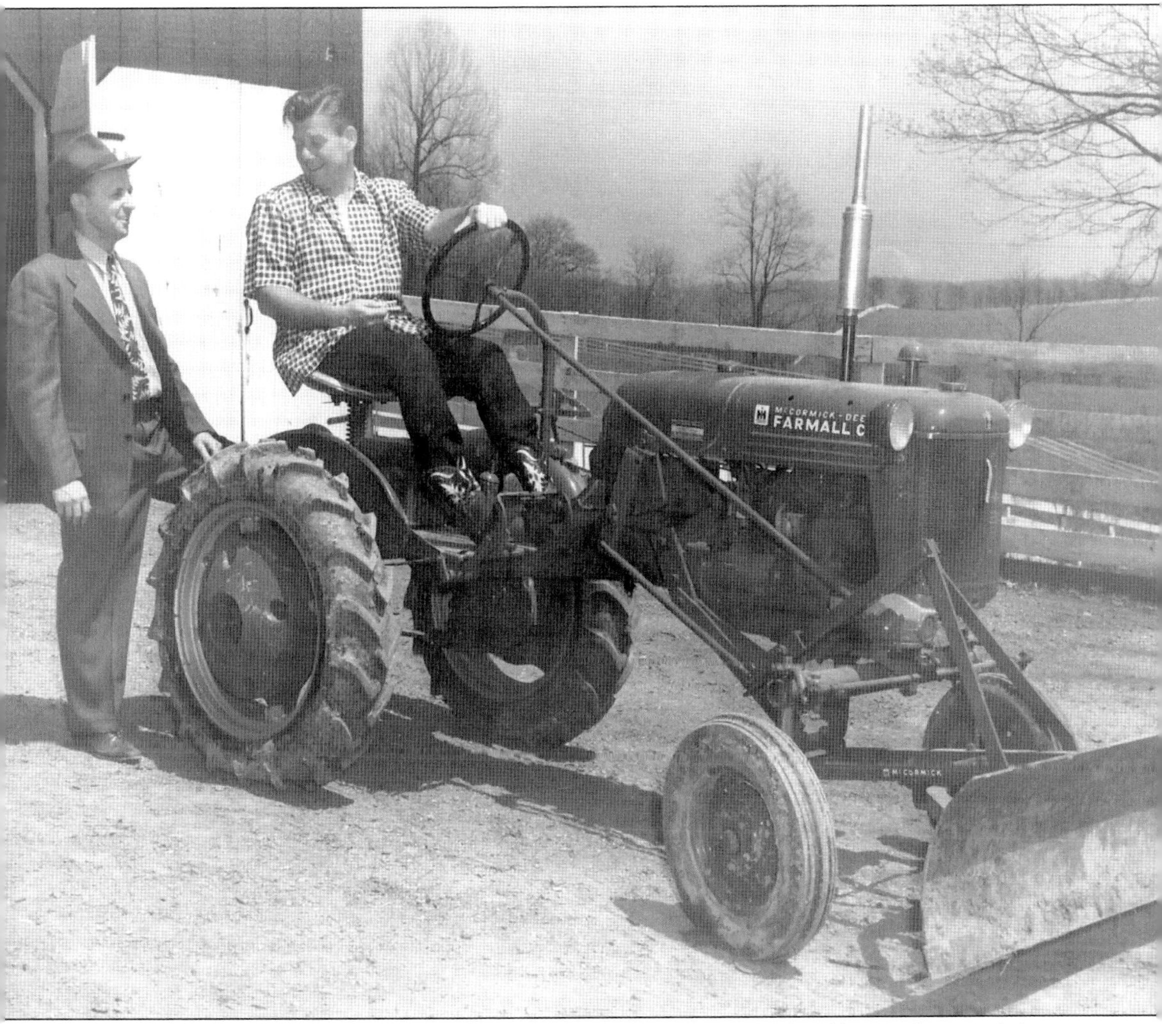

In the 1950s, music legend and radio host Arthur Godfrey was one of William Whitmore's best customers in Loudoun. Godrey was often seen on one of his tractors at his nearby farms, Meadow Hill and Beacon Hill. (Courtesy of Mary Whitmore.)

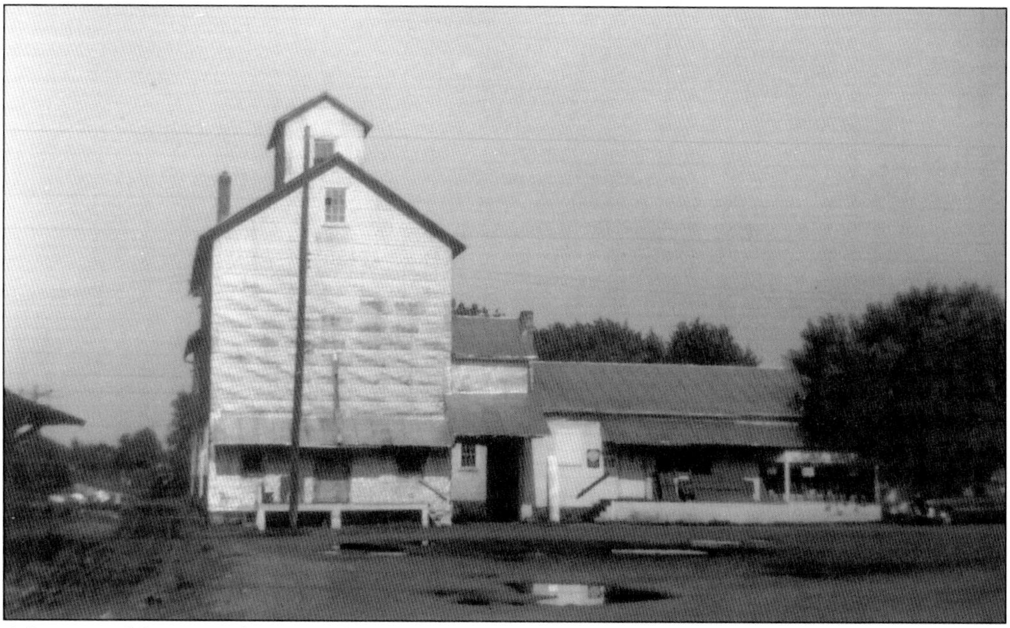

After several fires, Smith & Hirst built a mill in 1905 and covered the building with metal flashing. In 1921, the mill, which is now Magnolia's Restaurant, was sold to the Adams family, who would rename the business Loudoun Valley Milling. By the late 1930s, with the growing prominence of hybrid corn and orchard grass, they began to concentrate solely on the cleaning of seed. In 1943, the Adams family sold Loudoun Valley Milling to Wilkins and Rogers. (Courtesy of Northern Virginia Regional Park Authority.)

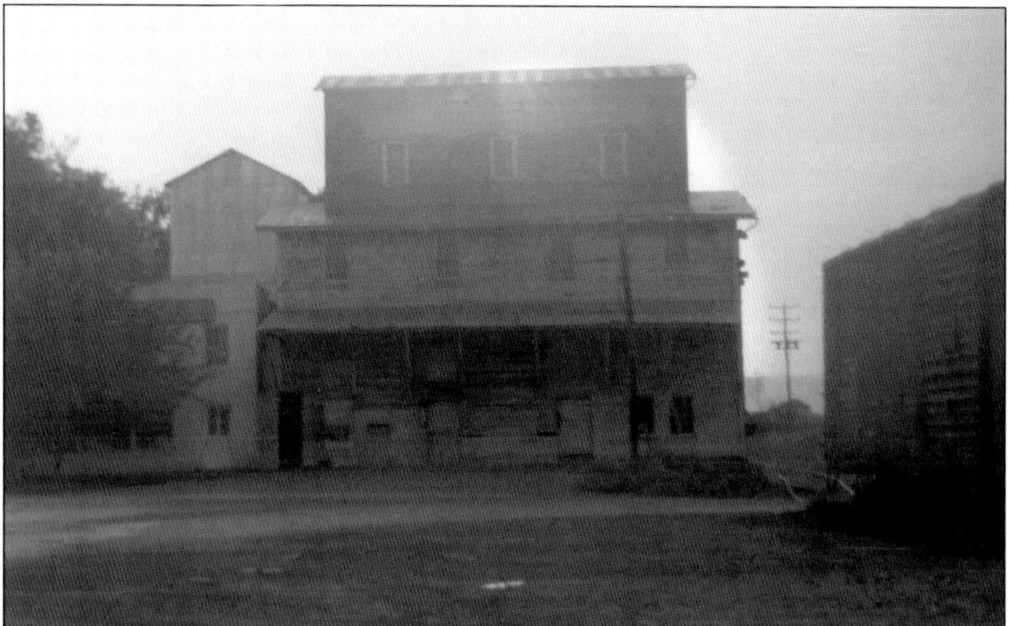

This photograph shows the seed-cleaning business Contee Adams Seed Company, which was still in operation in 1956. The mill bears the builder's name, Dillon, and the year built, 1874. (Courtesy of Paul McCray.)

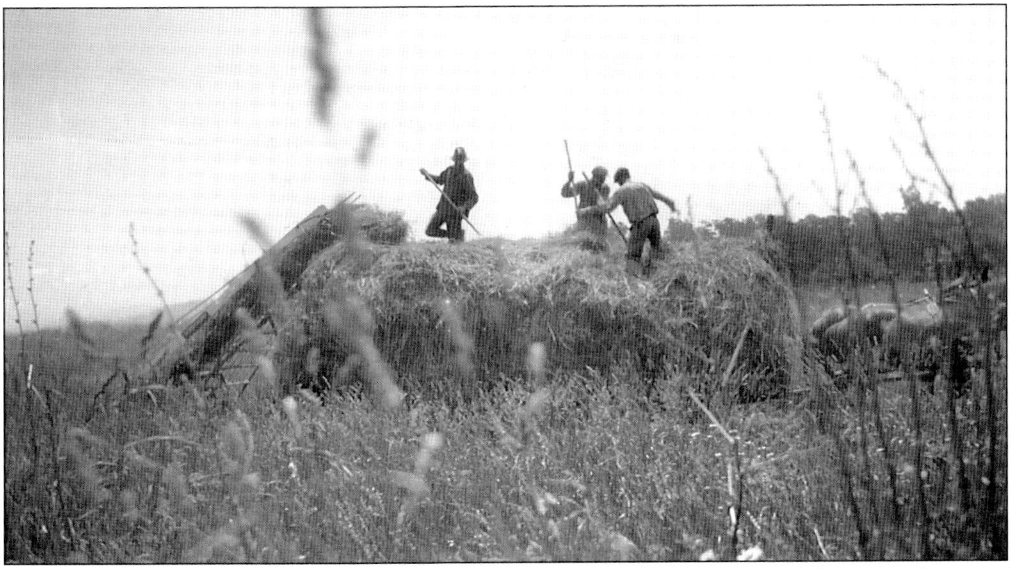

Orchard grass is a versatile and high-quality grass that was excellent feed for most classes of livestock. Virginia's production rose from 1.7 million pounds in 1940 to 2.7 million pounds in 1943. Loudoun produced 400,000 pounds of orchard grass in 1943. In this 1930 photograph, farmhands are haying in the fields at Black Oak Farm. (Courtesy of Robert Lyon.)

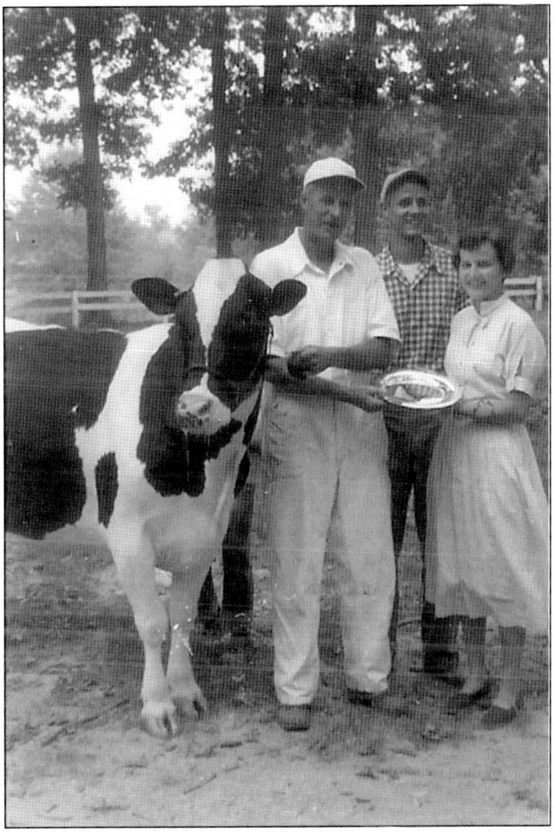

In 1955, Curtis "Slim" Cole (left) stands proudly with his winning Guernsey at Purcellville's dairy show with Mr. and Mrs. Kent Roberts. For much of the 20th century, Loudoun County retained its predominantly agrarian character. In 1945, Loudoun had 2,015 farms, and whole milk production increased by 1,200 percent since 1909. Today, Purcellville's Dogwood Farm, owned by the Potts family, is the last operating dairy farm in the county. (Courtesy of Henry Cole.)

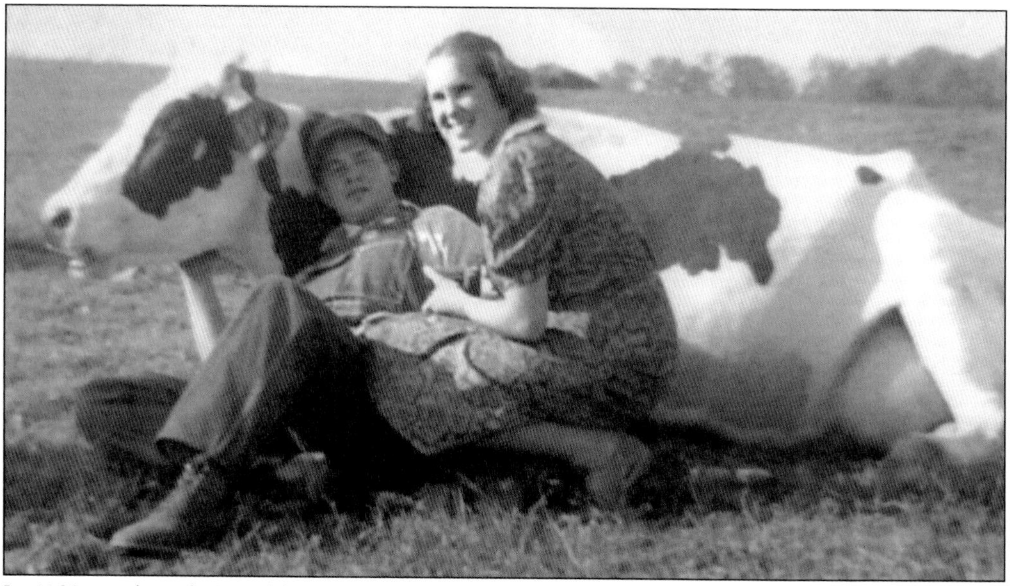

In 1939, newlyweds Ronald and Marjorie Hope posed with their Holstein Millie at their Round Oak Farm, which was southwest of Purcellville. Ronald and his father, Charles, established an outstanding herd. During this time, Millie produced a national record in milk production. Ronald's sharp eye and vast knowledge of pedigrees would come to fruition in the birth of Purcellville's famous bull, Round Oak Rag Apple Elevation, or "RORA Elevation" for short. (Courtesy of Donnie and Lindsay Hope.)

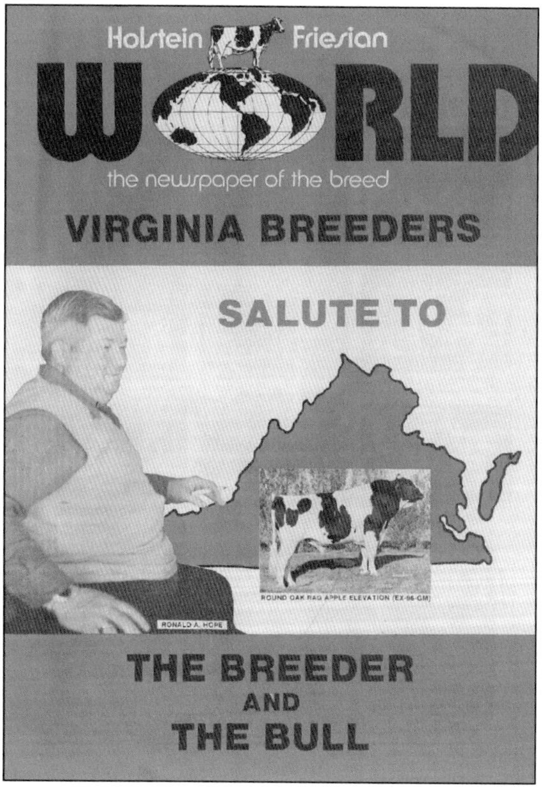

RORA Elevation produced so many offspring, an estimated 8.8 million, through artificial insemination and modern technology, that just about every American has consumed some of the bull's product. The Holstein International Association voted him the "Bull of the Century," comparing him to Secretariat in the horse industry. Ronald Hope and his prized bull were featured on the front page of this issue of *Holstein Friesian World* in April 1978. (Courtesy of Donnie and Lindsay Hope.)

George Simms served in World War II when orchard grass was not just the choice feed for the livestock, but also the perfect choice for munitions experts. With the war in full swing in the 1940s, experts were looking for a stable packing material to transport ammunition and small arms. Loudoun County was a top producer of the dense orchard-grass seed, which was safer than the wood chips that had a tendency to shift, sometimes causing the shells or arms to rub against the packing crate. (Courtesy of Reginald Simms.)

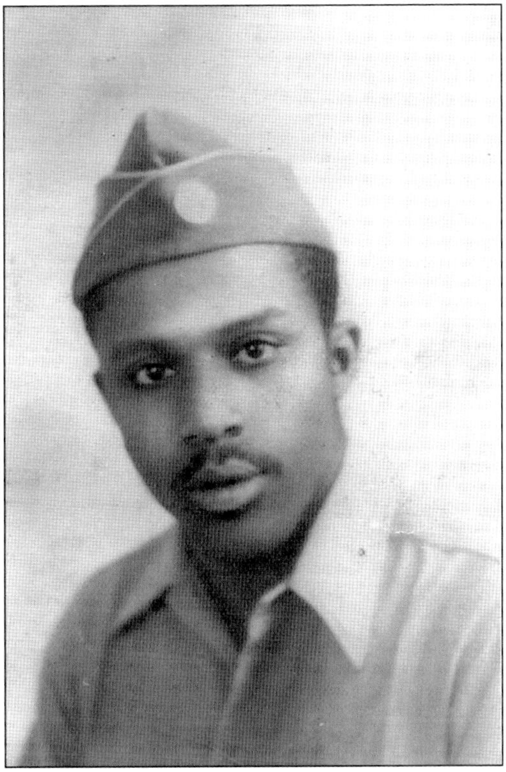

This 1931 photograph was presumably taken from the top of the new water tower. The lumberyard, mills, businesses, and farms along this stretch were conveniently located by the railroad tracks, and all of them took advantage of the train service. (Courtesy of Purcellville Preservation Association.)

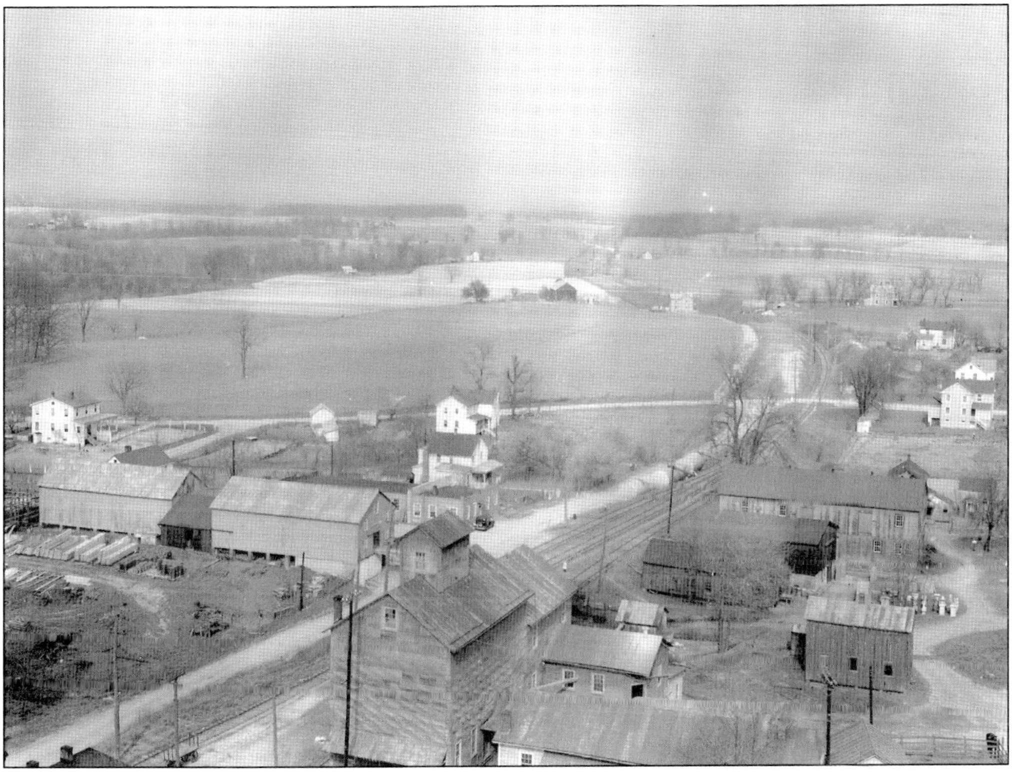

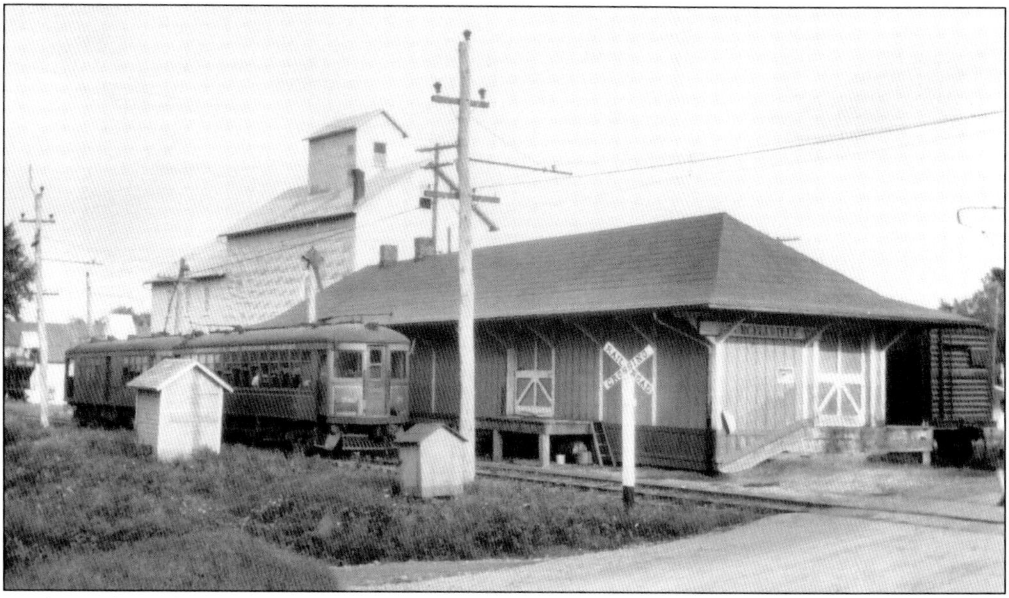

In the early 20th century, the valley at the foot of the Blue Ridge was the perfect place for Washingtonians who looked for a respite from the heat and congestion of the city. Passengers make their way west through Purcellville in this 1942 photograph. (Courtesy of Northern Virginia Regional Park Authority.)

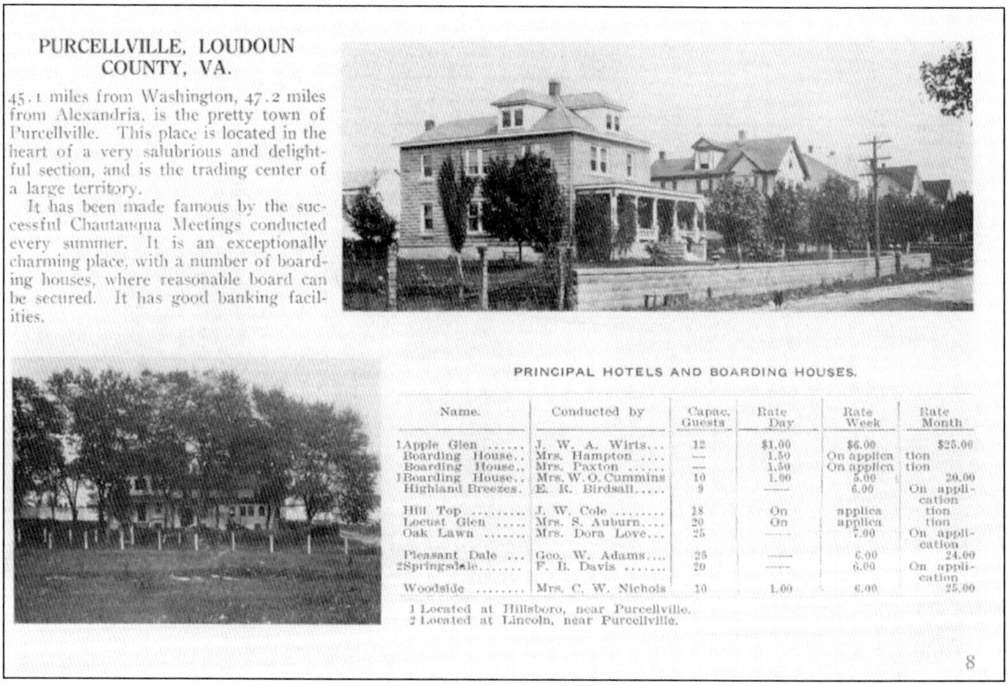

PURCELLVILLE, LOUDOUN COUNTY, VA.

45.1 miles from Washington, 47.2 miles from Alexandria, is the pretty town of Purcellville. This place is located in the heart of a very salubrious and delightful section, and is the trading center of a large territory.

It has been made famous by the successful Chautauqua Meetings conducted every summer. It is an exceptionally charming place, with a number of boarding houses, where reasonable board can be secured. It has good banking facilities.

PRINCIPAL HOTELS AND BOARDING HOUSES.

Name.	Conducted by	Capac. Guests	Rate Day	Rate Week	Rate Month
1Apple Glen	J. W. A. Wirts...	12	$1.00	$6.00	$25.00
Boarding House..	Mrs. Hampton	—	1.50	On applica	tion
Boarding House..	Mrs. Paxton	—	1.50	On applica	tion
1Boarding House..	Mrs. W. O. Cummins	10	1.00	5.00	20.00
Highland Breezes.	E. R. Birdsall.....	9	——	6.00	On application
Hill Top	J. W. Cole	18	On	applica	tion
Locust Glen	Mrs. S. Auburn....	20	On	applica	tion
Oak Lawn	Mrs. Dora Love...	25	——	7.00	On application
Pleasant Dale ...	Geo. W. Adams....	25	——	6.00	24.00
2Springsdale......	F. B. Davis	20	——	6.00	On application
Woodside	Mrs. C. W. Nichols	10	1.00	6.00	25.00

1 Located at Hillsboro, near Purcellville.
2 Located at Lincoln, near Purcellville.

8

Homes along the western route of the railroad opened as inns during the summer because of their proximity to the mountains. Nearly a dozen inns and boarding houses were available in Purcellville during the time of this advertising pamphlet, which was published by the railroad in 1916. (Courtesy of Paul McCray.)

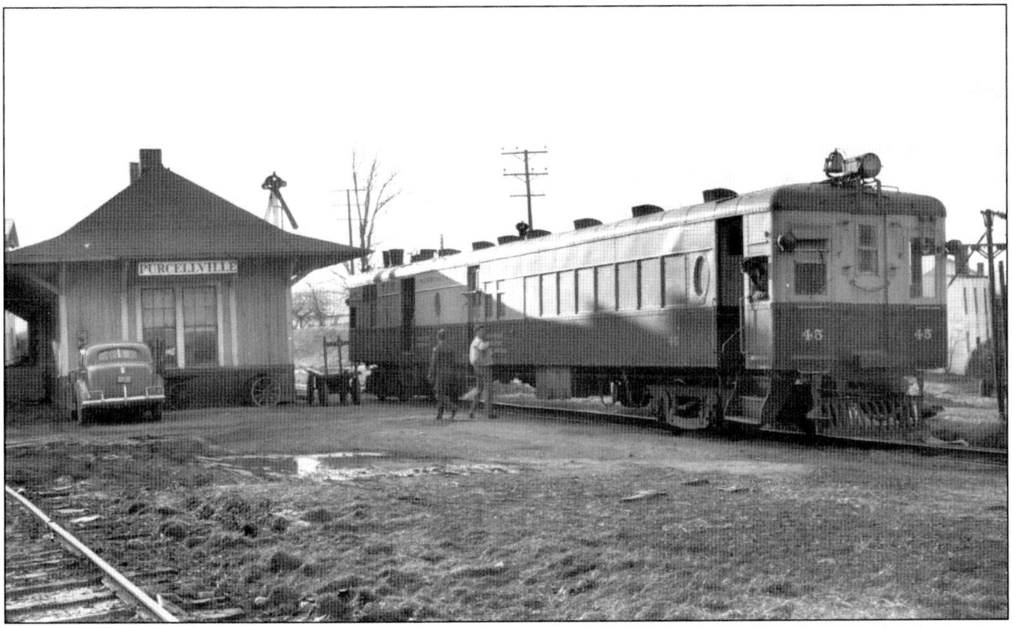

The rail terminus remained at Round Hill until 1900, when the line was extended a few more miles to Bluemont. Taken in 1951, this photograph shows the W&OD's diesel-electric motorcar no. 45, with its load of mail and passengers headed east to Rosslyn Station. (Courtesy of Northern Virginia Regional Park Authority.)

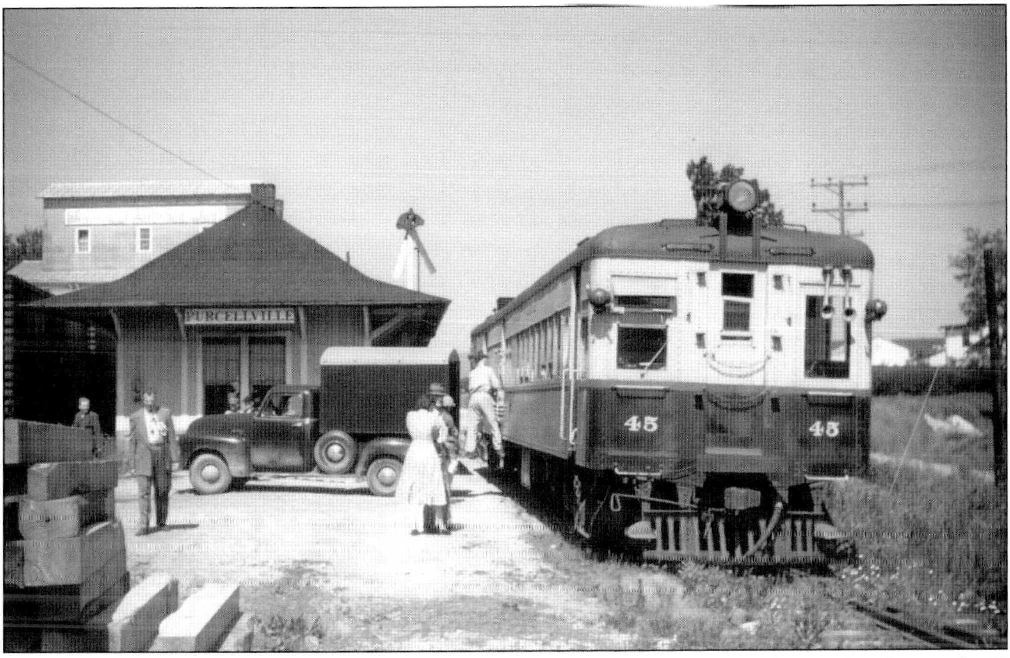

This 1951 photograph shows the mail truck backing up to the train as the mail is dropped off. Passenger service had dwindled drastically as automobiles and roadways improved. The final straw was when the W&OD lost its contract with the postal service, which was the only thing that kept the passenger service from losing money. (Courtesy of Northern Virginia Regional Park Authority.)

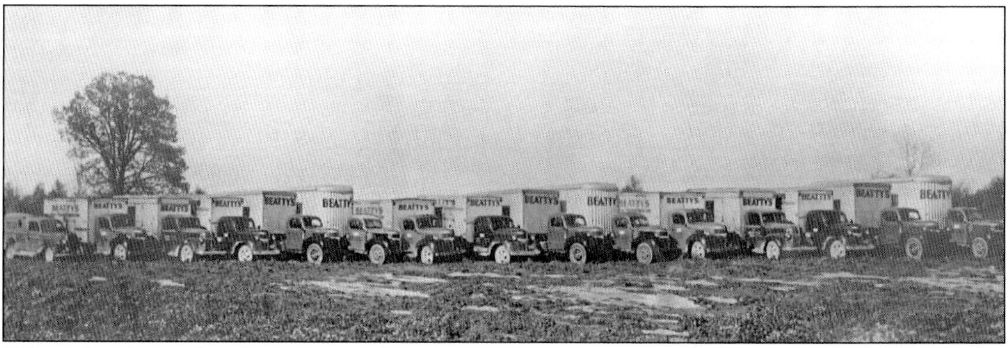

When the Beatty family first started hauling milk, the double-decker straight truck was loaded with 10-gallon milk cans, which were stamped with the initials of the farm and not refrigerated. In 1952, when tanker trucks started to be used, canned milk became nonexistent. Foley Rust bought the business from the Beatty family in 1940, and it remains in the Rust family today. As the main hauler of milk for Loudoun's dairymen, Loudoun Transport was once one of the county's biggest businesses. (Courtesy of Donnie and Lindsay Hope.)

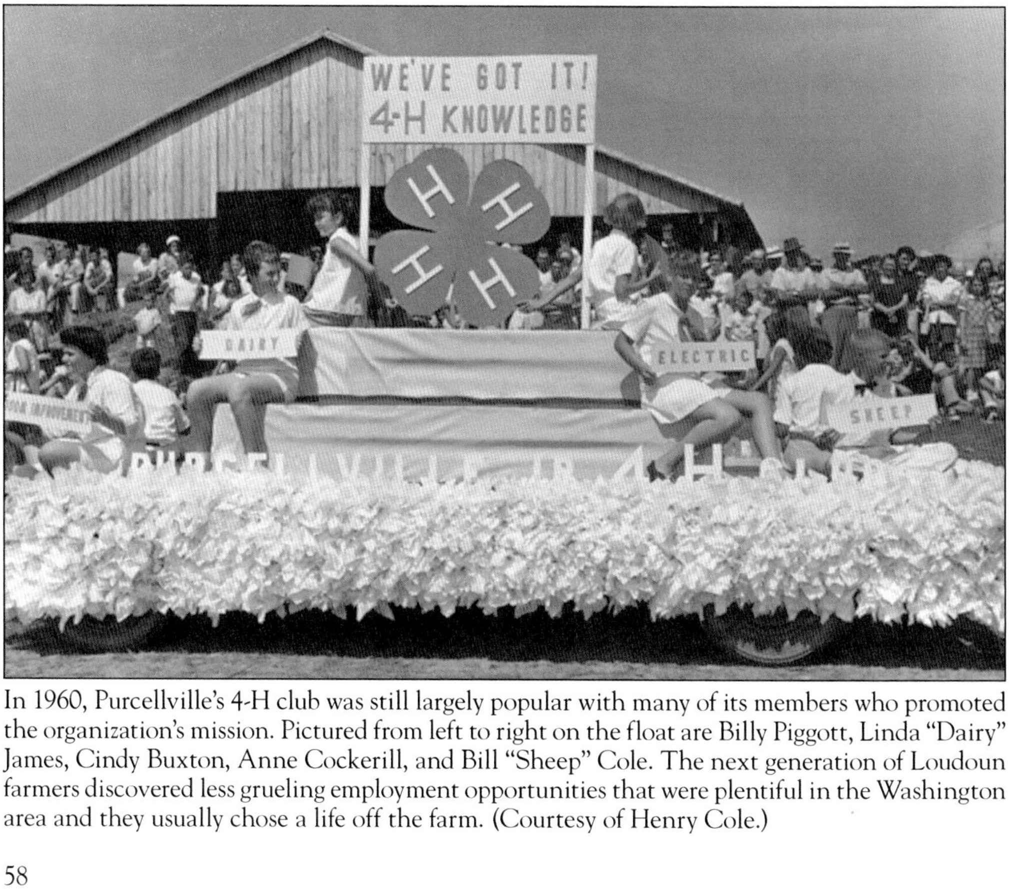

In 1960, Purcellville's 4-H club was still largely popular with many of its members who promoted the organization's mission. Pictured from left to right on the float are Billy Piggott, Linda "Dairy" James, Cindy Buxton, Anne Cockerill, and Bill "Sheep" Cole. The next generation of Loudoun farmers discovered less grueling employment opportunities that were plentiful in the Washington area and they usually chose a life off the farm. (Courtesy of Henry Cole.)

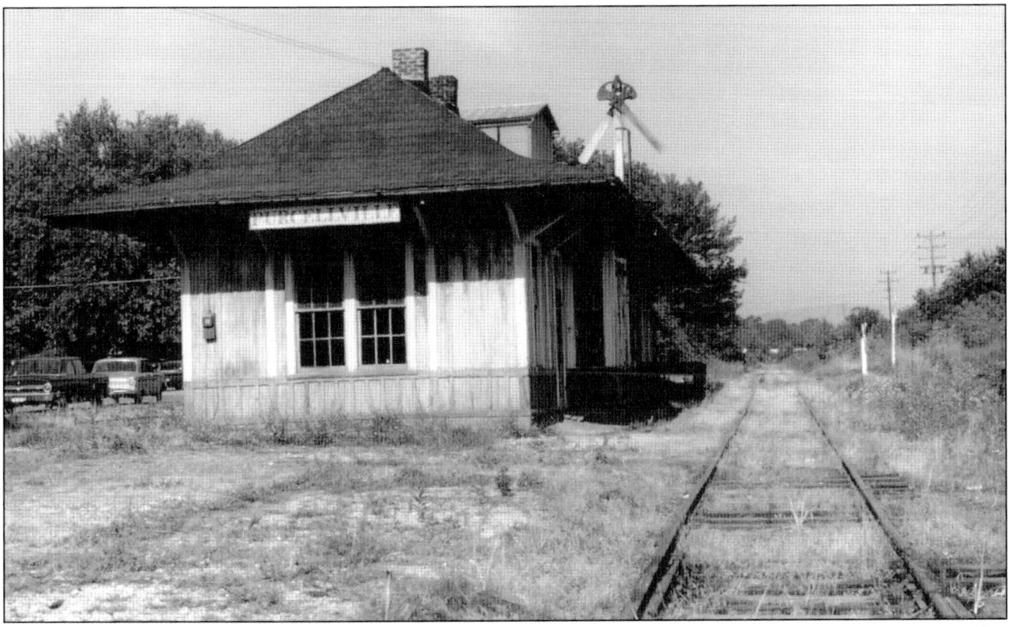

By 1984, the train station had lost its luster and was no longer a hotbed of activity. Over the years, travel by train waned. In 1968, users, local politicians, and railroad fans fought their way through the largest abandonment case heard by the Interstate Commerce Commission. (Courtesy of Northern Virginia Regional Park Authority.)

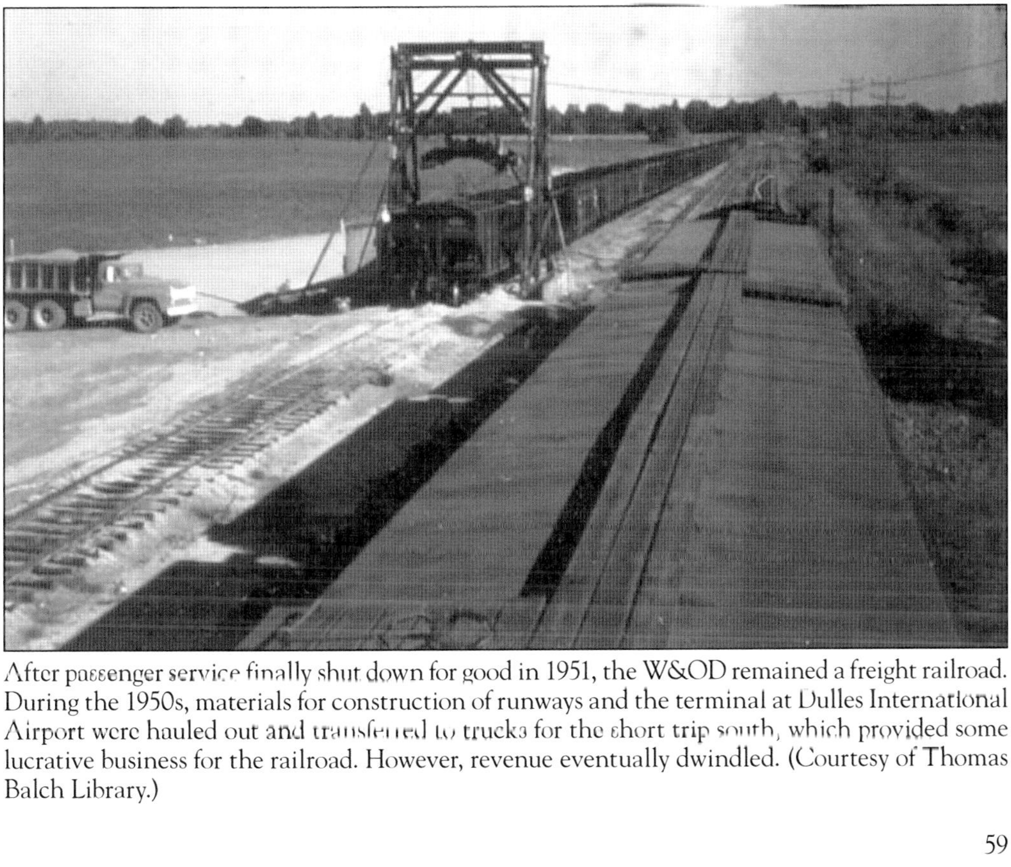

After passenger service finally shut down for good in 1951, the W&OD remained a freight railroad. During the 1950s, materials for construction of runways and the terminal at Dulles International Airport were hauled out and transferred to trucks for the short trip south, which provided some lucrative business for the railroad. However, revenue eventually dwindled. (Courtesy of Thomas Balch Library.)

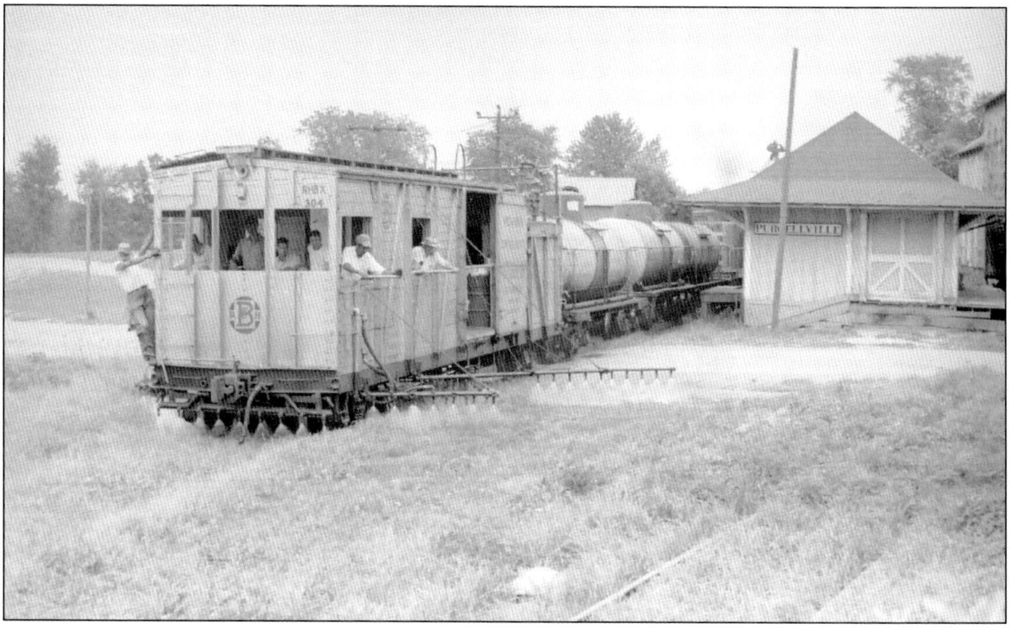

By 1958, activity at the Purcellville Station had slowed down when this train came through, spraying weed control on the tracks. The owners were beginning to pursue abandonment because the railroad was losing money and the line included valuable real estate. Ten years later, after a drawn out legal battle with a number of commercial and industrial users of the railroad, including many in Purcellville, an Interstate Commerce Commission judge approved the entire shutdown of W&OD. (Courtesy of Northern Virginia Regional Park Authority.)

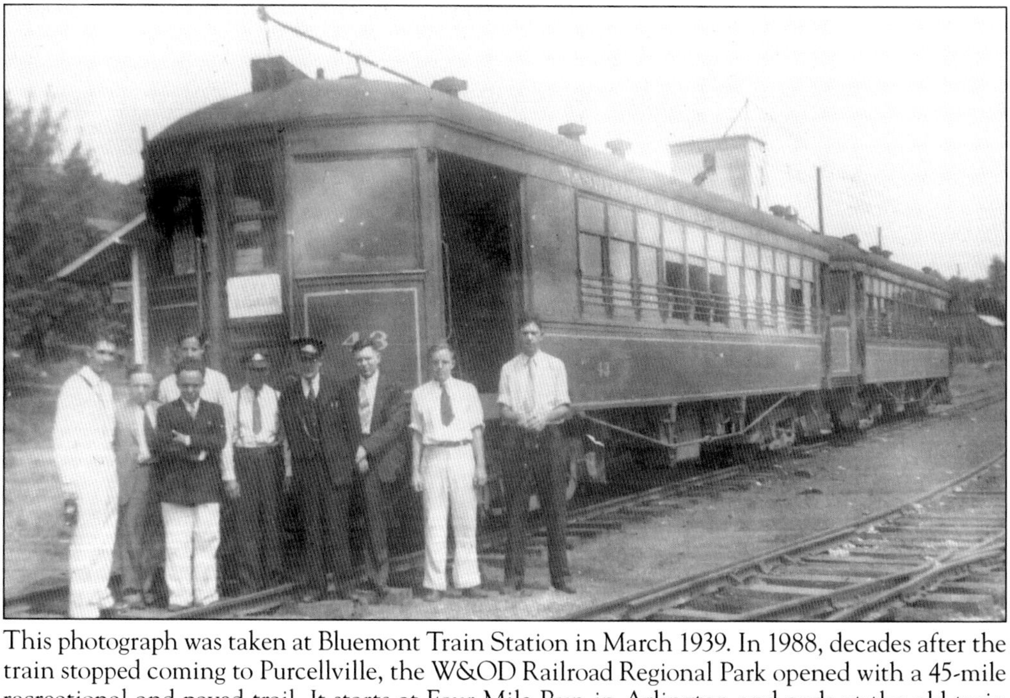

This photograph was taken at Bluemont Train Station in March 1939. In 1988, decades after the train stopped coming to Purcellville, the W&OD Railroad Regional Park opened with a 45-mile recreational and paved trail. It starts at Four Mile Run in Arlington and ends at the old train station in Purcellville. (Courtesy of Electric Railway Association/Railfan Organization.)

Four

At Home

Because most of the action in town took place at the train station, it makes sense that most residences and farms were built nearby. After the war, Loudoun County was a first-class farming community, ranking near the top of the entire Eastern Seaboard. Townspeople were looking forward to many decades as a peaceful, quiet model for country living. The forces for change, however, were already in place by the 20th century, which converted the scene of a bucolic lifestyle into suburbia.

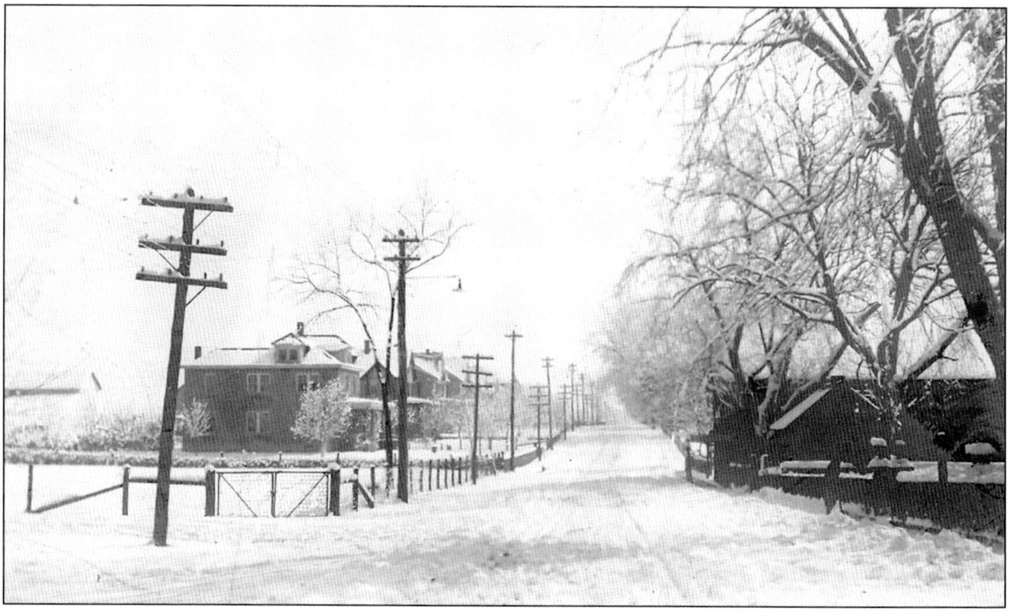

Main Street was home to most of Purcellville's residents. Even the farms were just down the way and on the outskirts of town, which allowed farmers to get their goods to the nearby train station for shipment. J.B. Hackley's family lived on Main Street, and their home (left) was built with formed concrete blocks from the Purcellville Foundry. The company also sold plows, stoves, farm bells, and sash weights. Cummings and Sons Livery Stable was located across from the Hackley home. This photograph was taken well after 1886, when Purcellville's first phone service was operating. (Courtesy of Jane Hirst Bogle.)

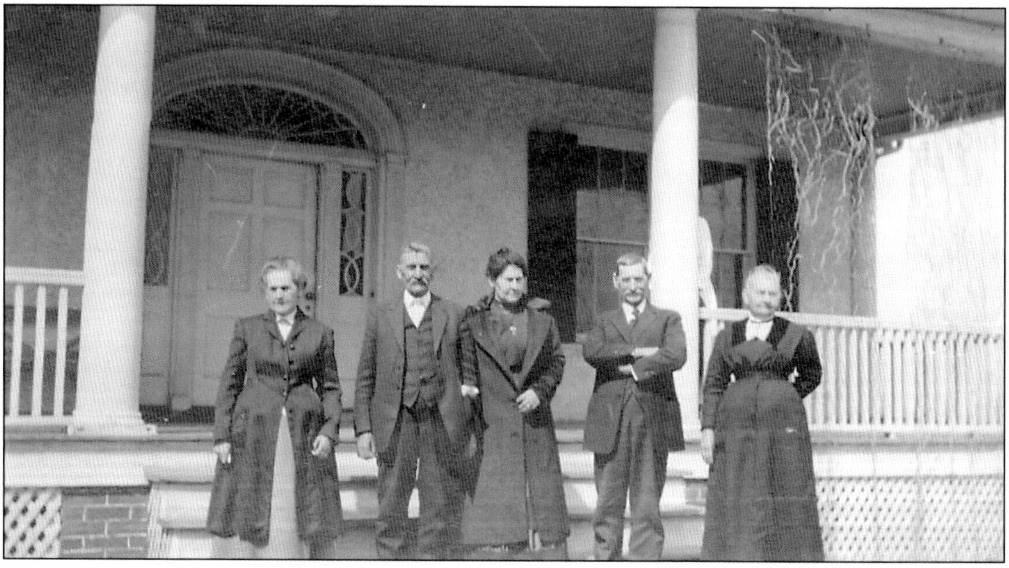

In this 1910 photograph, friends and family gather on the porch of Sue Gregg's home on Main Street. Pictured from left to right are Sarah D. Grubb, Daniel J. Gregg, Luola L. Dillion, Albert Gregg, and Tammie Dillion. The house sits in its original location, now surrounded by the Blue Ridge Shopping Center. (Courtesy of Beverly Bowman Chiasson.)

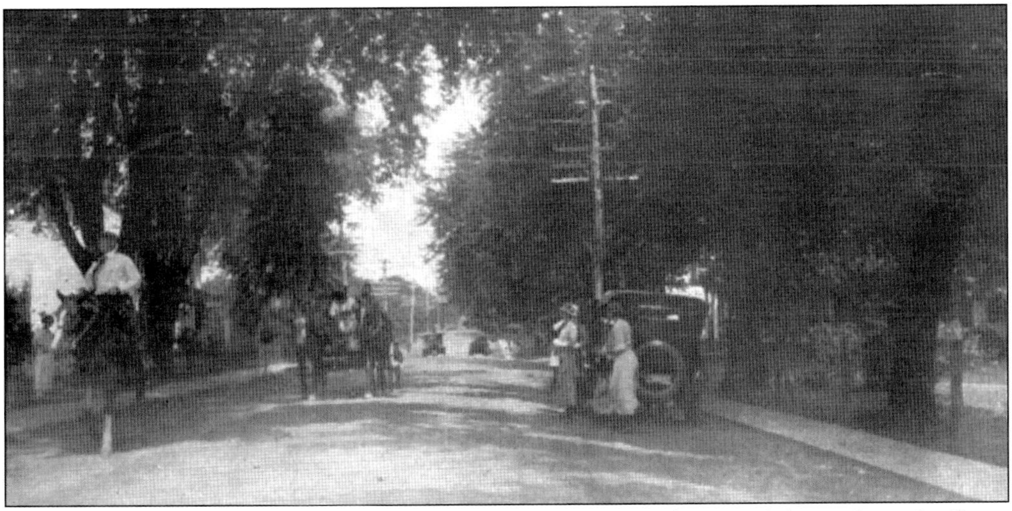

At the turn of the century, it was not uncommon for horses and automobiles to share the Great Road. Many people drove cars, but people also rode their horses around town. In 1904, the first automobile was seen in Purcellville. The town council voted to approve the first speed limit of 8 m.p.h. in 1910. (Courtesy of Elaine Virts.)

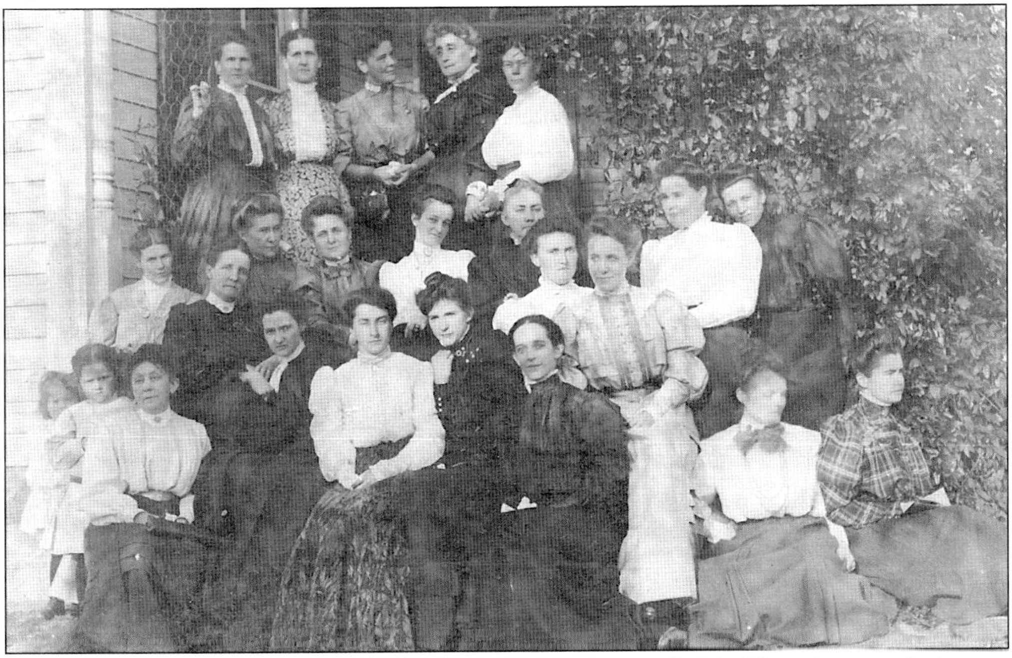

The Home Interest Club is Purcellville's longest running social club. This photograph shows a gathering of members and friends on the front porch of one its members in November 1906. Among those pictured are Mrs. Smith, Mrs. Charles Nichols, Mrs. Ed Nichols, Mrs. S.N. Brown, Mrs. Thomas Brown, Mrs. Dan Hughes, Mrs. J.T. Hirst, Mrs. Henry Janney, Mrs. L. Welsh, Mrs. Edgar Gregg, Mrs. W.P. Pancoast, Mrs. Henry Piggott, Mrs. Bently Gregg, Mrs. Hugh Piggott, Rachel Hoge, Miss Stables, Mrs. Charles Hoge, Mrs. Will Welsh, Mrs. Joe Shumate, Lula Pancoast, and Julia Hoge. The club has been composed of twenty four members since its inception in 1902, and it continues to meet to exchange recipes, discuss politics and prose, and share town happenings. (Courtesy of Jane Hirst Bogle.)

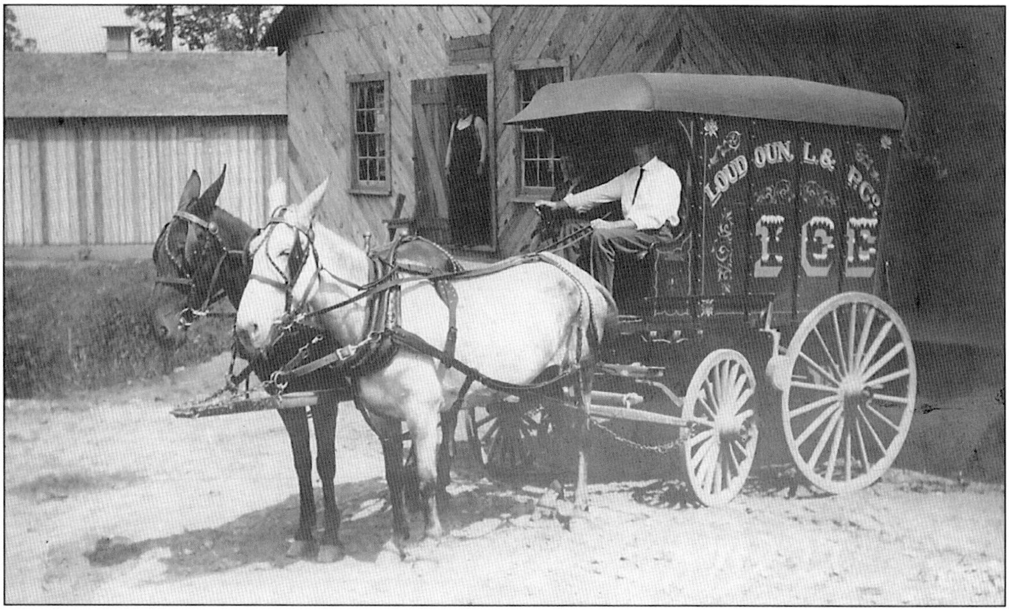

Despite the overall progress of daily life, there were still challenges. In 1912, Moncure Lyon decided he had had enough of water-born illnesses such as typhoid fever, that resulted from lack of electricity for cooling. With Ned Cockey as his partner, Lyon founded the Loudoun Light and Power Company. (Courtesy of Robert Lyon.)

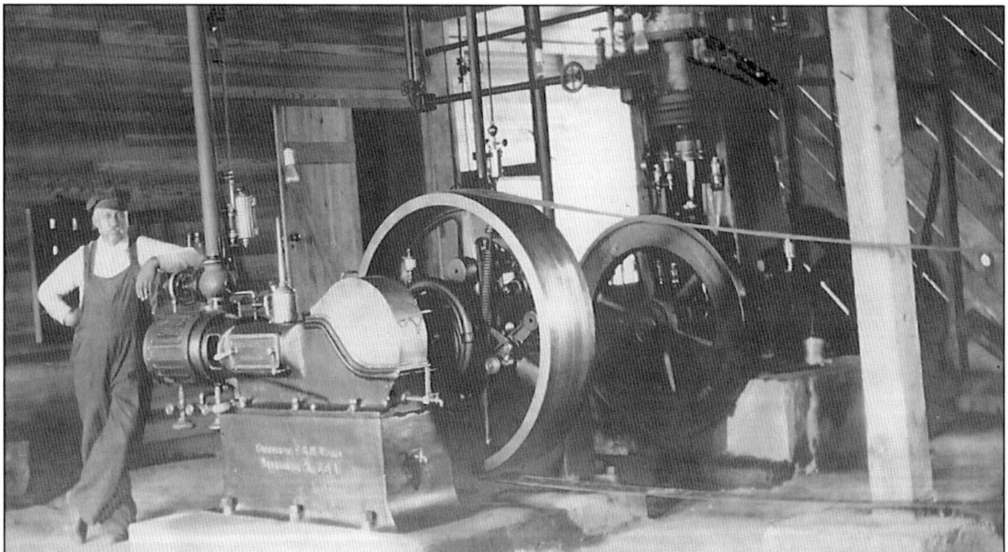

The Loudoun Light and Power Company brought electricity to Purcellville, provided by a diesel-powered plant that also manufactured six tons of ice daily. The company was in operation from 1912 to 1927, transferring hands over many years, and is now owned by Dominion Virginia Power. (Courtesy of Robert Lyon.)

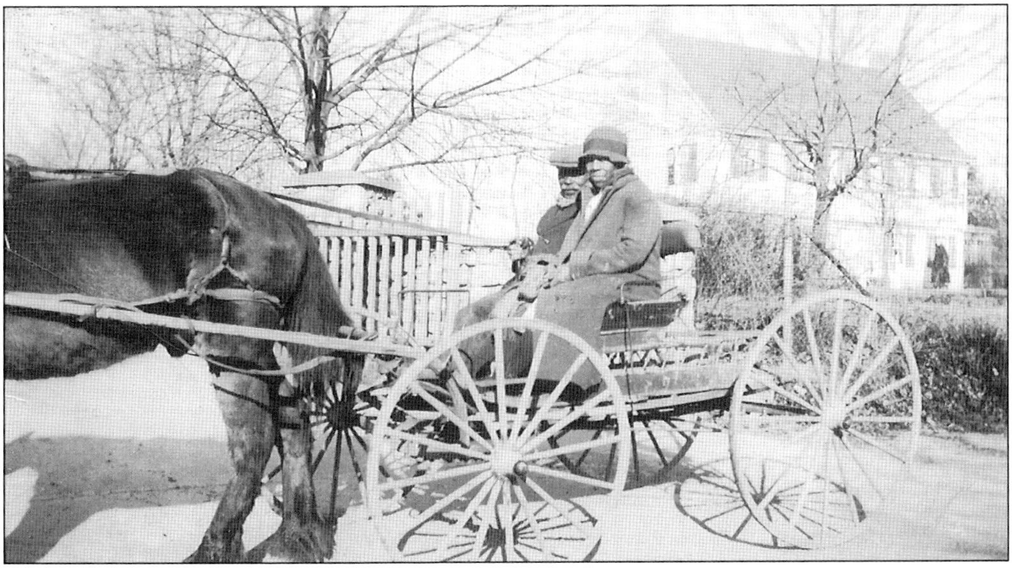

In this 1936 photograph, Hulda Marsh heads east to her family's home on a horse-drawn wagon on Main Street as automobiles slowly drive past her on their way into town. Hulda was the housekeeper for Moncure Lyon's family, whose home is in the background. (Courtesy of Robert Lyon.)

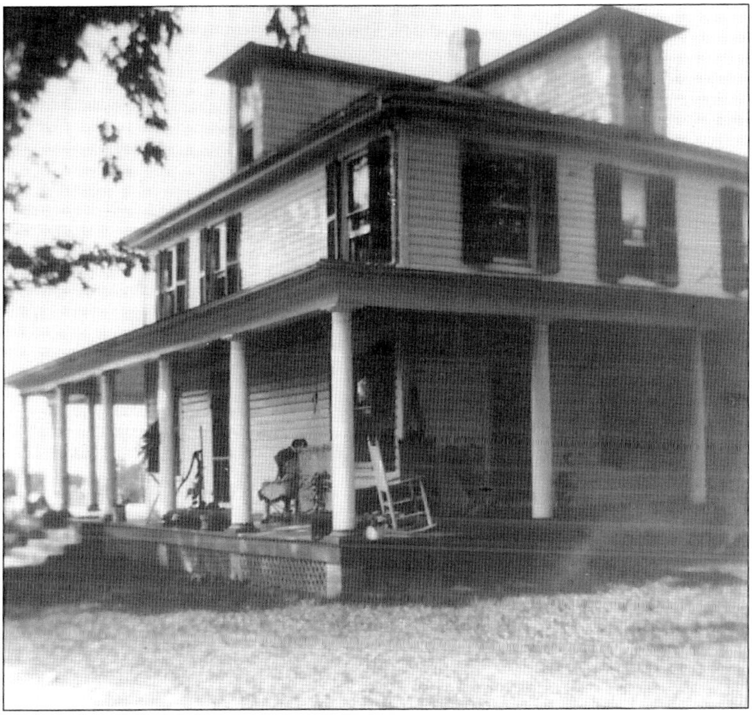

Jake Cornwell's home was among several in town to add electricity by Loudoun Light and Power Company in 1914. In the 1920s, Cornwell operated Purcellville's movie theater, which played silent movies and was accompanied by a piano player. (Courtesy of Robert Lyon.)

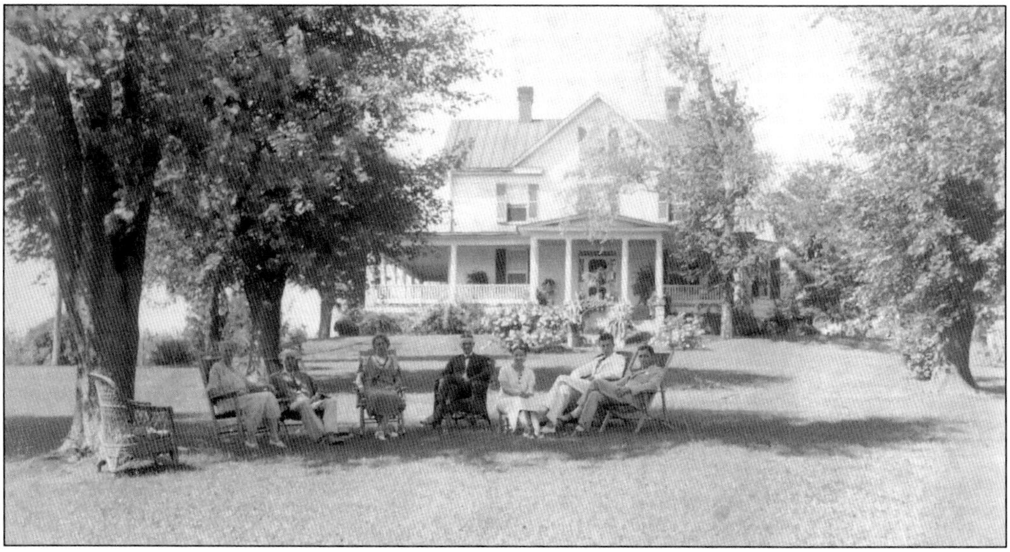

In this 1928 photograph, the Cole family relaxes in the shade in front of their home on Shadowlawn Farm, which was on the east end of Main Street where Purcellville Gateway is located. Pictured from left to right are Kate Cole, W.S. Cole, Wihela Cole, Jim Cole, Betty Cole, Curtis "Slim" Cole, and Frank Cole. (Courtesy of Henry Cole.)

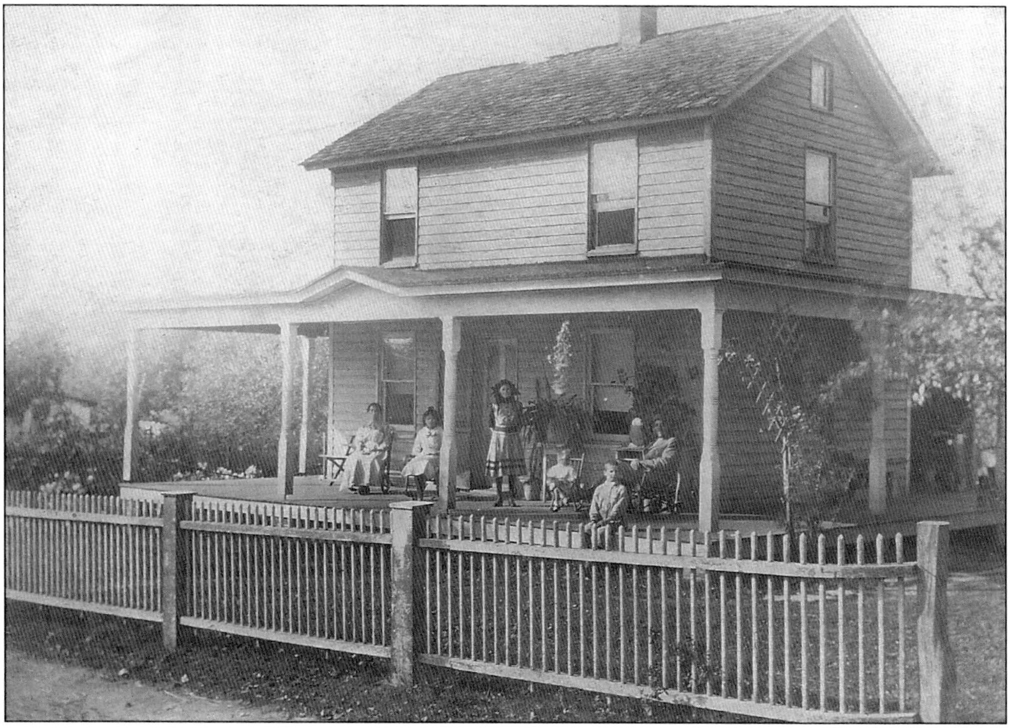

This 1912 photograph shows Joseph and Lena Cook gathering with their family on the porch of their home on G Street. Their house is still owned by descendants of the Cook family. Because the Quakers significantly influenced Purcellville, they were the first settlers in town and the first to integrate. The Quakers showed early support for land and business ownership by African Americans. (Courtesy of Sheila Pinkney Kelly.)

This photograph shows George W. Lee (left) standing with his employee Will Lucas. George W. Lee owned and operated the only barbershop in Purcellville from 1904 to 1956. His son George E. Lee managed a barbershop nearby in Round Hill. (Courtesy of Shirley Lee Washington.)

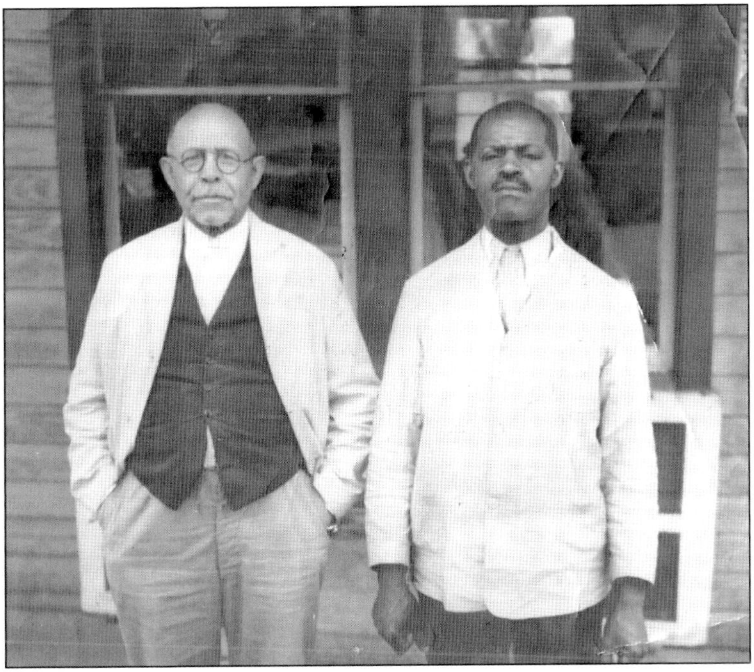

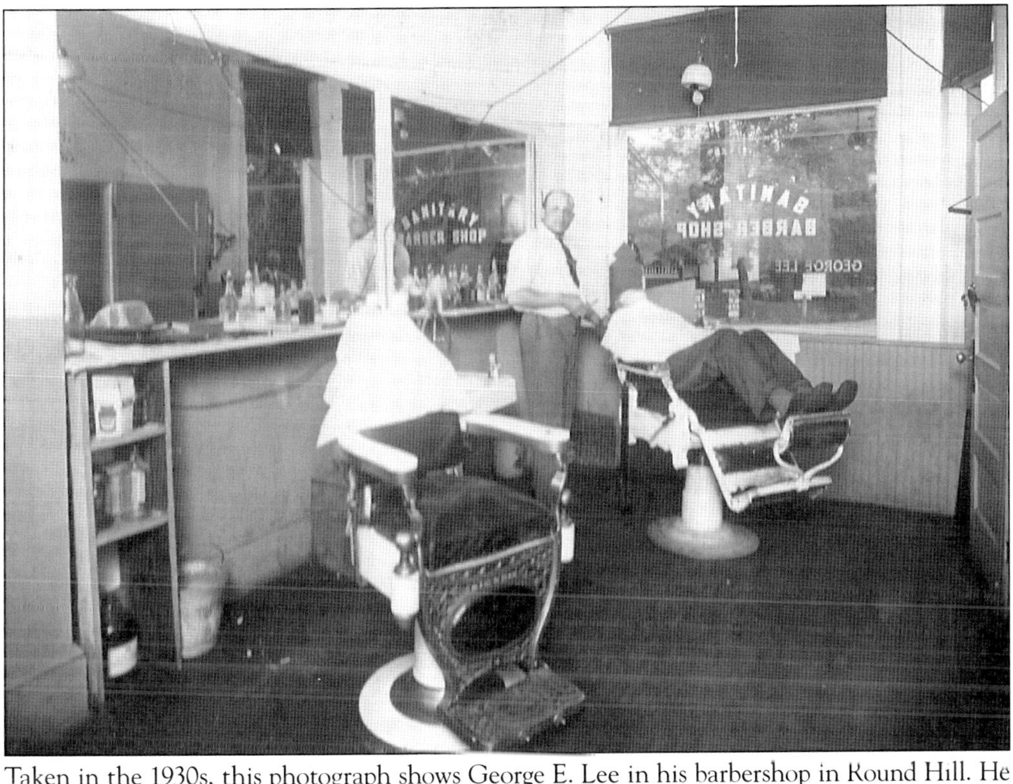

Taken in the 1930s, this photograph shows George E. Lee in his barbershop in Round Hill. He and his father, George W. Lee, ran their barbershops during an era when most businesses were reserved for white customers, most of whom insisted upon segregation. Both barbers served African American customers in their own homes. (Courtesy of Purcellville Preservation Association.)

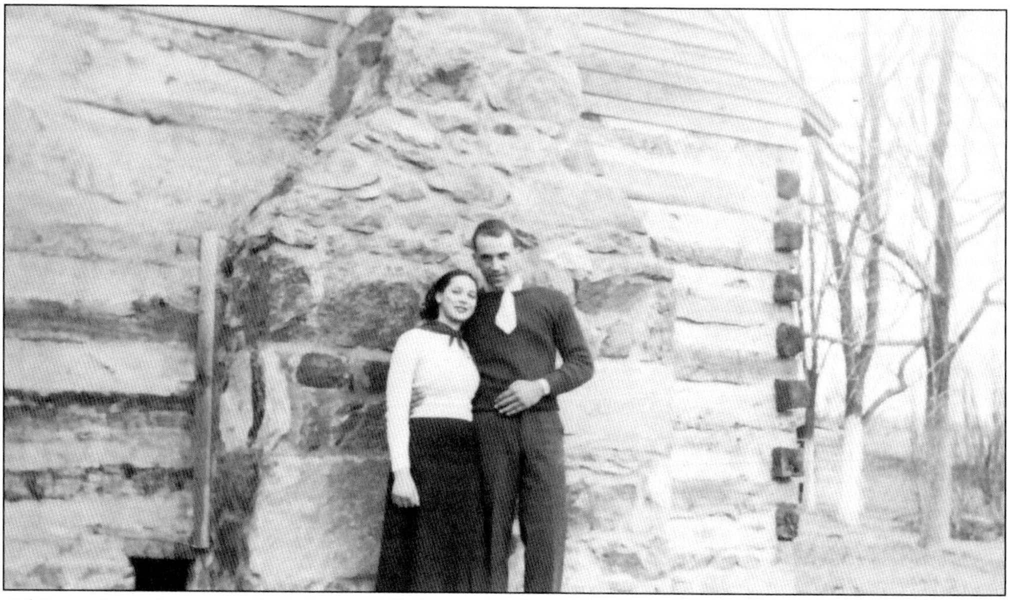

African Americans settled along Hill Street, today's G Street, which was commonly referred to as the "color line" by townspeople through the mid-20th century. The neighborhood was conveniently located near the Emancipation Grounds. The area was purposely excluded when Purcellville incorporated in 1908. Taken in the early 1930s, this photograph shows Vivian Cook Pinkney and her cousin Claude Brown outside of the log cabin that served as an office on the grounds. (Courtesy of Reginald Simms.)

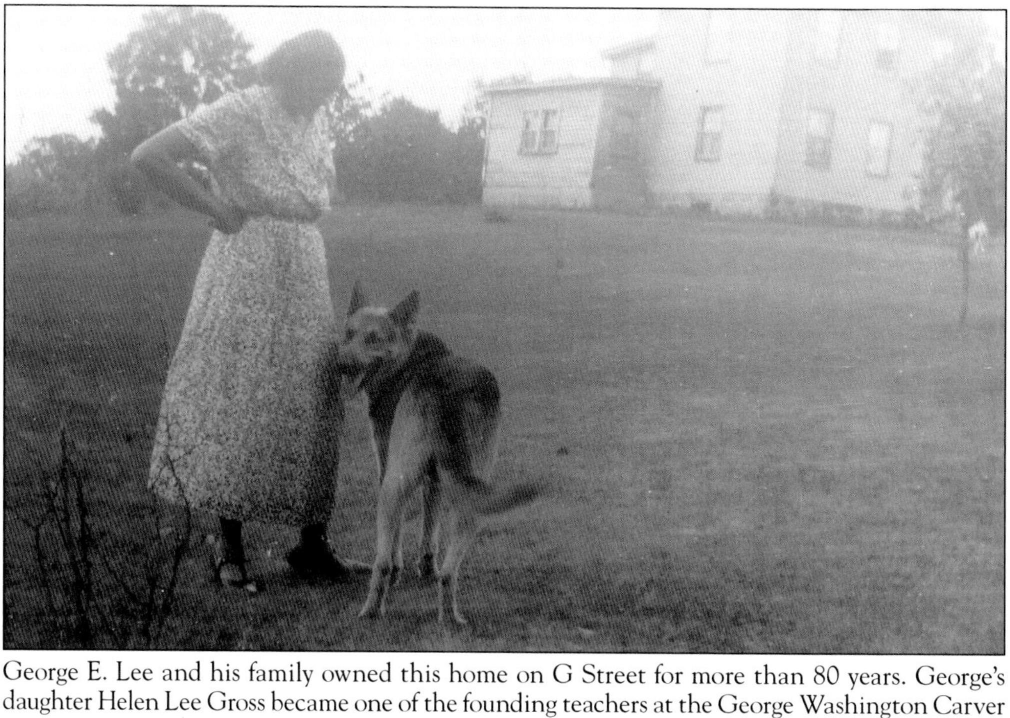

George E. Lee and his family owned this home on G Street for more than 80 years. George's daughter Helen Lee Gross became one of the founding teachers at the George Washington Carver School. This 1935 photograph shows Helen's mother, Nancy Lee, outside of their home. (Courtesy of Purcellville Preservation Association.)

The Clark family settled in the former home of celebrity resident Billy Pierce. Before the Clarks purchased the Pierce home in 1935, legendary dancer and choreographer Billy Pierce grew up in the house, later bringing his wife, Nona, and son to Purcellville. This portrait of the Pierce family was taken in 1930. Pierce was a dance teacher in the Theater District in New York City who adapted local African American dance moves with Broadway choreography during the Harlem Renaissance. Some say he introduced the Charleston and Black Bottom, teaching Fred Astaire, Ethel Barrymore, and other famous white clients his choreography. (Courtesy of Charles Clark.)

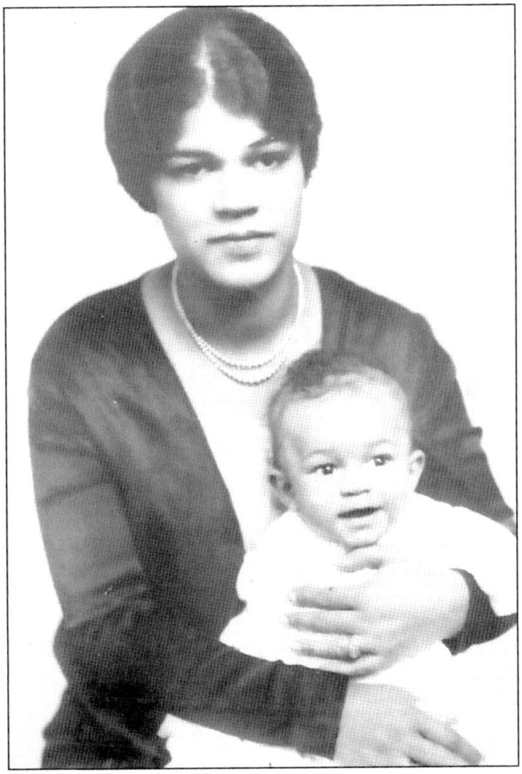

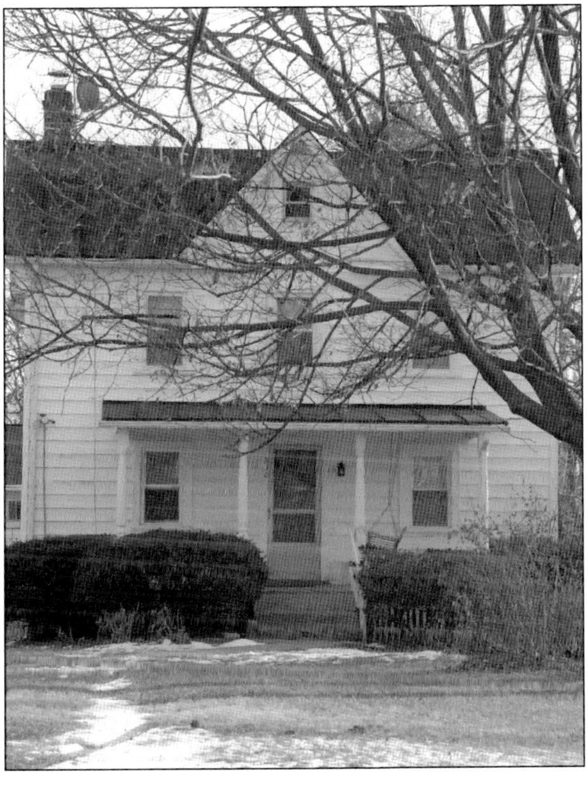

Across the street from the Pierce home on G Street was the Elks Lodge, where Billy Pierce's father, Dennis, was a captain. In 1933, Billy Pierce died suddenly at age 43. Hundreds of people from all over the world attended his funeral in Purcellville. The lodge is still standing and is now a private home. (Courtesy of Cathy Darby.)

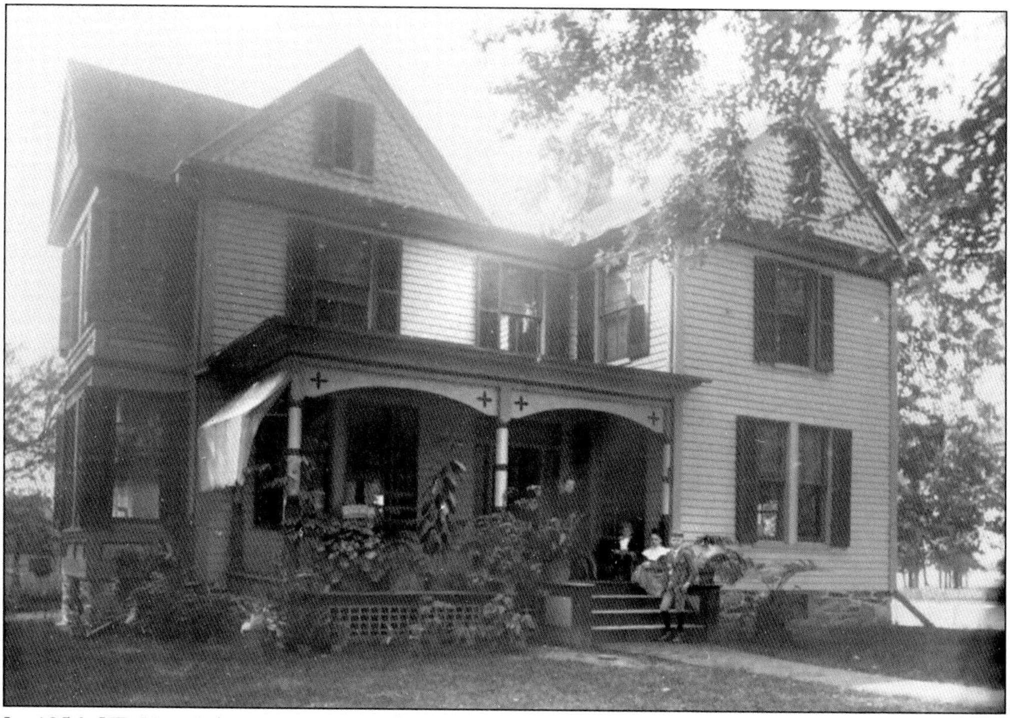

In 1956, J.T. Hirst's home was moved from its original location on Main Street to its present location behind the Purcellville Library. It made way for the building of an all-brick Safeway. In 1992, the Safeway building would become Purcellville's town hall and police station. (Courtesy of Jane Hirst Bogle.)

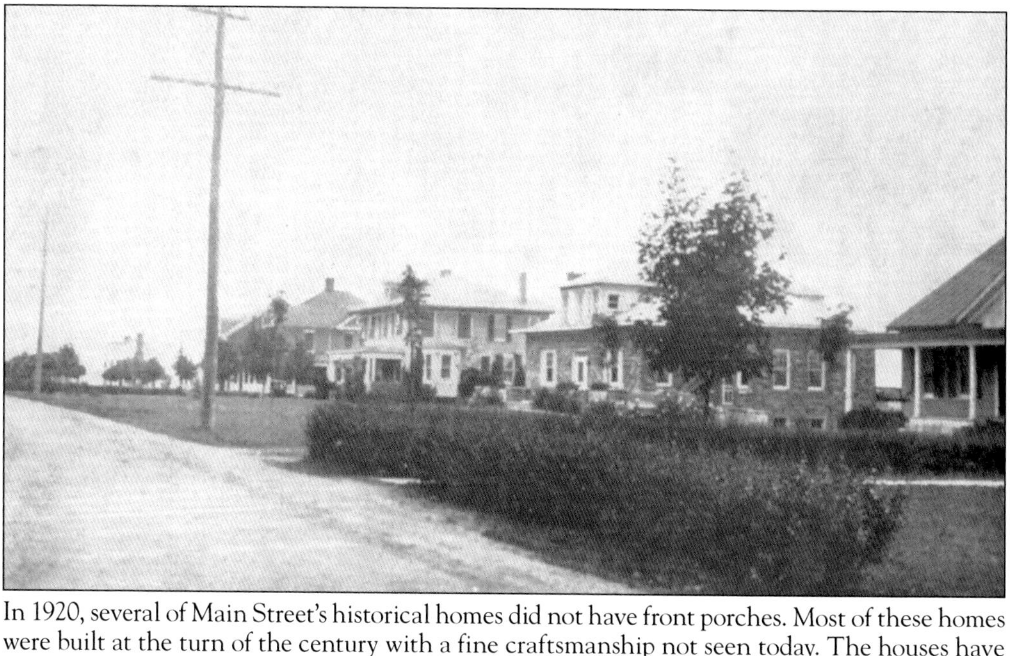

In 1920, several of Main Street's historical homes did not have front porches. Most of these homes were built at the turn of the century with a fine craftsmanship not seen today. The houses have wooden floors throughout, lovely oak paneling in the foyer, and a grand front staircase, beautiful light fixtures, built-in bookshelves, and tall ceilings. (Courtesy of Thomas Balch Library.)

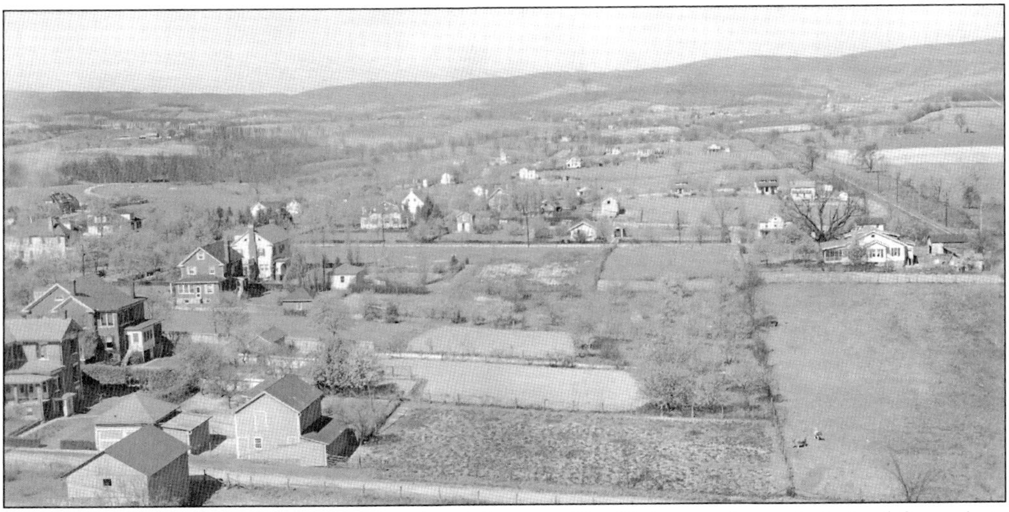

Most families throughout Loudoun preferred being self-sufficient and got their food from their farmettes. Extra livestock and crops went to the market for profit. Townspeople remember when everyone had a vegetable garden, hogs, sheep, chicken, and a few fruit trees. This aerial photograph was taken in 1932. (Purcellville Preservation Association.)

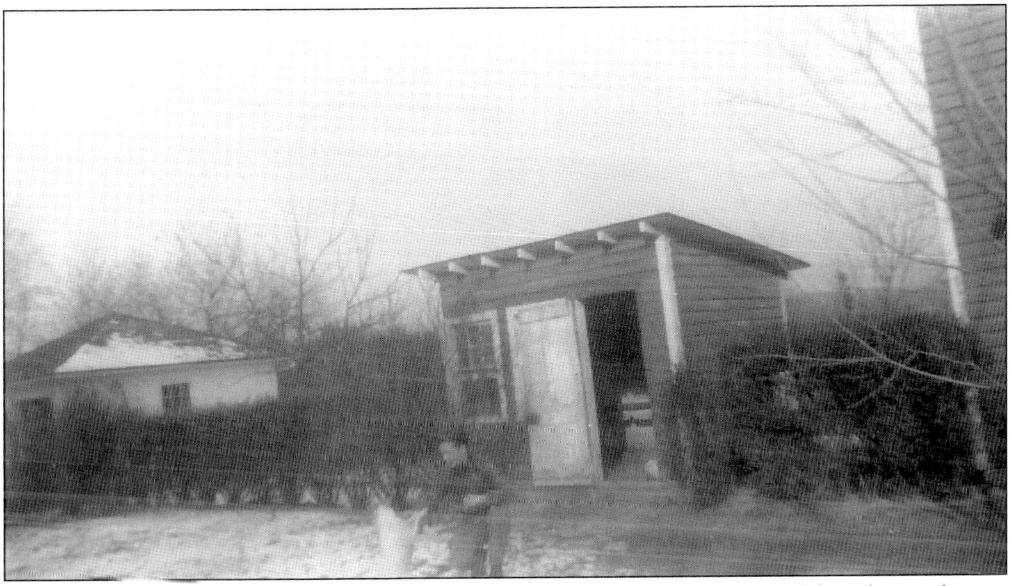

Many of Purcellville's families started with a small farm behind their homes, although most homes sold and subdivided their land over the years. Several homes still have remnant farmettes, such as a chicken coop that many townsepeople now use as a storage shed. This 1932 photograph shows the chicken coop behind the Kilgore home on Main Street when it was still in full operation. (Courtesy of Brad Kilgour.)

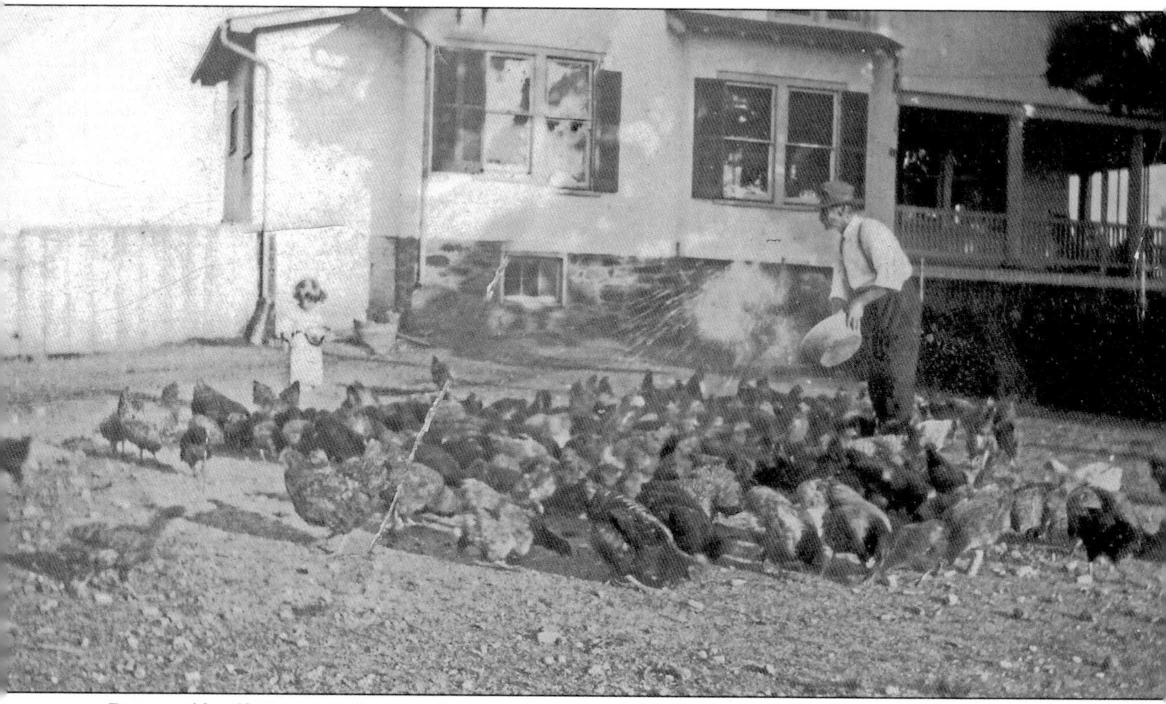

Being self-sufficient was the goal for most families in the 1900s. Recently, roosters became prohibited to own in Purcellville, while hens and chickens were allowed if they were contained. In 1920, a young Ruth Gregg and her grandfather Daniel Gregg feed the chickens at their home on Twenty-Eighth Street. The home remains in the family today. (Courtesy of Carnell Bowman.)

Five

A Village Grows into a Town

Train service was lucrative to farmers and became a huge convenience to townspeople because it shortened travel time between the big city and rural town. The village experienced its boomtown era during the period of the railroad and began to feel the effects of its growth. However, the roads were a mess because of increased traffic, and wagon wheels were constantly getting stuck in the mud and manure. The townspeople wanted to incorporate their village, which would generate tax revenue to pay for better roads. On March 14, 1908, the village officially became a town at the general assembly, and its first act was to improve the streets and sidewalks. During this time, much of what we see in Purcellville today was built. The past workings of the town can still be seen vividly today.

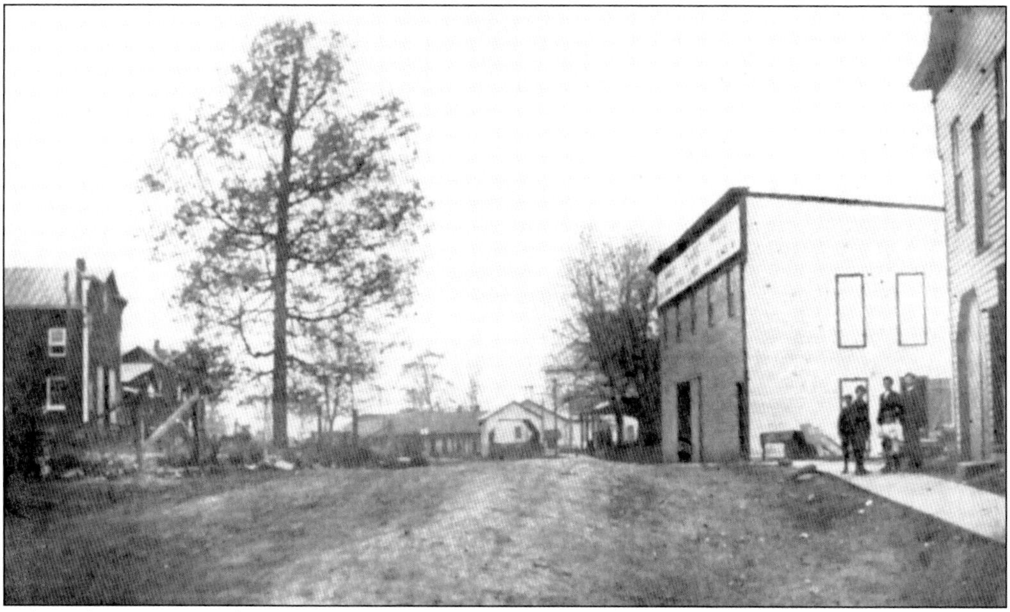

When the W&OD railroad was built, the need for stagecoaches ended. On Twenty-First Street, there was a livery stable that provided horse-drawn taxis for Purcellville residents. The stable is in the foreground on the right. They rented out horses for 50¢ a day, or a driver with a horse-drawn wagon for $2 a day. The livery stable advertised that their "vehicles are substantial and in good order, the horses gentle and true, and the drivers careful, attentive and polite." (Courtesy of Thomas Balch Library.)

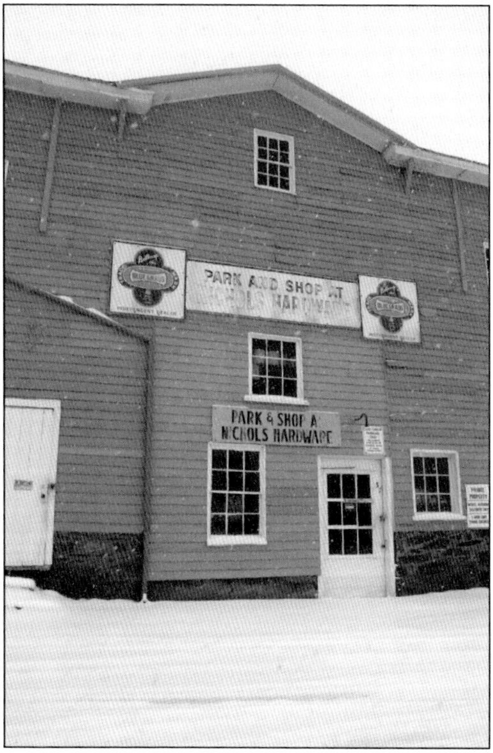

Tillett and Gregg's livery stable was designed with high ceilings, which provided ample overhead space to accommodate the stagecoaches. Nick Hampton built the stable in 1908. Today, Nichols Hardware uses the space for storage. (Courtesy of Cathy Darby.)

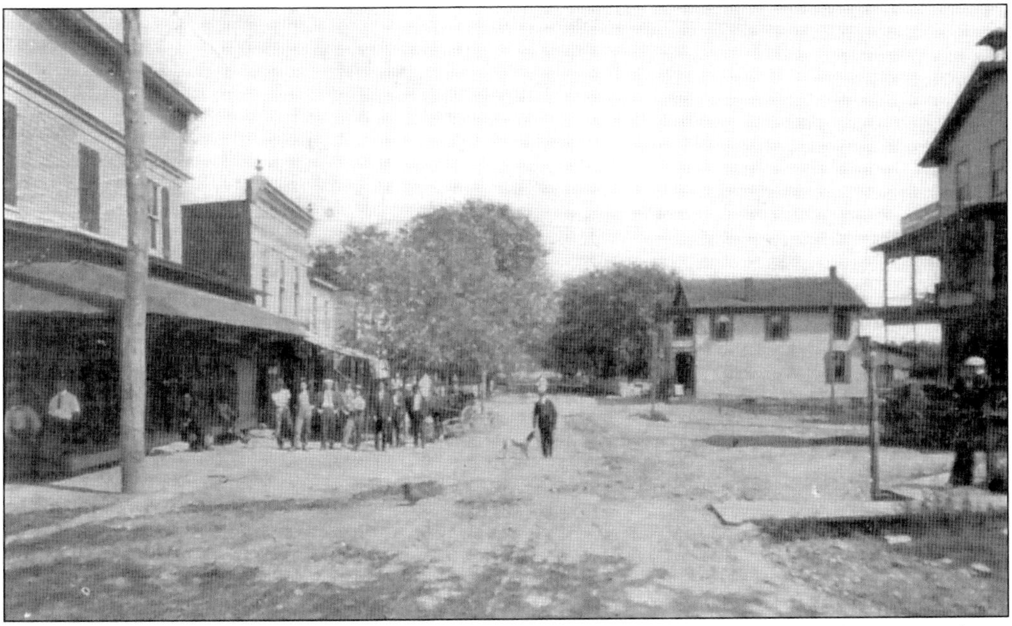

In 1908, the hub of Purcellville was located conveniently near the train station. This postcard was sent from Purcellville to Paeonian Springs (five miles away) on January 25, 1908. The crowd on the left is standing at the business block that was commonly referred to as "Ward's Corner" after Frank Ward had taken over William Pancoast's store at the corner in 1906. Today, Wards Corner is commonly referred to as the "Teardrop" because of the teardrop-shaped island that separates the cross streets on the south side. In the distance, to the south (on the right), is Edwin T. Hirst's store (1893–1917), run by Clarence K. Davis until about 1950. (Courtesy of John Fishback.)

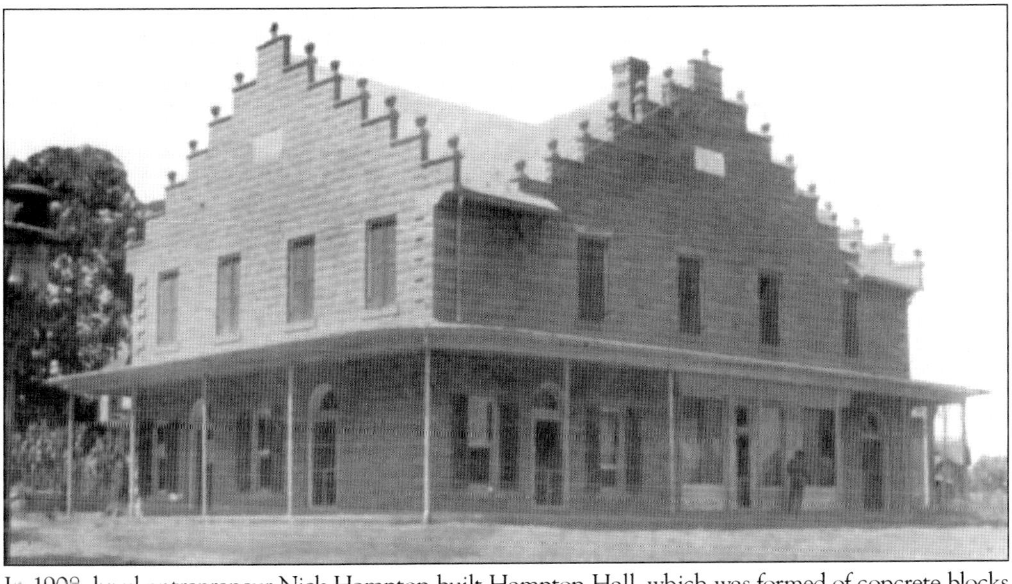

In 1908, local entrepreneur Nick Hampton built Hampton Hall, which was formed of concrete blocks from the Purcellville Foundry in the heart of downtown. Today, the building houses the White Palace Restaurant. After Purcell's Store closed, Hampton Hall served as the location of the post office and other businesses, with a few meeting rooms upstairs. The upstairs also served as an entertainment hall where townspeople remember Cab Calloway performing in the 1930s. (Courtesy of Thomas Balch Library.)

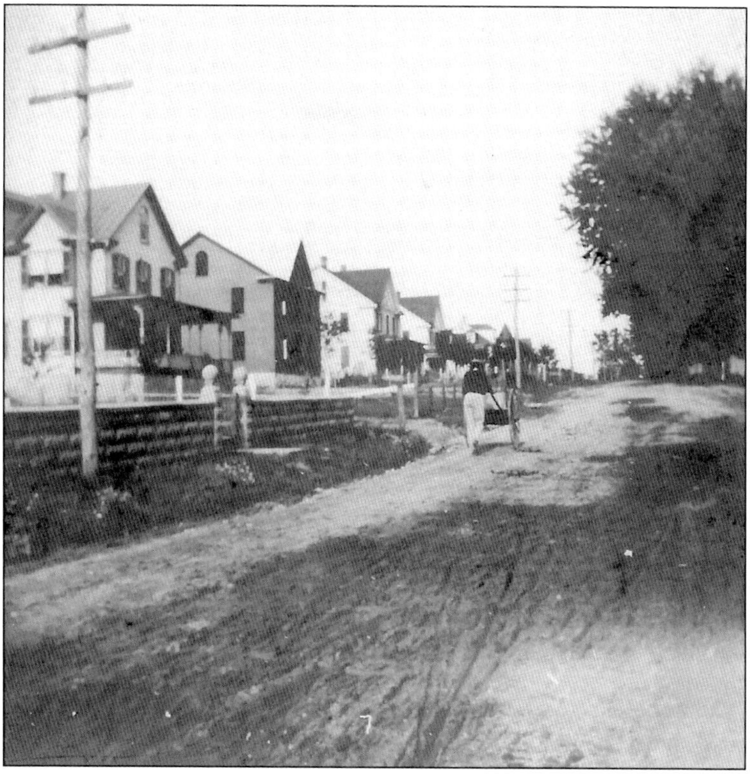

In 1908, the town council addressed the urgency of improving the dirt streets and sidewalks. Rocks were dumped on the Great Road, and the streets were lined with logs, which kept the rocks in place. Purcellville did not build a paved road until 1927. (Courtesy of Thomas Balch Library.)

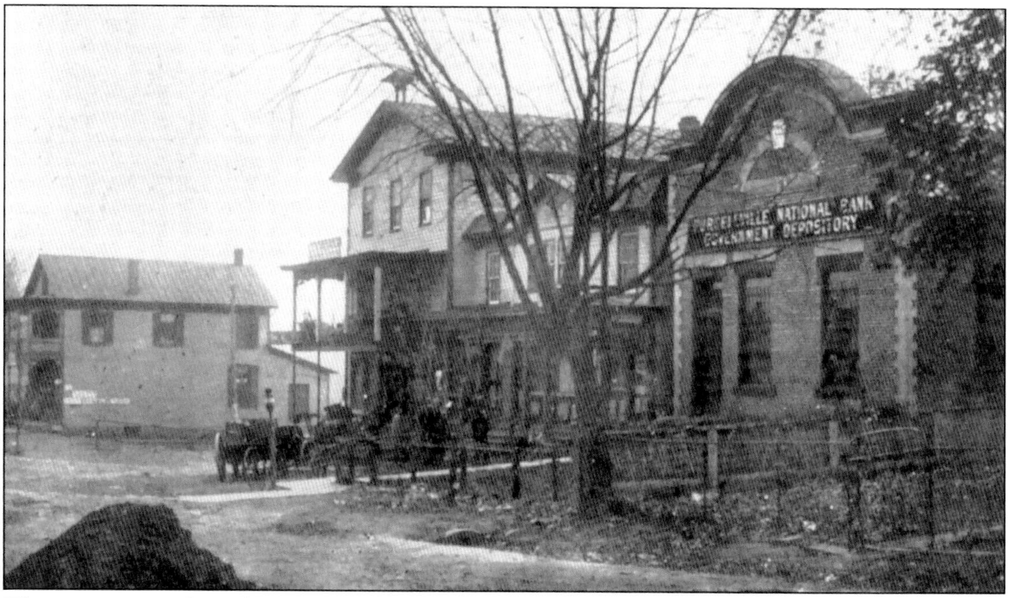

This 1908 image shows horses being hitched up outside of the original business block on the south side of Main Street and Nursery Avenue, referred to as Taylor's Mill Road in the early 1900s. Arch Simpson built the bank on the far right in 1901. After the town council addressed infrastructure issues, they addressed the issue of dogs and hogs. Farmers saw canines as a nuisance because they often attacked sheep and calves. The town council mandated that canines would be taxed $1 per year, plus an extra $1 if the dog was unspayed. (Courtesy of Thomas Balch Library.)

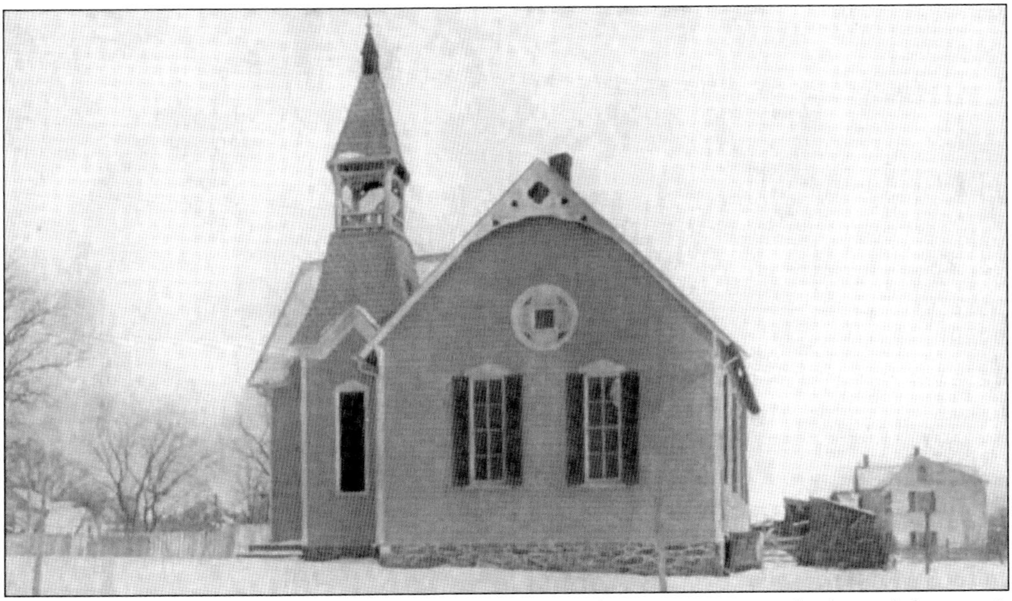

The Free Church on Nursery Avenue was opened to all denominations, and it hosted the town's earliest religious services. Today, the church building now houses the Hall Funeral Home. In 1824, the first religious ceremony was in James Dillon's log schoolhouse. This beginning of an organized religious instruction created a mild sensation in the town, with many attending more out of curiosity than a desire for instruction. (Courtesy of Thomas Balch Library.)

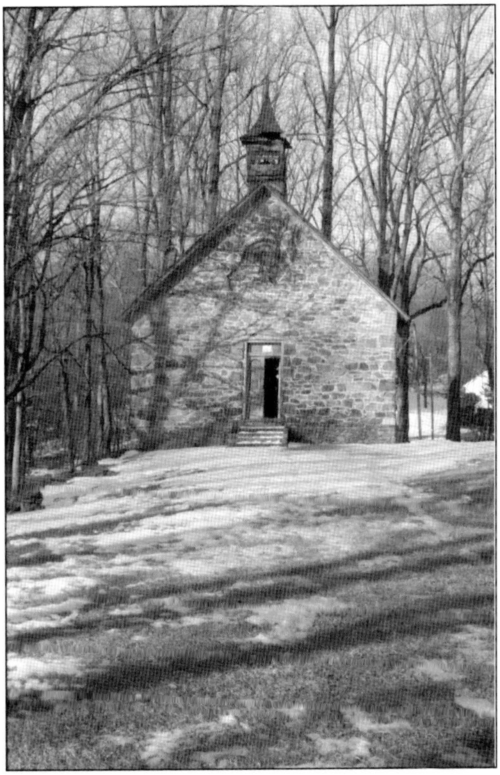

Grace Methodist Episcopal Church was first conceived in the Old Lincoln Schoolhouse. The church was first organized in 1872. The Quakers and Freemen built the existing church near the "school house under the hill" in 1884. Services were originally held on the second and fourth Sundays, and the basement was used as a vocational school where Quakers taught sewing, cooking, shoe repair, and other skills to the African American community. Today, Lincoln Preservation Foundation is renovating the church building to its original luster. (Courtesy of Sarah Huntington.)

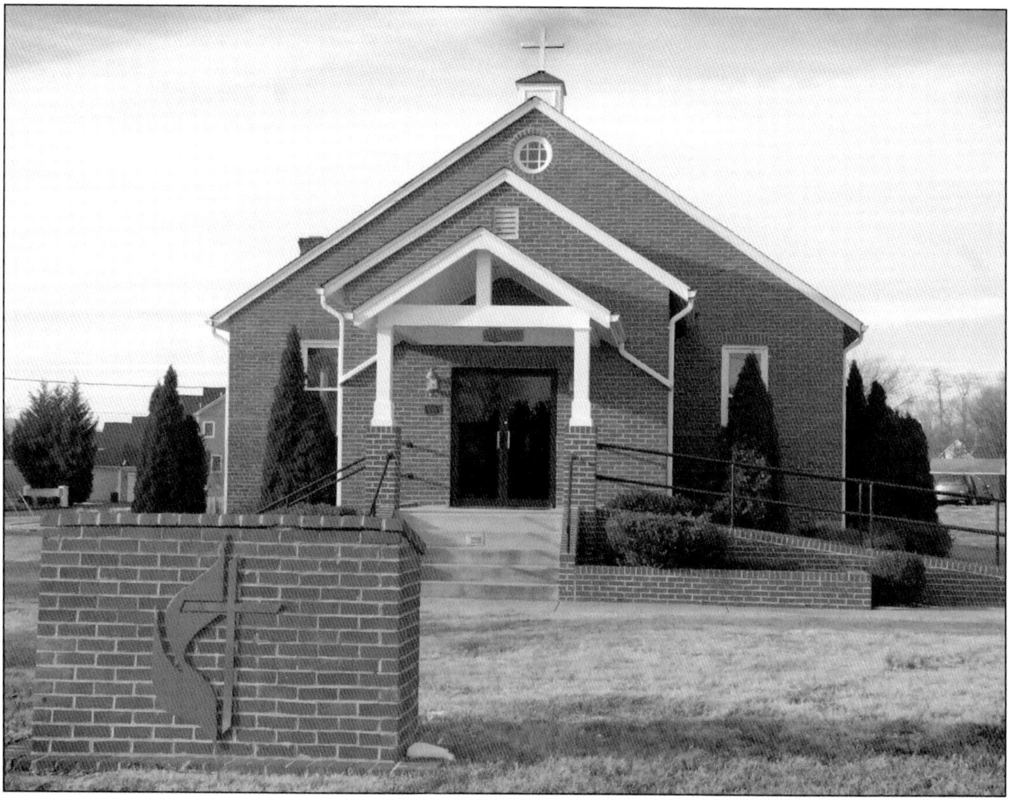

By 1915, most of Grace Methodist Episcopal Church's congregation resided in Purcellville, and had to walk to Lincoln for church services. In Lincoln, the church served as an anchor and stabilizing force until 1942. In 1949, the Grace Annex Methodist Episcopal Church broke ground for a new building on G Street in Purcellville, and the old stone church in Lincoln was eventually abandoned. (Courtesy of Cathy Darby.)

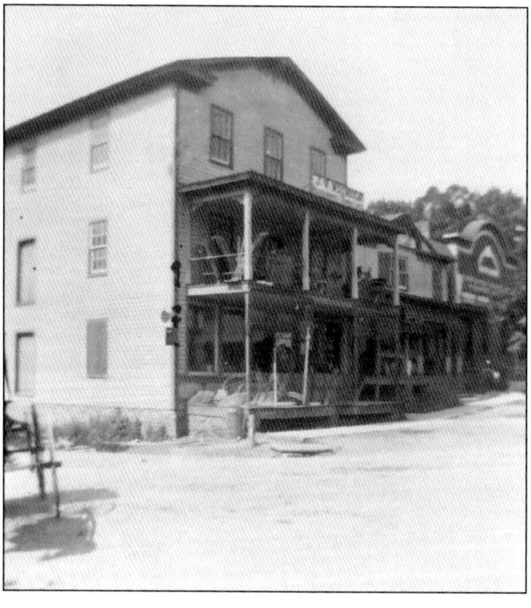

J.V. Nichols Hardware store was at the corner of Nursery and Main Streets where upstairs was Pancoast's Hall and in 1908 the town hall. Today, this corner is where the Purcellville Family Restaurant is. In 1901, Arch Simpson built the Purcellville National Bank at the far end of this business block. However, the entire block was destroyed in the great fire of November 1914, which burned a good deal of downtown Purcellville. (Courtesy of Thomas Balch Library.)

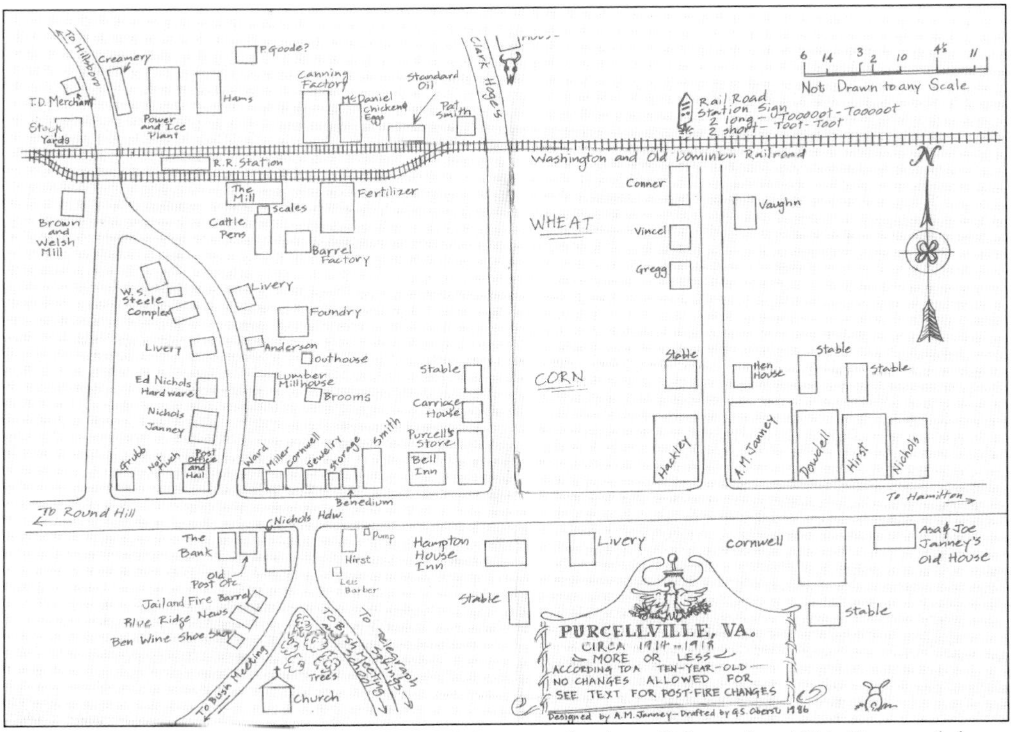

Most of Purcellville's business block burned down in the fire of November 1914. One week later, a second fire took the other buildings on the east side of downtown. This map was designed by Asa Moore Janney, one of Loudoun's best storytellers, historians, shopkeepers, map makers, postmasters, and unofficial mayors. A native son of a family that helped to settle and shape Loudoun County, Janney passed on a great deal of history based on what his forefathers shared since the early 1700s. (Courtesy of Asa Moore Janney.)

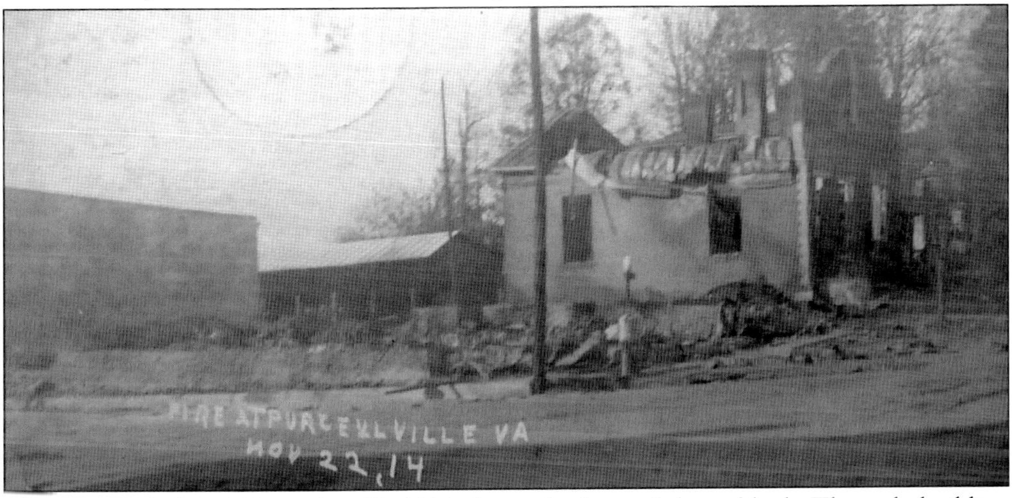

This postcard, dated November 22, 1914, shows the burned-down block. The only building remaining is the bank at the far right, but it was badly damaged and eventually gutted. When the fire bell rang in the building, some residents ran to pull the hand-pumper, and others grabbed ladders and buckets at the tin shop across the street in an effort to save one of Purcellville's few business blocks. (Courtesy of Thomas Balch Library.)

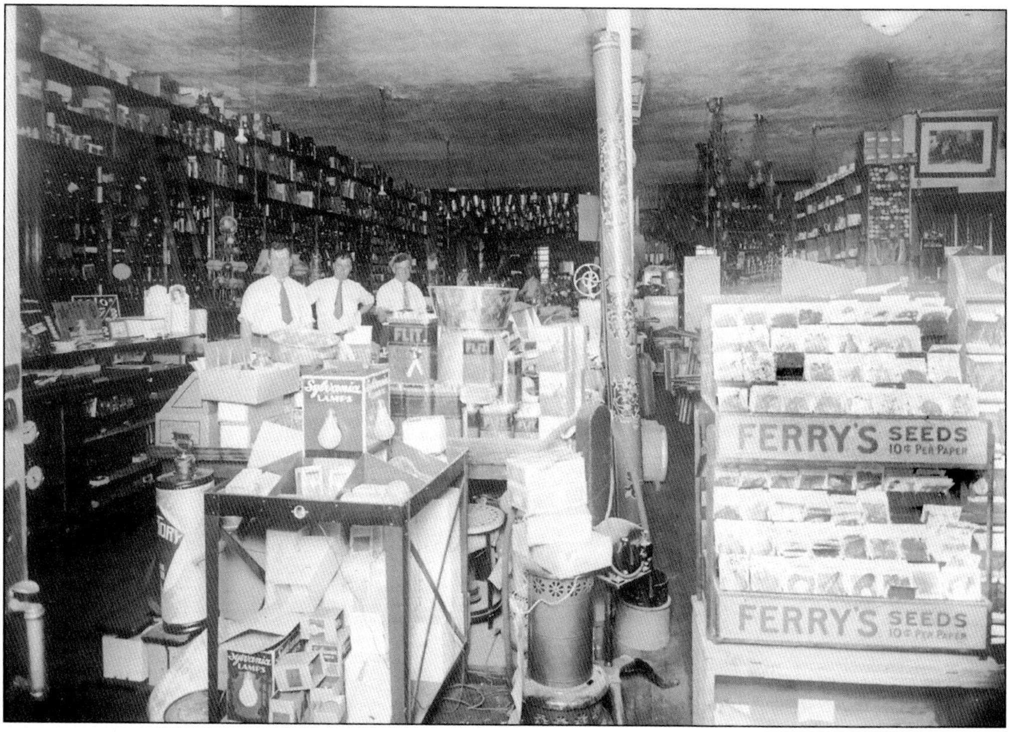

In 1914, Edward Nichols and Ambrose Warner opened Nichols Hardware near the train station, which accommodated the farmers who brought their milk for transport to Roslyn. They would open up early and work until midnight, when the town's electricity was shut off. As the store stocked more and more merchandise, the aisles became narrower. Asa Moore Janney remembered that his father gave Nichols advice: "Don't worry; if they fall over it they might buy it." Today, the retail store is one of the oldest in the Virginia Piedmont, and is still owned by its founding family. (Courtesy of Kenneth Nichols.)

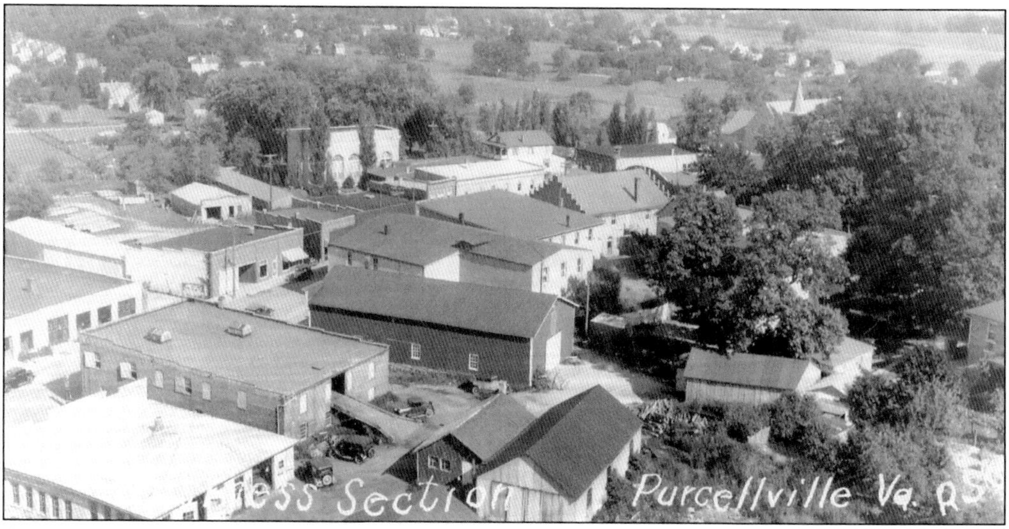

On Twenty-First Street, most of Purcellville's offices and businesses can be traced back to 1874. Almost all of these buildings are still standing. (Courtesy of Sue Russell.)

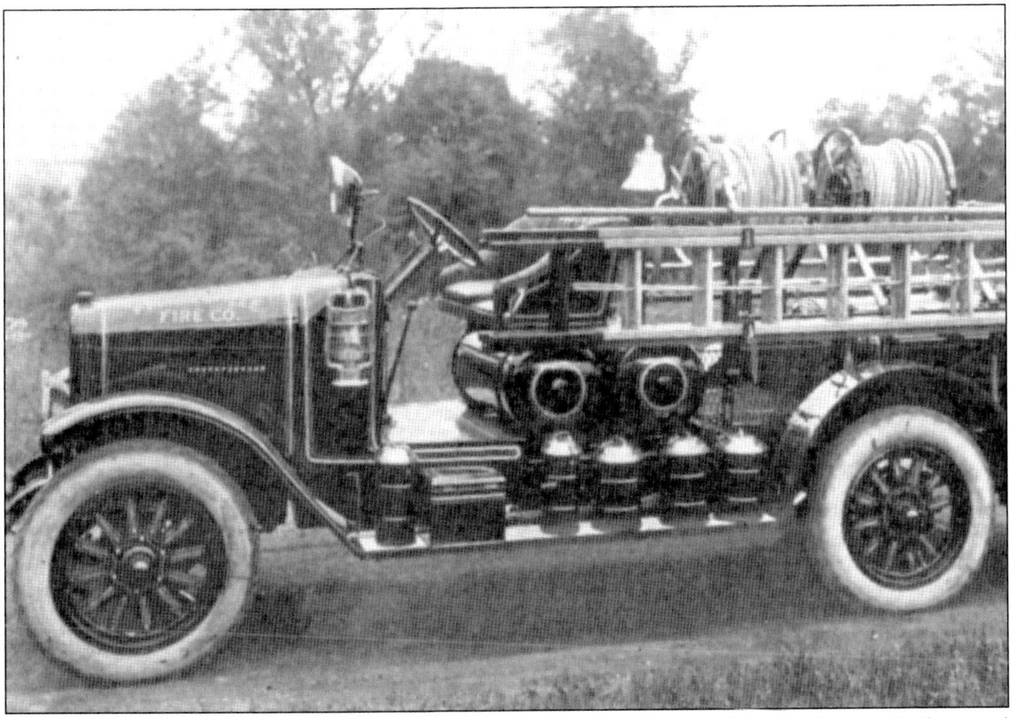

The town organized its first fire company in 1923. The first fire truck had a four-tank chemical engine that was mounted on a one-ton harvester chassis. (Courtesy of Thomas Balch Library.)

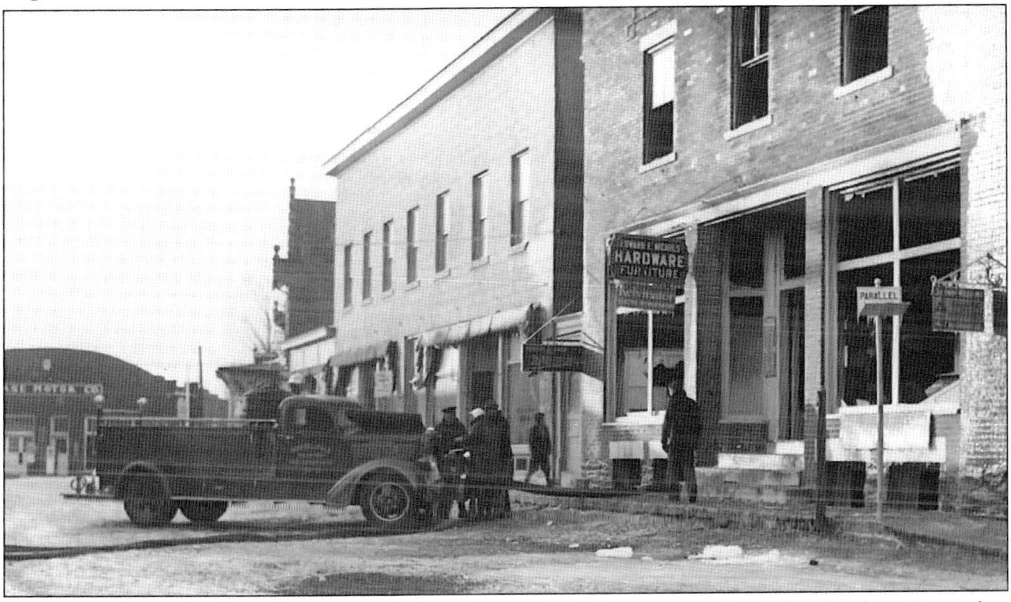

Several fires nearly destroyed Nichols Hardware store. The first occurred in 1914. Two late November fires destroyed the business district on both sides of Main Street. The heat was so intense that it blew out the front windows of Nichols Hardware, which was under construction at the time. Fortunately, the bricks acted as a protection against the fires, and the store survived both fires. This photograph was taken the day after the store experienced its third fire on January 26, 1940. (Courtesy of Kenneth Nichols.)

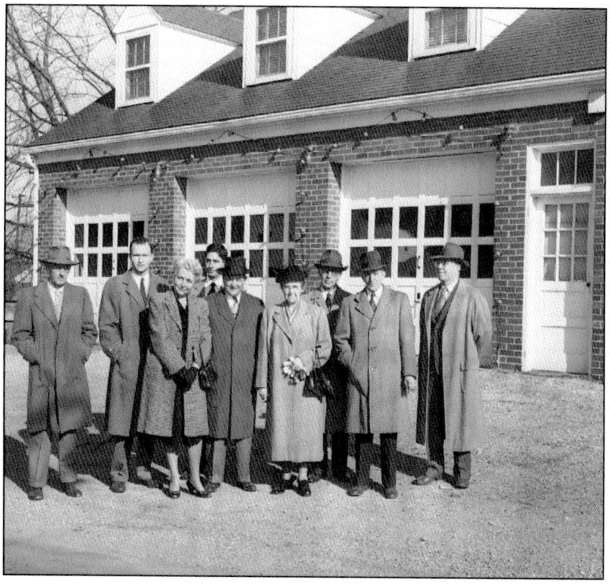

In 1931, the Purcellville Volunteer Fire Company was finally organized and eventually built a brick firehouse on Twentieth Street. The town council meetings would sometimes be held here. This photograph was taken in 1951. Pictured from left to right are Linden McDaniel, Edward Nichols Jr., Helen Hirst Marsh, Robert Grubb, Mayor Albert Anderson, Margaret Edmondson, George Grille, Derry Tribby, and Charles Graham. (Courtesy of Thomas Balch Library.)

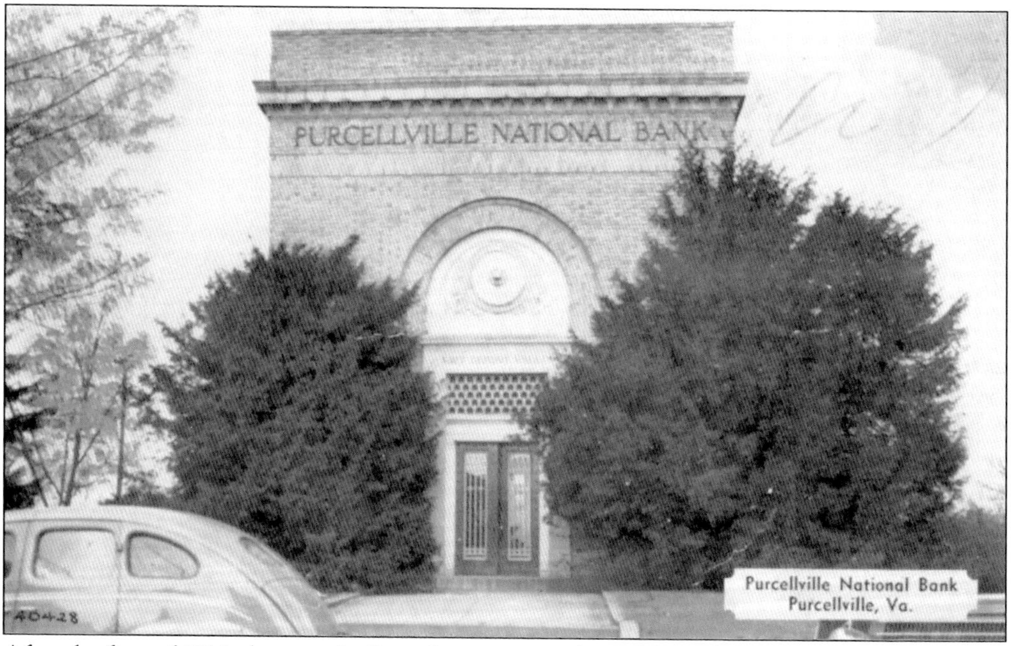

After the fires of 1914, the town built its downtown with guidelines from Virginia's first building codes. In 1915, the design team of Dennison and Hirous built the new Purcellville National Bank building to simulate a vault. The building is now owned by Valley Energy. Clarence Robey was the president of the new bank. He and his wife, Gertrude, greatly influenced the cultural, educational, and business development of Purcellville. (Courtesy of Thomas Balch Library.)

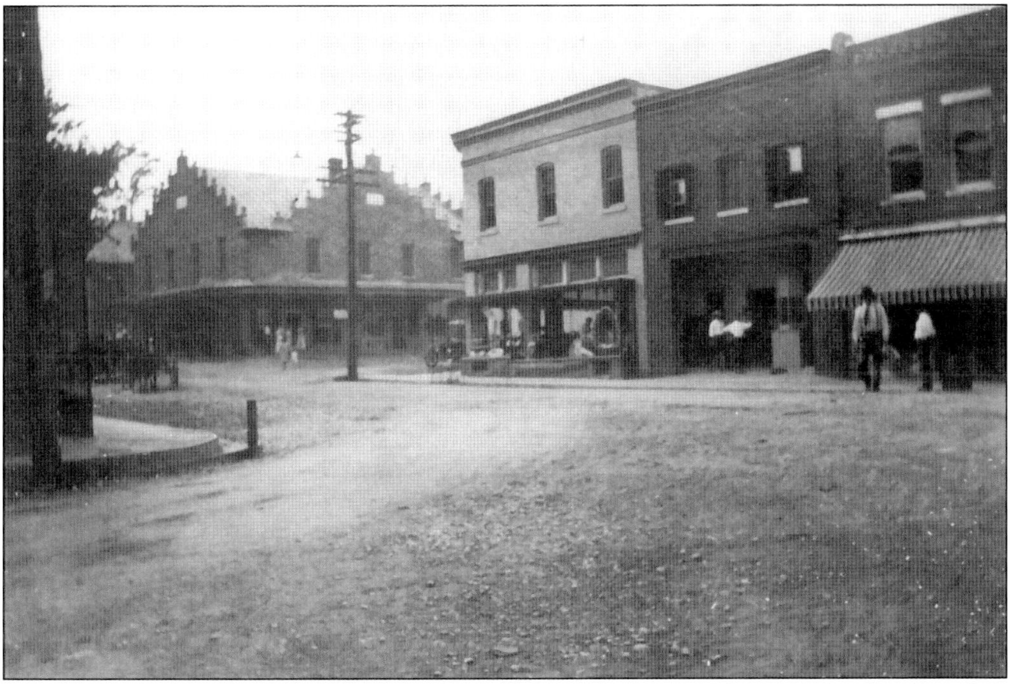

After the fires of 1914, the new building code stated, "No building is to be erected within boundary of the business district except same that it be built of stone, brick or concrete with mettle Cornish and fire proof roof." (Courtesy of Thomas Balch Library.)

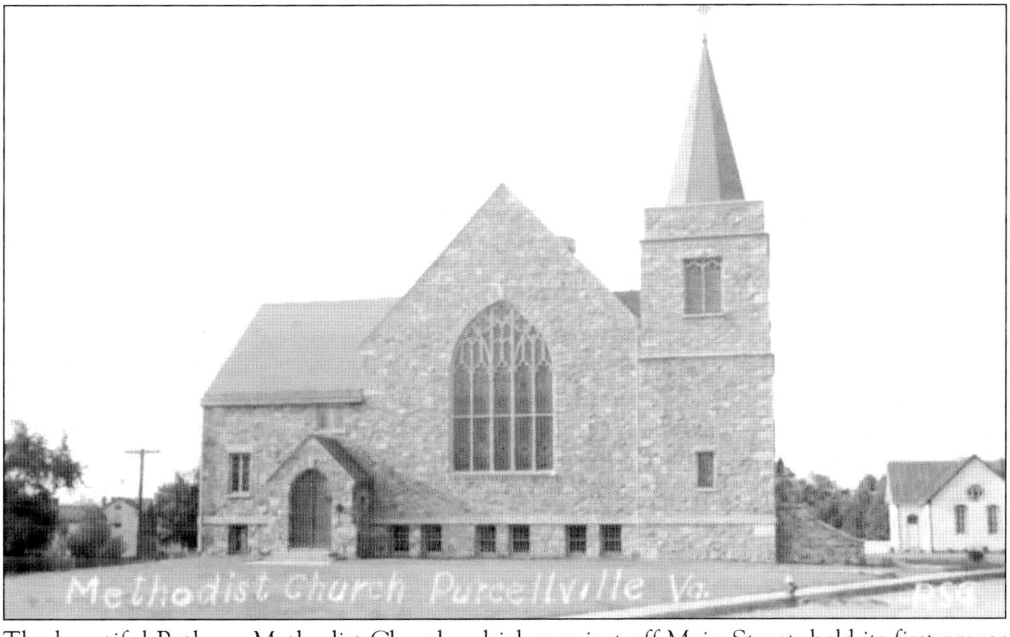

The beautiful Bethany Methodist Church, which was just off Main Street, held its first prayer meeting in 1929. In 1919, members of the Dillon family donated land for the new building, and in 1925, contractor Clarence Case and stonemason Wilmer Baker began building the new church. The Free Church can be seen in the background on the right where many of Purcellville's churches first met for services before building their own. (Courtesy of Thomas Balch Library.)

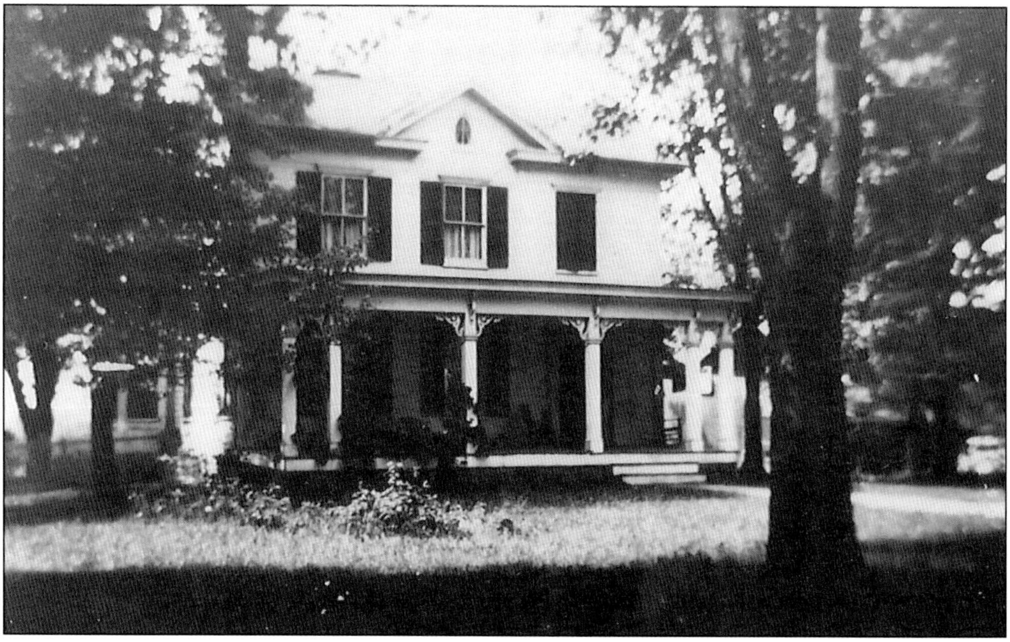

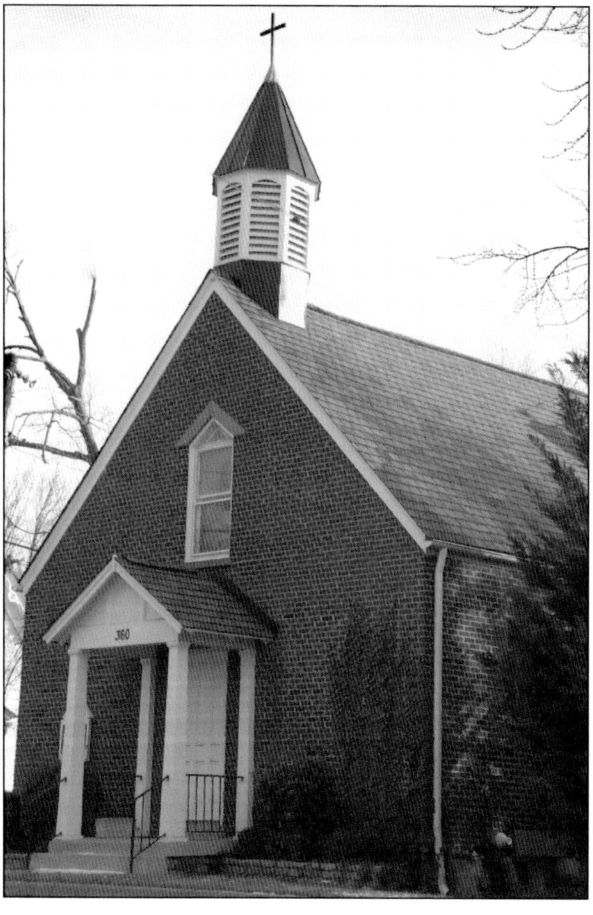

Before 1920, Father Van Inglemgam held the first Catholic service in Purcellville at the home of Gertrude and Notley Ball. Once or twice a month, Father Inglemgam would buggy in from his Falls Church home. Later that year, the Balls donated land for the church, which was built next door to their home on Main Street. (Courtesy of Robert Lyon.)

Clarence Case built the Catholic Church on Main Street and engraved on its cornerstone "A.D. 1921." Bishop O'Connell dedicated the church in 1921 and took Father Inglemgam's suggestion to name it St. Francis de Sales, after the noted bishop who lived from 1567 to 1622. In the early 1990s, a new and larger church for the parish was built north of town near the Berlin Turnpike, and the original building was turned over to the Diocese of Arlington. (Courtesy of Cathy Darby.)

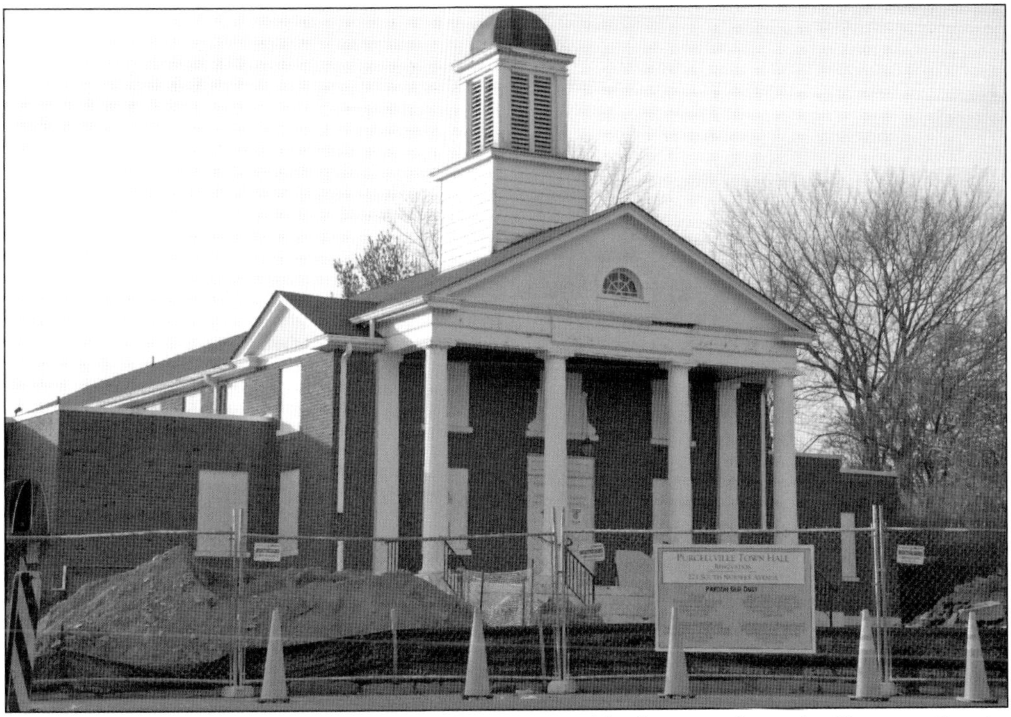

The Purcellville Baptist Church organized in 1924 and broke away from the Ketoctin Baptist Church. In 1928, the congregation held its first baptismal service in its new sanctuary. Because of the spread of polio in 1935, all public gatherings, including worship services, were closed for a time. In 2008, Purcellville purchased Purcellville Baptist Church for its town hall, which is under construction in 2011. (Courtesy of Purcellville Preservation Association.)

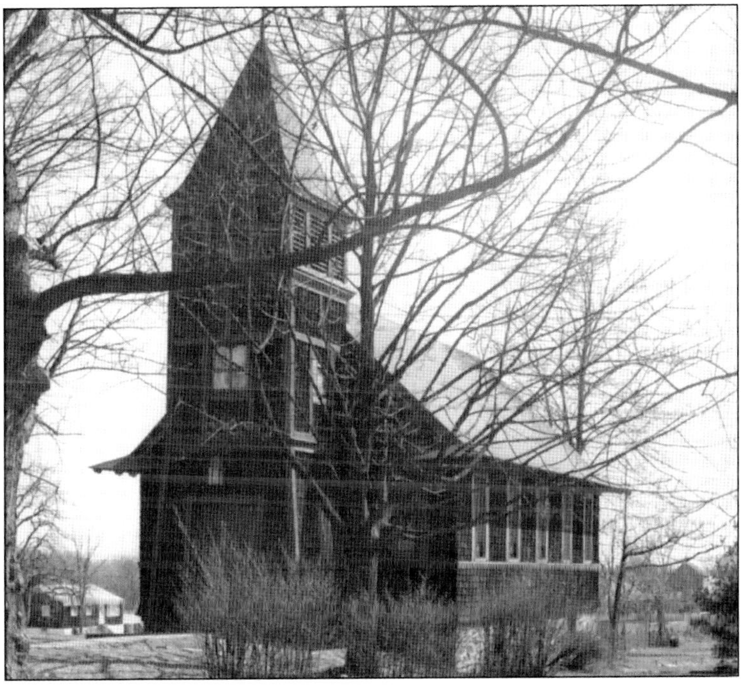

In 1911, St. Peters Episcopal Church's original building was built on Main Street. Arch Simpson designed it with a pitched roof like a Norwegian stave church. When the Episcopalian parish moved out in 1963, the Presbyterians would meet here until their new church, St. Andrews, was built in 1967 on Main Street, west of town. The building is now a Masonic lodge. (Courtesy of Courtesy of Brad Kilgour.)

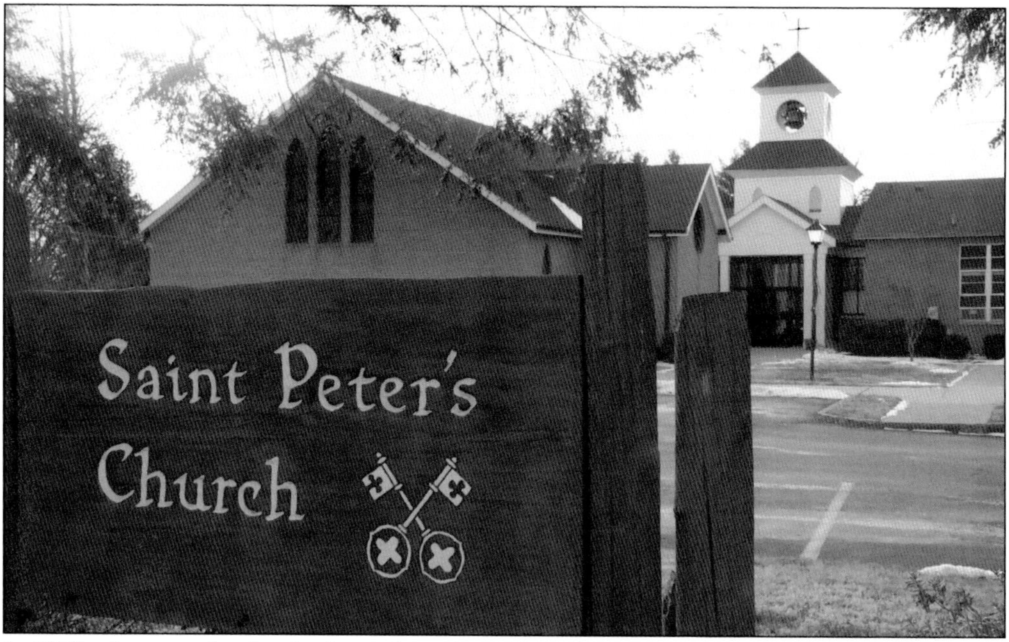

In 1963, when membership had significantly increased, a new St. Peter's Episcopal Church was built on the southwest of town. The bronze bell, which dedicated the church in 1922, was moved to the new church's tower. The bell is engraved with the names of many Loudoun men who served in the Great War. (Courtesy of Cathy Darby.)

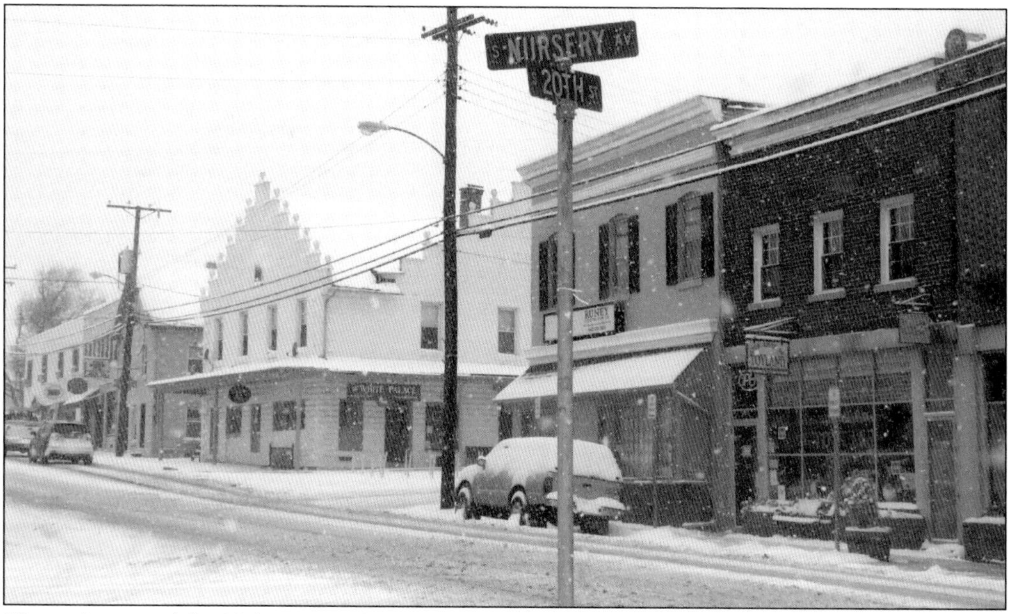

Through most of the 20th century, business was still bustling in Purcellville's downtown area near the train station. About 1921, Albert Cornwell, seller of musical instruments and jewelry, opened a soda fountain, which in 1927 became The White Palace, named by its owner-cook George Stavrakas. In 1955, George Kakouras arrived in Purcellville from Greece to help his uncle. The White Palace is one of Loudoun's oldest continuous operating restaurants and continues to be one of the best places in town to get a delicious home-cooked meal. (Courtesy of Cathy Darby.)

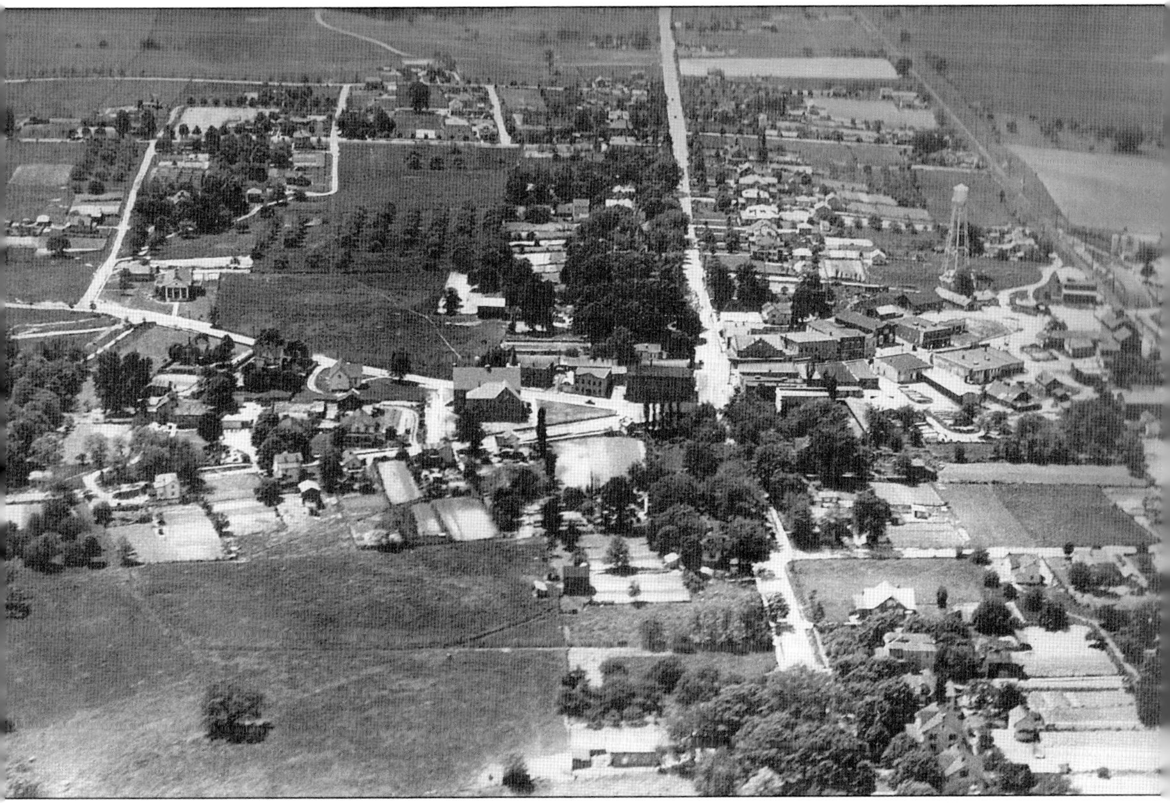

This aerial photograph shows western Purcellville when the W&OD Railroad was in full operation. The land was very undeveloped, and an orchard grew right in the middle of town. (Courtesy of Sue Russell.)

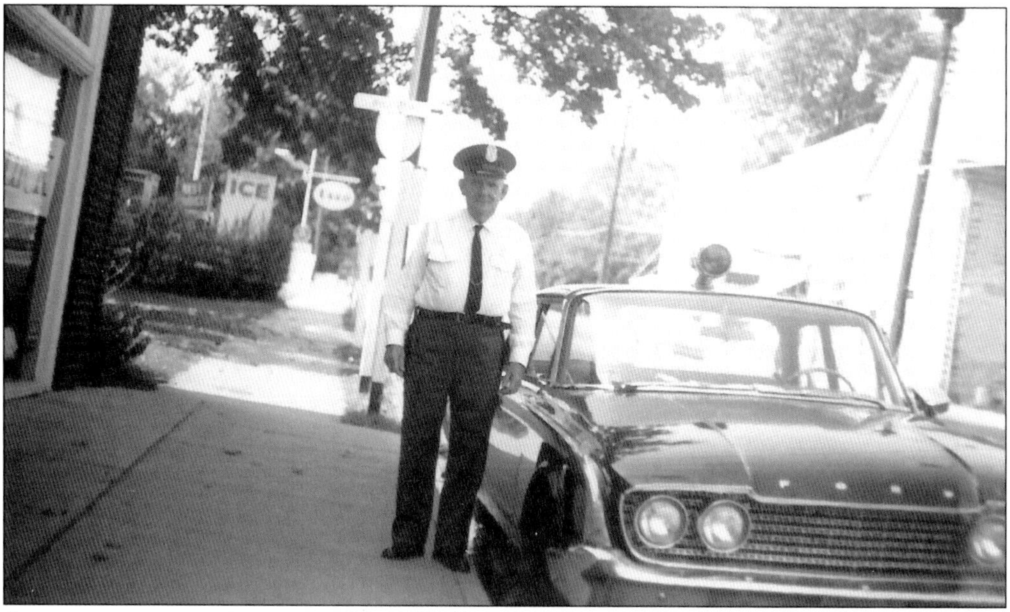

As town sergeant on the streets of Purcellville, officer John Dwyer put many trainees through his individual "police school." Dwyer was best known for working with town youth, and his discipline and practice continue in the department to this day. This 1960 photograph shows a western view of Main Street when Purcellville's population was 1,419. (Courtesy of Thomas Balch Library.)

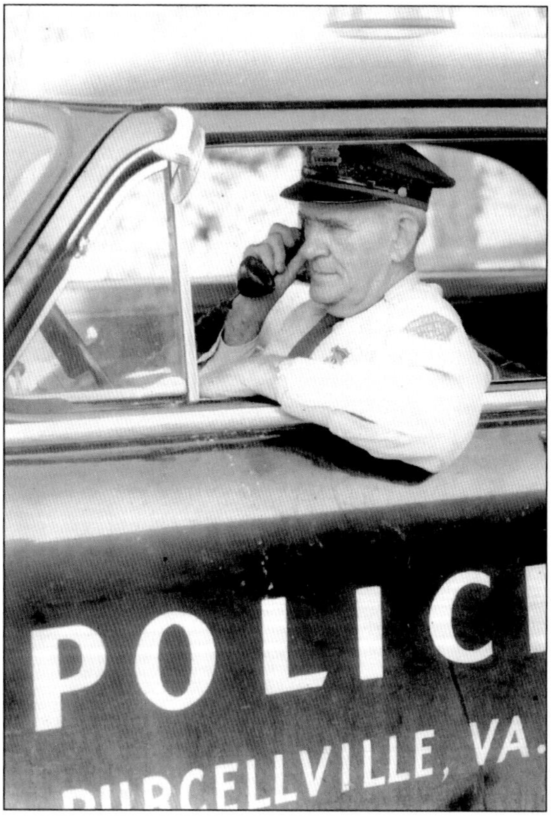

In 1956, Dwyer joined the force to fill in temporarily at the town's police department, but his temporary assignment stretched to 10 years. (Courtesy of Thomas Balch Library.)

In 1967, Basham Simms, a World War II veteran, ran for a seat on the town council when there were no African Americans in the county's public office. "Segregation was still so prevalent," recalled Simms. "I figured prejudice had horns that would stick me . . . I guess I didn't get stuck." With support of both white and black voters, Simms won the election. (Courtesy of Reginald Simms.)

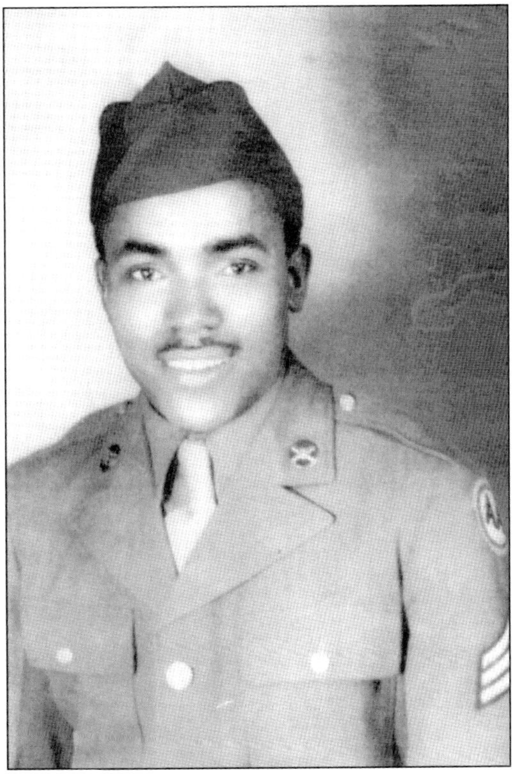

In 2002, Basham Simms Water Treatment Plant broke ground with former mayor John Marsh, councilman Basham Simms, and town manager Rob Lohr. The plant was a $6.9 million state-of-the-art wastewater treatment plant. In his 27 years on the town council, Simms served on the Public Works Committee, becoming an expert on the town's water and sewer facilities. (Courtesy of Town of Purcellville.)

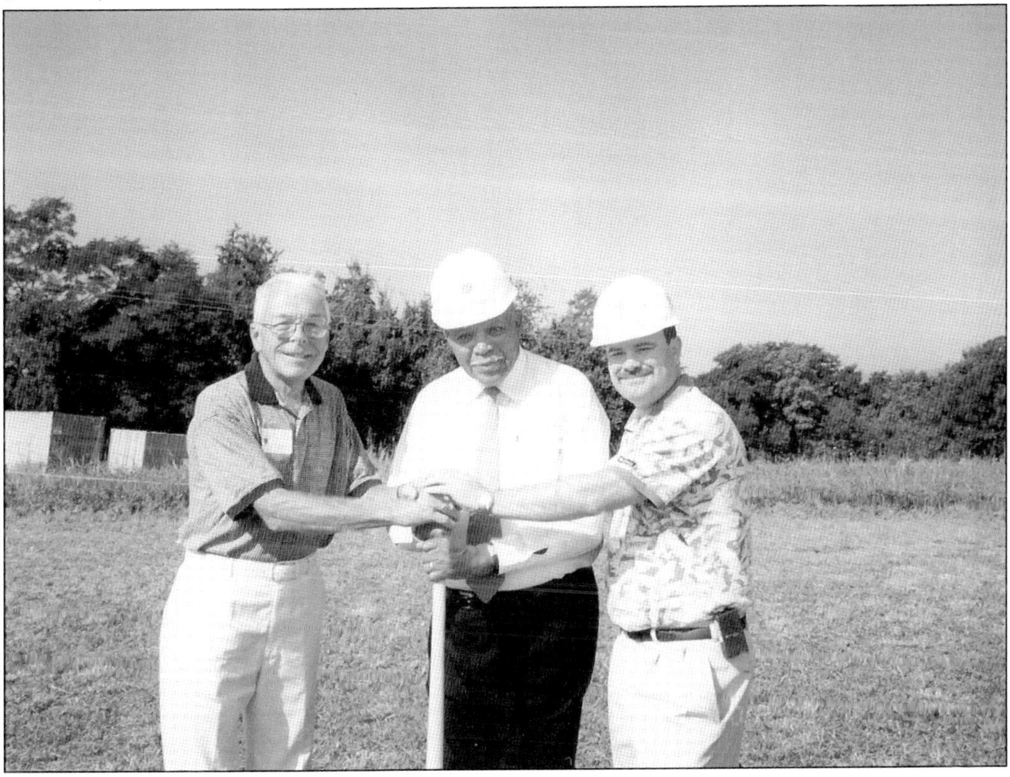

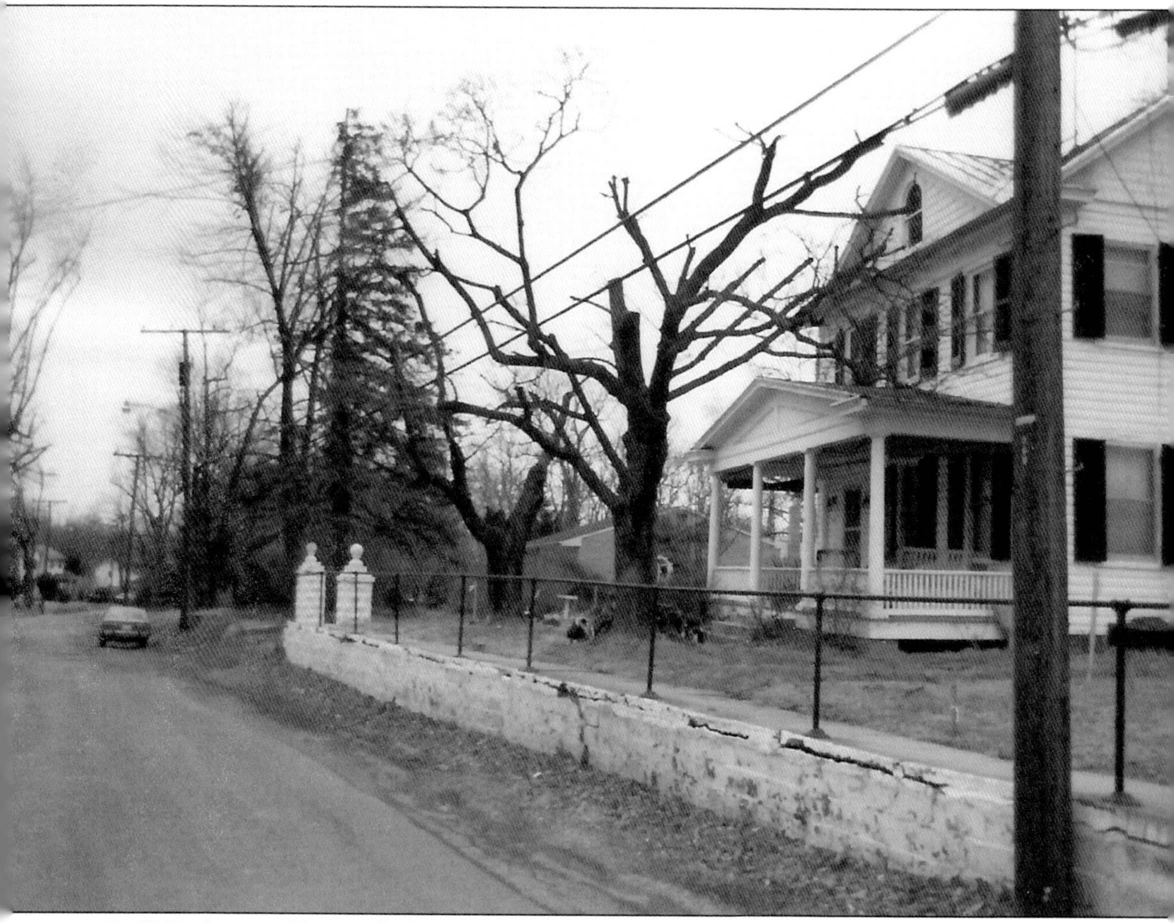

In 1981, the crumbling wall along Twentieth Street was a sign of how the town was experiencing growing pains, showing the wear and tear of age. With fewer labor demands on farms, residents sought higher-paying work elsewhere. Workers discovered that they could experience a bucolic lifestyle in Loudoun but still commute to the city. Newly subdivided tracts of land were being developed, and a population explosion was on the brink while Purcellville was trying to keep up. (Courtesy of Sue Russell.)

Six

At Play

For centuries, Purcellville residents have been strong in their religious faith, family values, education, hard work, and their time for play. One of the town's earliest annual events was the corn pull, where farmers "pulled" their corn, hauled it to a convenient spot, and made a tall pile of it. On a Saturday night, friends and neighbors would take their places along the pile, and every man took about two feet. Whoever could husk his way through the pile the fastest would win. Dillons Woods was west of town, and in 1901, Nick Hampton's portable sawmill began felling trees. The area would eventually be the central site for the town's entertainment. When the horn blew for leisure time, townspeople would go to the movie house, baseball field, the dance hall, or just "set for a spell" on a neighbor's porch. Country living was good and no one was in a hurry for change.

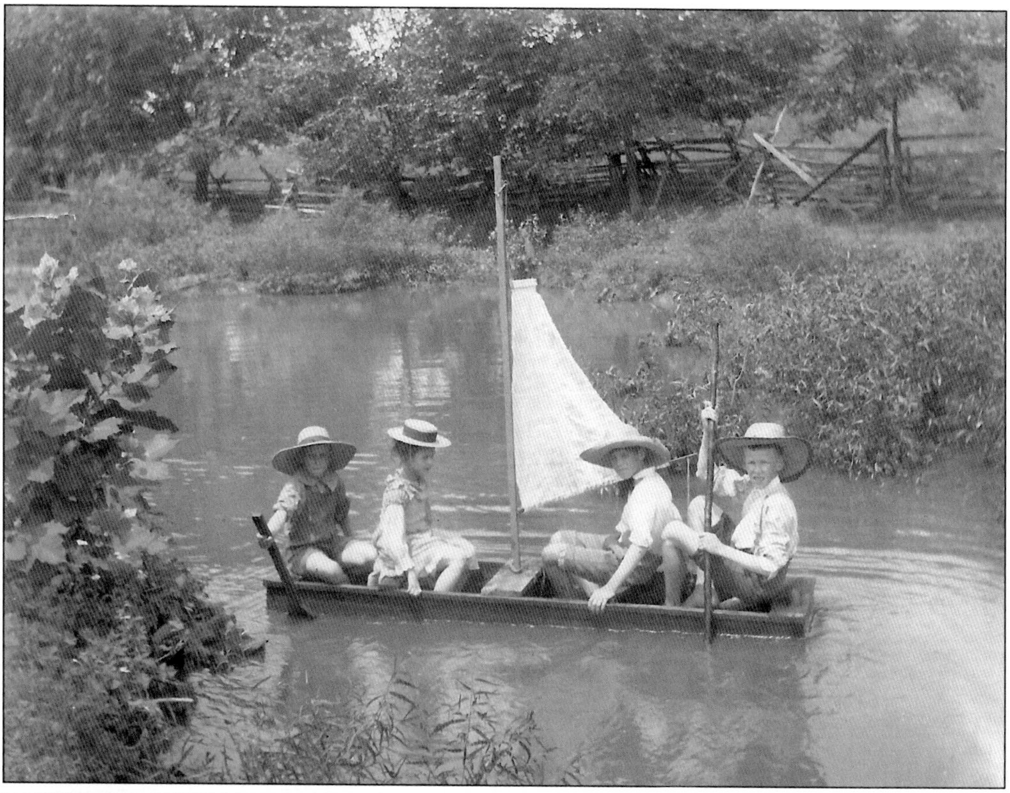

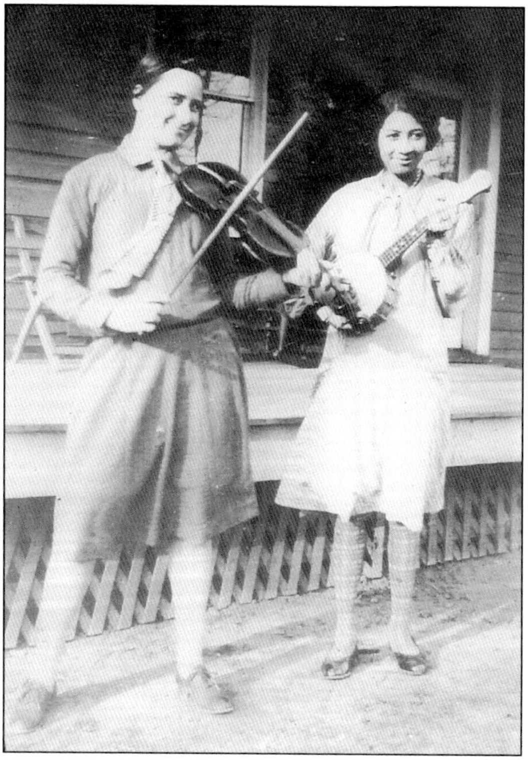

On a warm day in 1899, Virginius "Jinks" Hirst, Louise Henderson, Harold Wismith, and Terry Hirst set sail on their handmade craft. They headed north of town on Catoctin Creek. (Courtesy of Jane Hirst Bogle.)

Although scarlet fever left her hearing impaired, Maxine Cook (right) had a great ear for music. This photograph shows her playing the banjo on her family's front porch on G Street. She also played the ukulele beautifully. (Courtesy of Sheila Pinkney Kelly.)

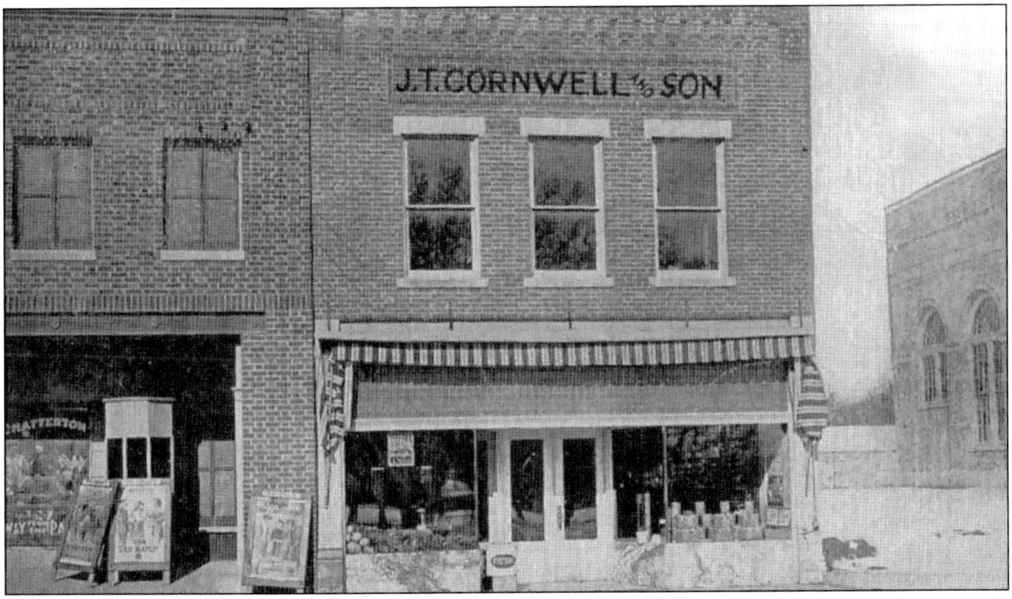

This business block on Main Street still exists today, but unfortunately, the theater does not. It was one of the most popular destinations in the 1920s. Most townspeople were coming off the farm and the movies took them "out of this world." Old timers remember watching their favorite stars up on the big screen, like Hopalong Cassidy and Alfred "Lash" LaRue, and how the best seat in the house happened to be the balcony, reserved for African Americans due to segregation laws. (Courtesy of Reginald Simms.)

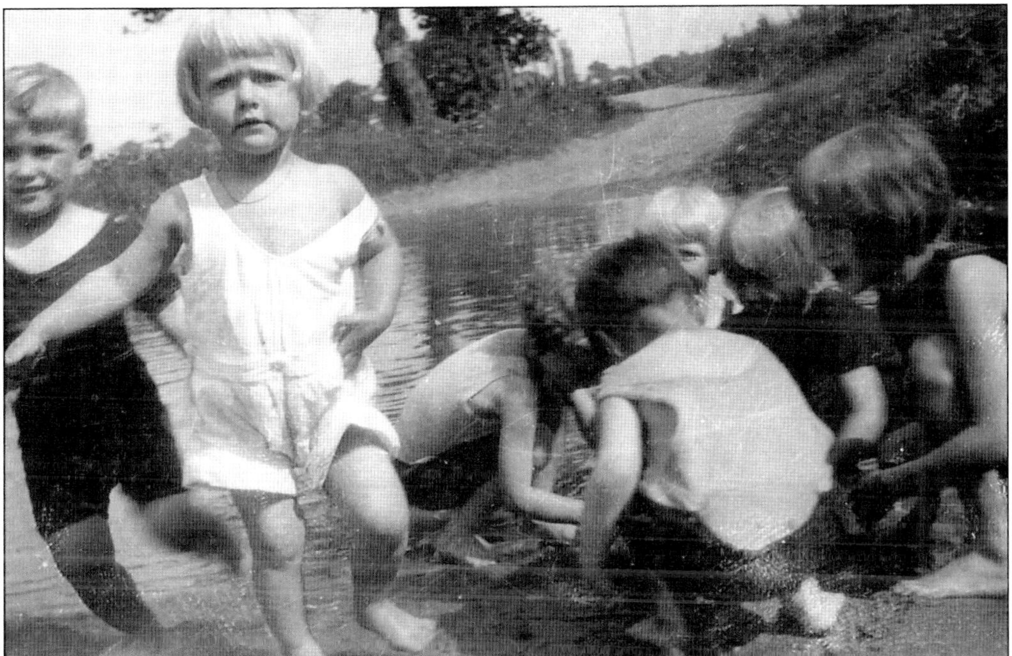

This 1926 photograph shows neighborhood children playing in a waterhole on a warm afternoon near Hillsboro Road. Pictured from left to right are Eddie Case, Betty Lyon Helen Case, Bob Lyon, Mary Owen Lyon, Constance Lyon, and Fanny Nelson Lyon. (Courtesy of Robert Lyon.)

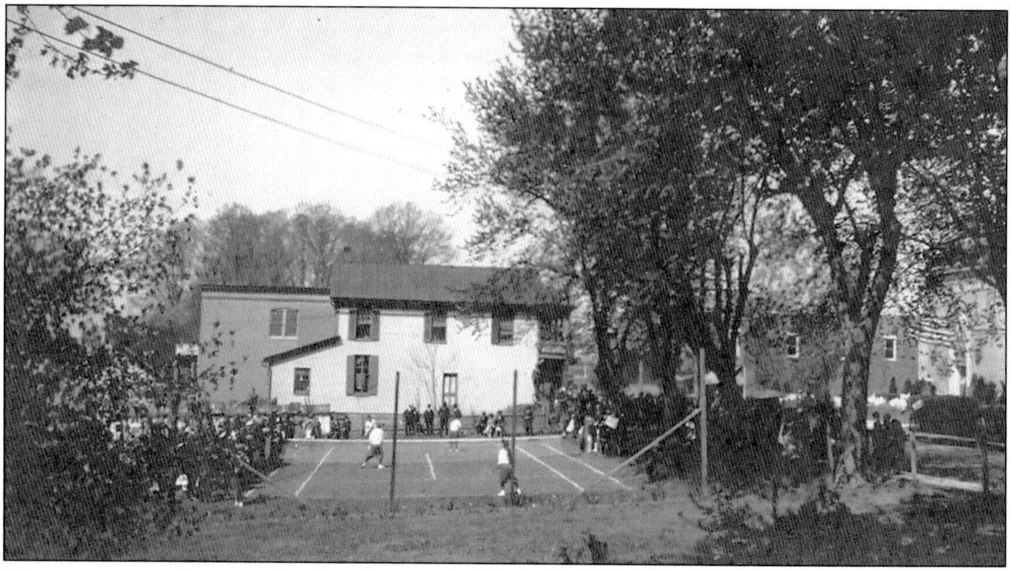

Many townspeople remember heading to the Hirsts' home on Main Street with its tennis court in the side yard. This 1925 photograph probably shows a competitive tennis match, based on the size of the crowd. The Hirsts' home was moved a few hundred yards away, which made way for the new Safeway Store. At that time, it was called the Sanitary Grocery Company. It would eventually become the town hall. (Courtesy of Jane Hirst Bogle.)

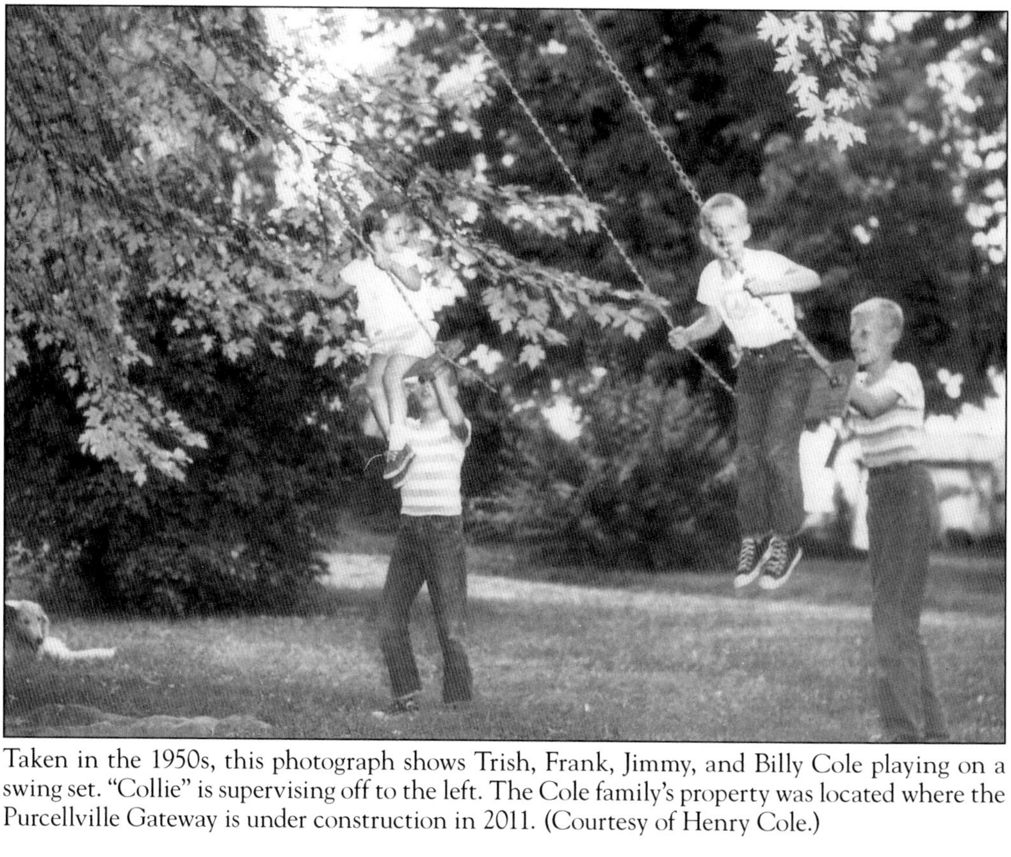

Taken in the 1950s, this photograph shows Trish, Frank, Jimmy, and Billy Cole playing on a swing set. "Collie" is supervising off to the left. The Cole family's property was located where the Purcellville Gateway is under construction in 2011. (Courtesy of Henry Cole.)

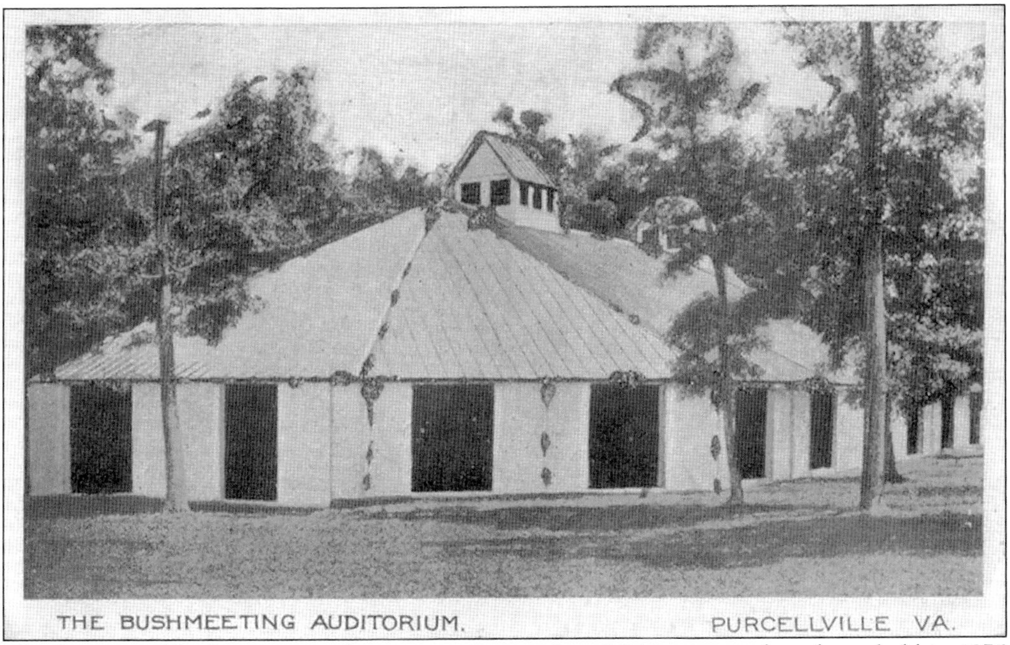

The first actual bush meeting where evangelists and prohibitionists gathered was held in 1876 near Lincoln. To shade the area, the organizers drove stakes in the ground, put on crosspieces, and placed bushes atop. This arbor was replaced by a tent, but the name stuck. The bush tabernacle auditorium in Purcellville was built in 1904 by Arch Simpson for $2,500 on land owned by Joseph Dillon. (Courtesy of Thomas Priscilla.)

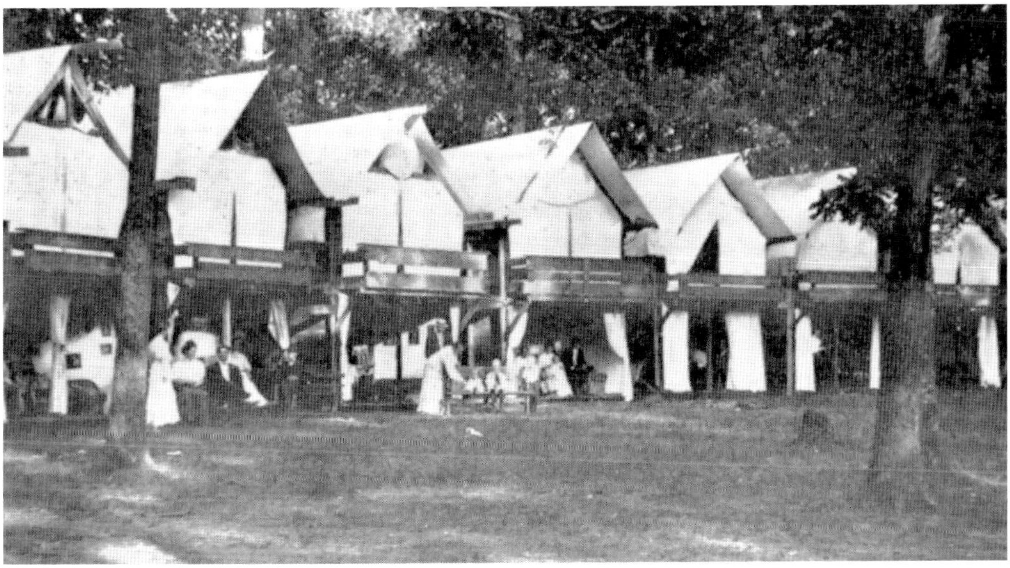

The first "temperance" picnic in Purcellville was held in June 1877 by the Good Templars of Loudoun County. The bush meetings began the following year. Every August, an annual gathering of speakers, entertainers, and evangelists would draw thousands of people. The day would end around an old-fashioned dinner on the grounds. This 1907 postcard shows the camp's meeting grounds where families would set up tents and camp for an entire week. (Courtesy of Thomas Priscilla.)

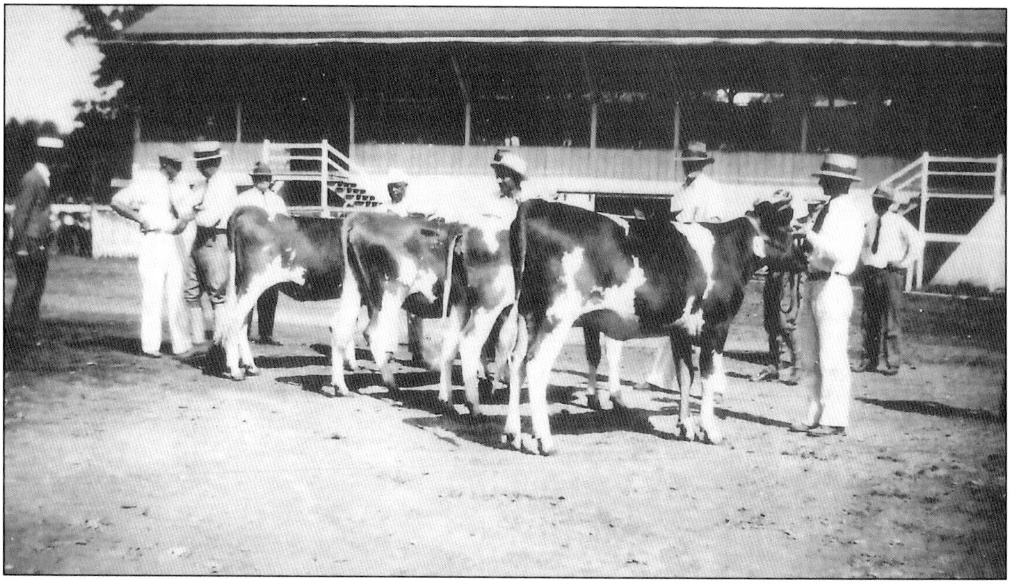

The Depression brought an end to the bush meetings and the property became a site for community events, such as the Loudoun County 4-H Fair, where cow shows and other competitions took place. The last bush meeting was in August 1931, when ex-baseball player and evangelist Billy Sunday delivered a sermon titled "Crooks, Corkscrews, Bootleggars and Whiskey Politicians." Townspeople remember politician and prohibitionist William Jennings Bryan coming to speak as well on the "evils of alcohol." (Courtesy of Robert Lyon.)

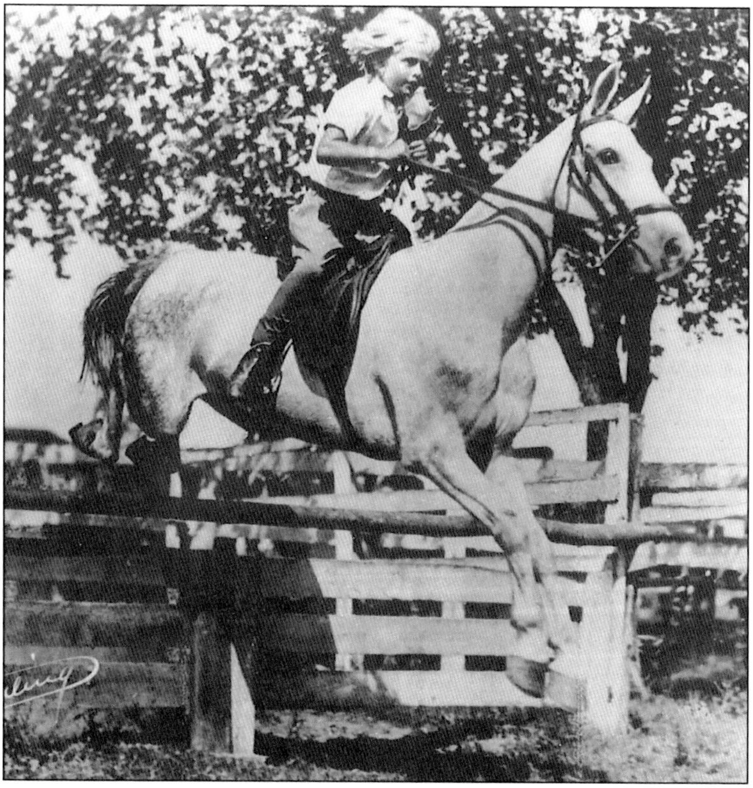

For a few years after the bush meetings ended, ownership of both the fair grounds and the auditorium changed hands because of weak financial support. However, leasing the grounds for events such as the 4-H Fair helped. This 1928 photograph shows Betty Lyon competing in the horse show. (Courtesy of Robert Lyon.)

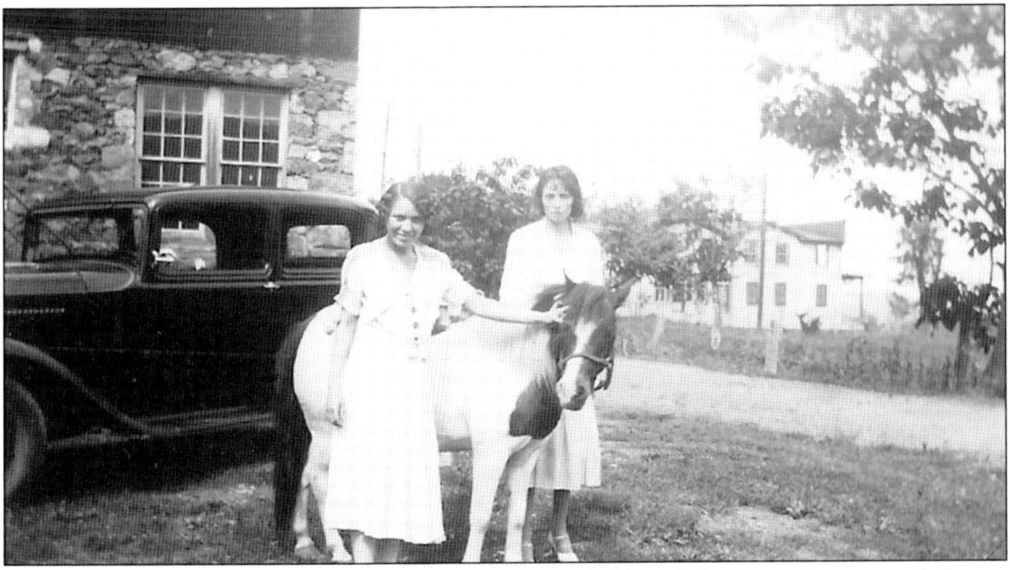

This 1930 photograph shows young Helen Lee Gross (left) with her prized pony on G Street. (Courtesy of Purcellville Preservation Association.)

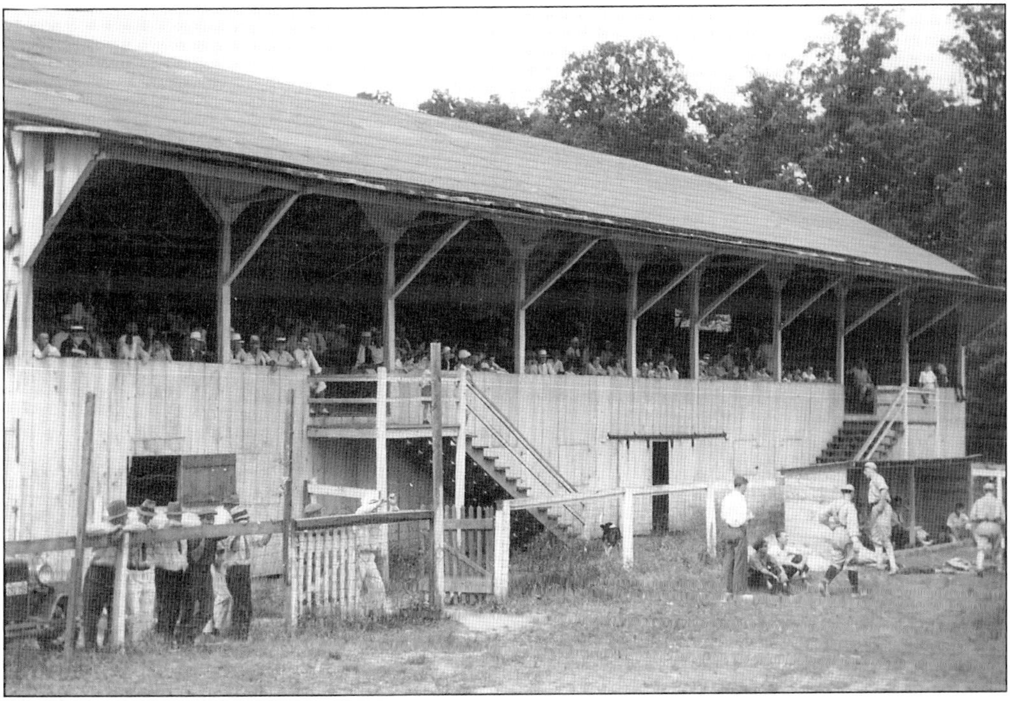

Many community events were held at Purcellville's stadium and on the grounds and auditorium nearby. The Purcellville Fire Department held their annual carnival here. There were athletic events and dog shows, and on one Mother's Day there was a meeting of the Klu Klux Klan. Taken on July 4, 1935, this photograph shows the doubleheader baseball game between the Kann's Department Store team of Washington, DC, and the Purcellville Baseball Club. (Courtesy of Mary Whitmore.)

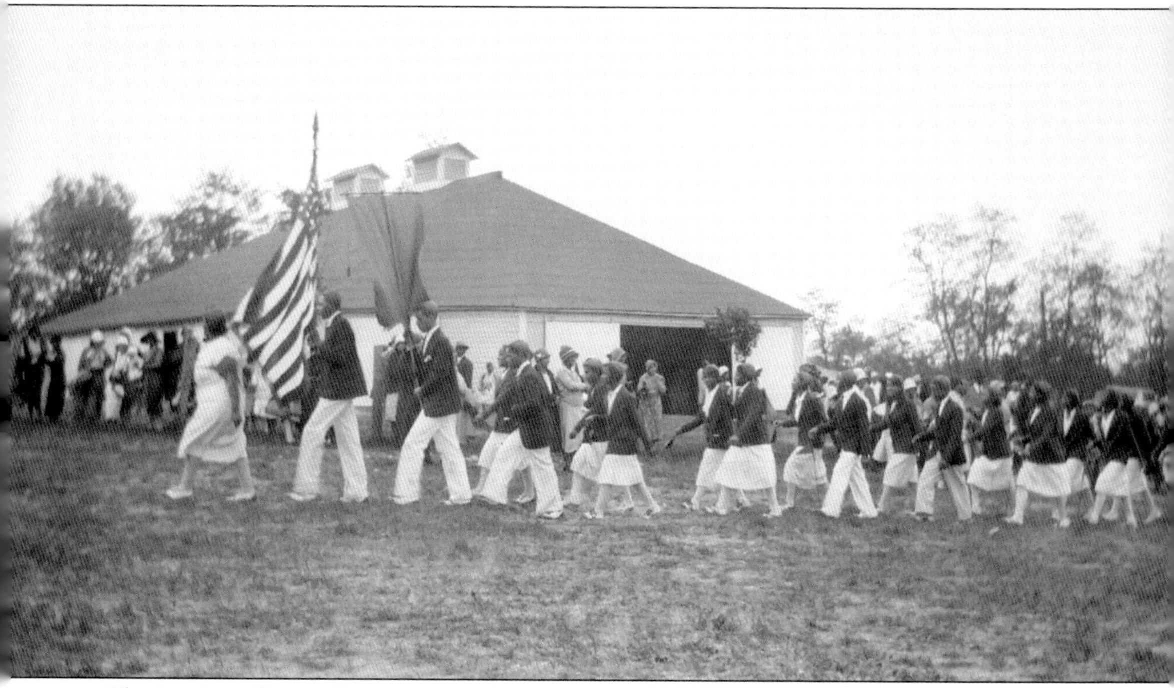

The Loudoun County Emancipation Association worked with the same builder who built the bush meeting tabernacle. Arch Simpson designed and superintended the tabernacle for the celebration of the Emancipation Proclamation in 1914. This 1950 photograph shows the tabernacle building behind the procession at the annual Emancipation Celebration. (Courtesy of Reginald Simms.)

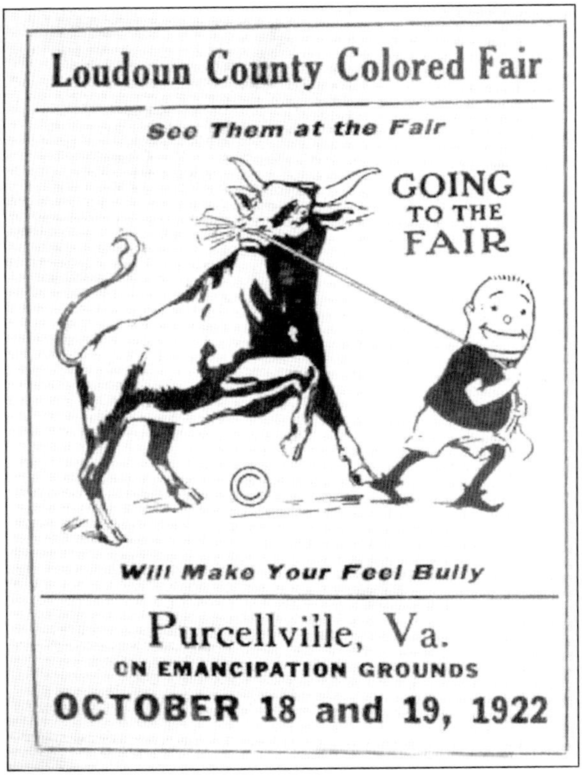

The Emancipation Grounds were used for many activities, including the Loudoun County Colored Fair that was held in October 1922. This is the front side of the admission ticket. (Courtesy of Reginald Simms.)

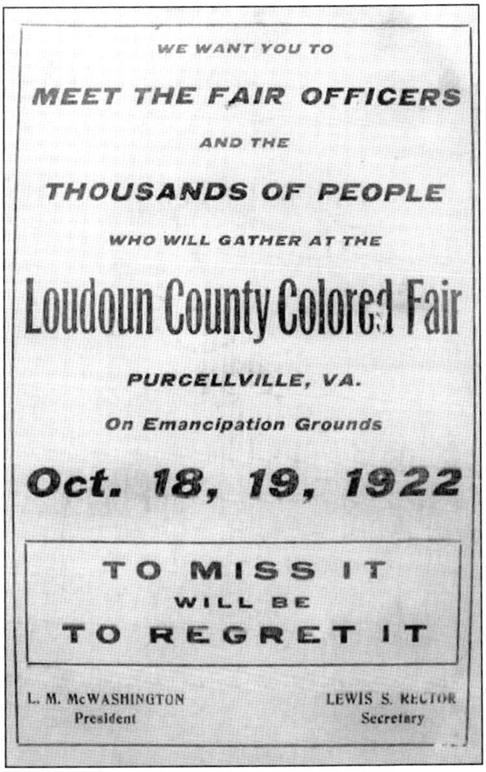

This is the reverse of the admission ticket to the Loudoun County Colored Fair in October 1922. (Courtesy of Reginald Simms.)

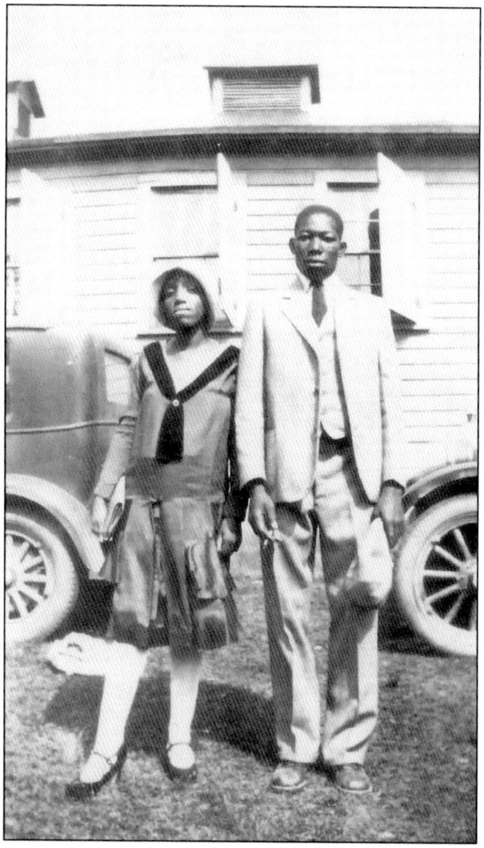

This 1930 photograph shows Anderson Simms and Ella Murray finely dressed for the annual Emancipation Celebration. The tabernacle is in the background. Attendees of the event wore their best clothes, and professional photographers were available for formal photographs. (Courtesy of Reginald Simms.)

The Lincoln's Cornet Band serenaded the fairgoers at the Emancipation Celebration. The midmorning parade would start the festivities as the crowds headed to the Emancipation Grounds. They celebrated with patriotic songs, flags, cheers of liberty, political addresses, religious sermons, and a picnic feast. (Courtesy of Reginald Simms.)

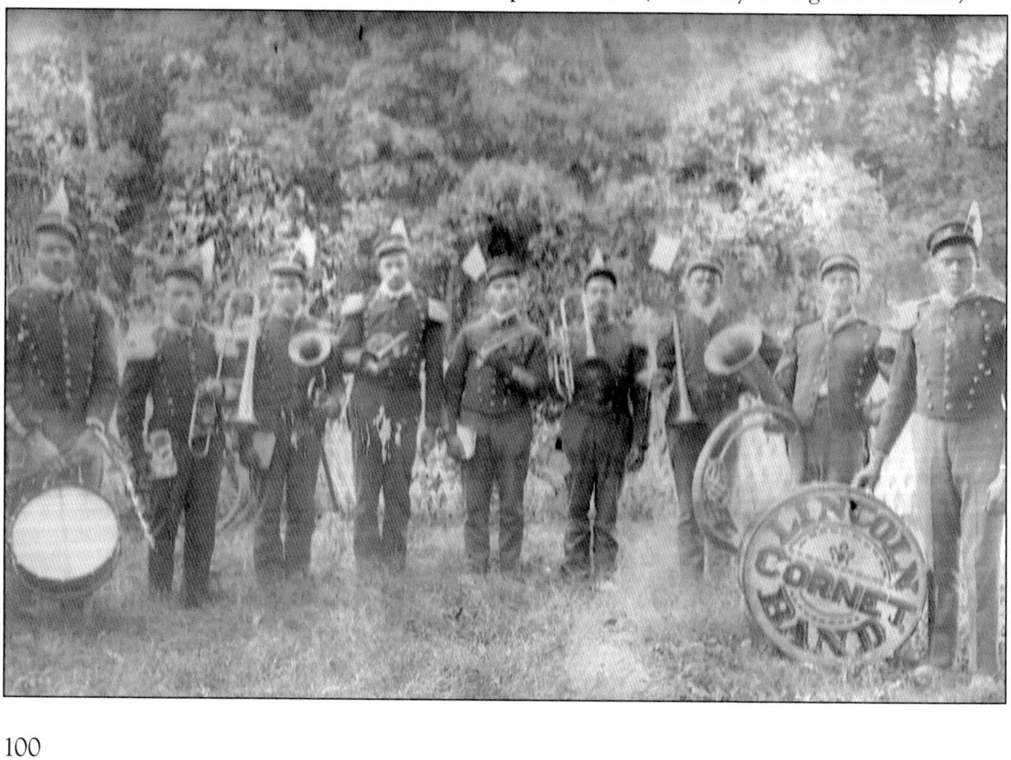

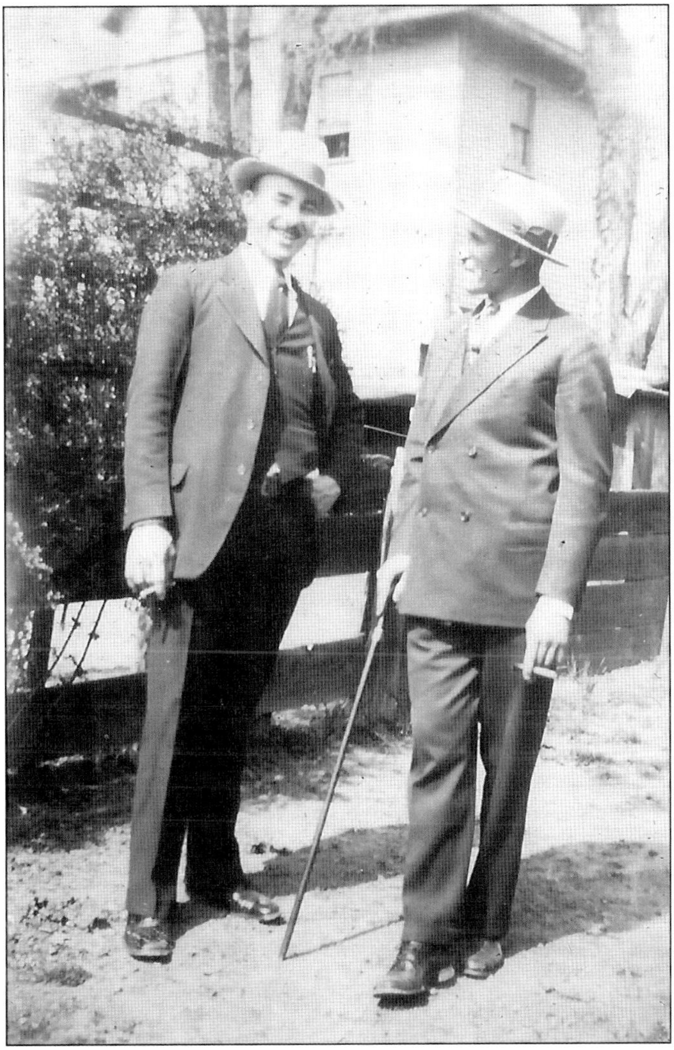

This 1930 photograph shows brothers Willie and Dooley Brown in their finest double-breasted suits. They were waiting for the festivities of the Emancipation Celebration to begin. (Courtesy of Reginald Simms.)

This 1933 admission ticket boasts the activities of the day, and describes that the event has "good music, good speakers, and amusement for all." (Courtesy of Reginald Simms.)

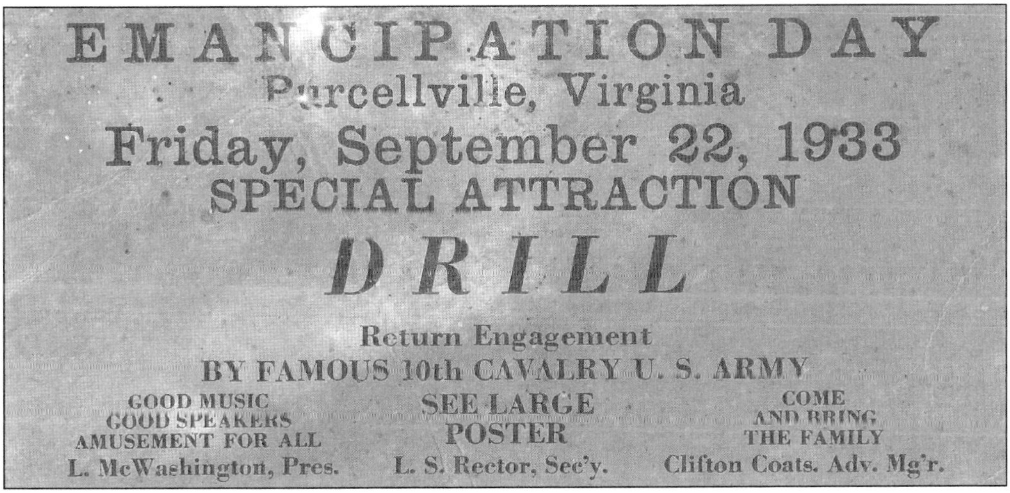

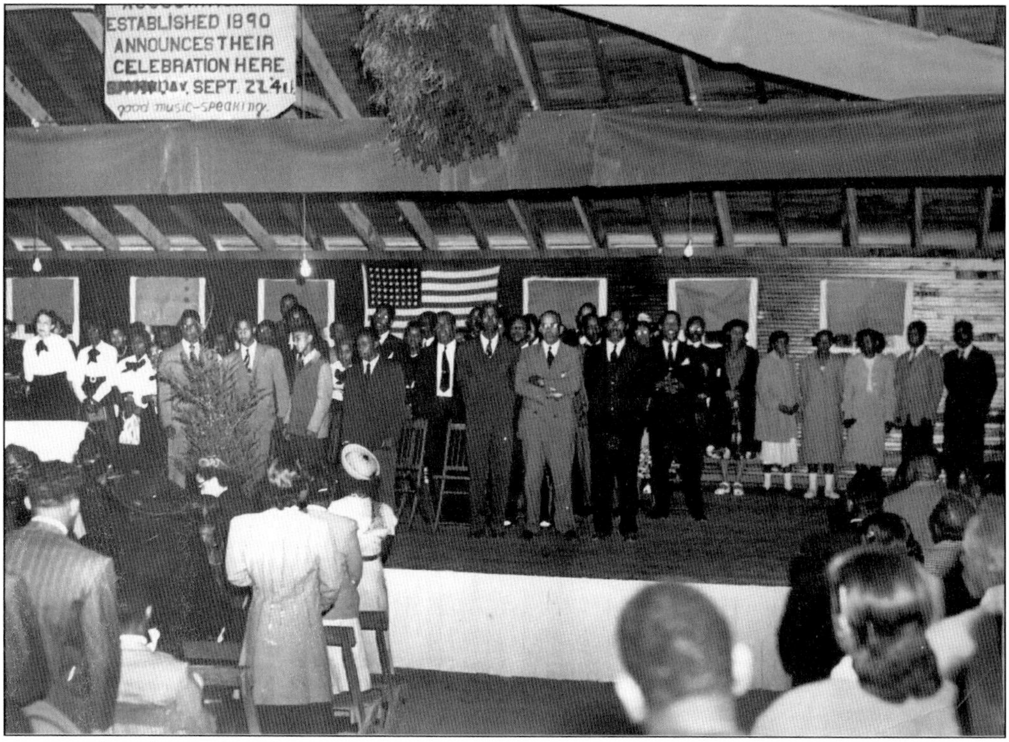

In 1941, the tabernacle auditorium on the Emancipation Grounds hosted orators who entertained and educated the crowds. Programs included preachers, politicos, and community leaders. In some years, 5,000 visitors would attend the exciting Emancipation Day Celebration. (Courtesy of Thomas Balch Library.)

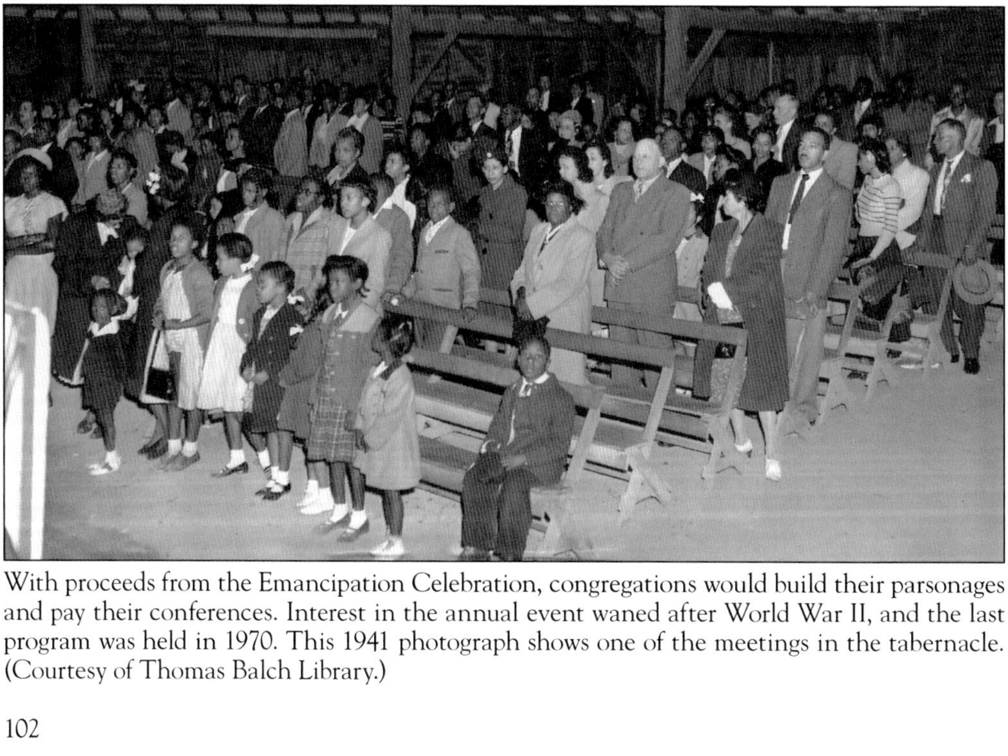

With proceeds from the Emancipation Celebration, congregations would build their parsonages and pay their conferences. Interest in the annual event waned after World War II, and the last program was held in 1970. This 1941 photograph shows one of the meetings in the tabernacle. (Courtesy of Thomas Balch Library.)

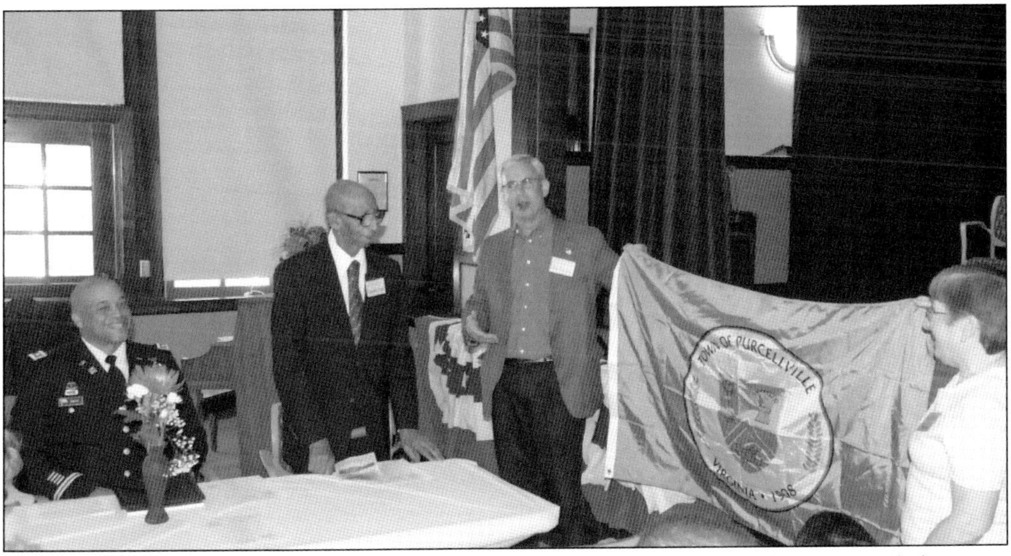

In September 2010, Mayor Robert Lazaro and Councilwoman Joan Lehr presented the town flag to Charles Clark, who is second from left, and Lt. Col. Spencer Smith at the Emancipation Celebration. In recent years, the celebration was held at the Carver Center. The event has evolved into a multicultural festival where people of all ethnicities celebrate Emancipation Day. The celebration is a family-oriented day full of history, reenactments, music, exhibits, motivational speeches, gospel, lunch, and fellowship. (Courtesy of Purcellville Preservation Association.)

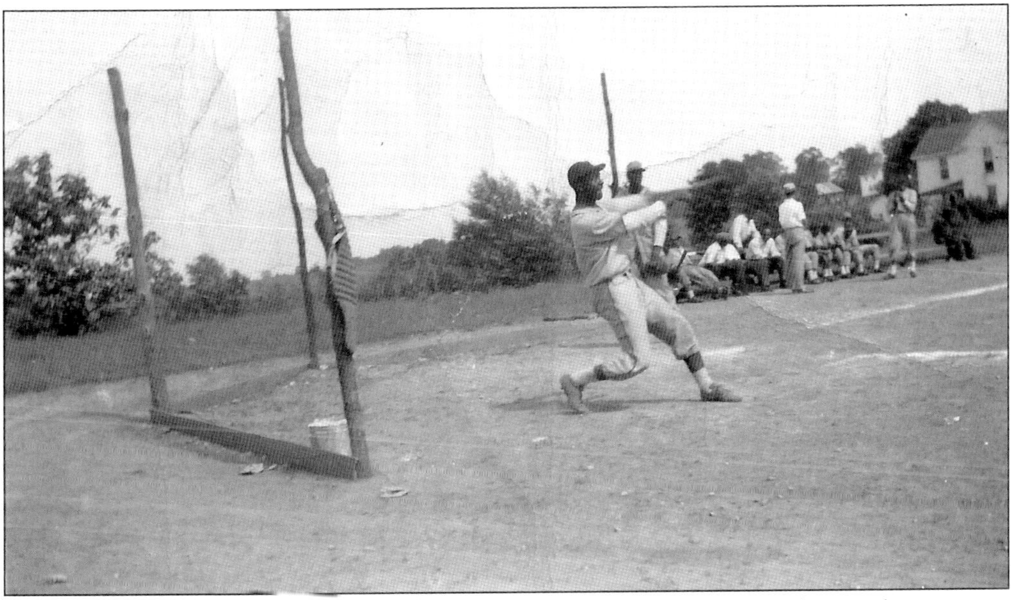

The popularity of baseball grew from the 1800s to become the focal point for social interaction among the residents of over 30 Loudoun communities. Friends, neighbors, and family would root for their local heroes and discuss the news of the day. These baseball games, where sometimes 3,000 fans would show, were where Loudoun residents socialized for decades. This 1932 photograph shows John Middleton, second baseman for the Purcellville Nationals. (Courtesy of Reginald Simms.)

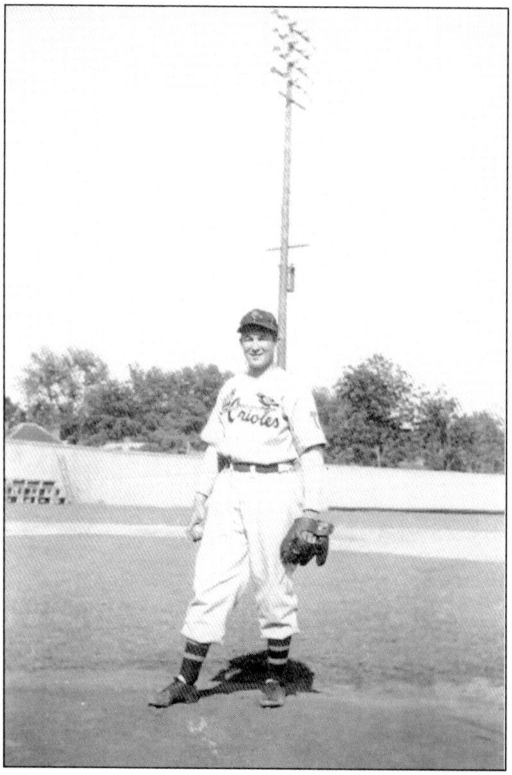

In the 1930s, one of Purcellville's greatest pitchers, Ronald Hope, would go on to play for the farm team in the Orioles minor league baseball program. The purpose of the system was to develop players who would participate in major leagues on demand. Hope would only play for one season because he wanted to return to his family's farm and marry his high school sweetheart Marjorie. (Courtesy of Donnie and Lindsay Hope.)

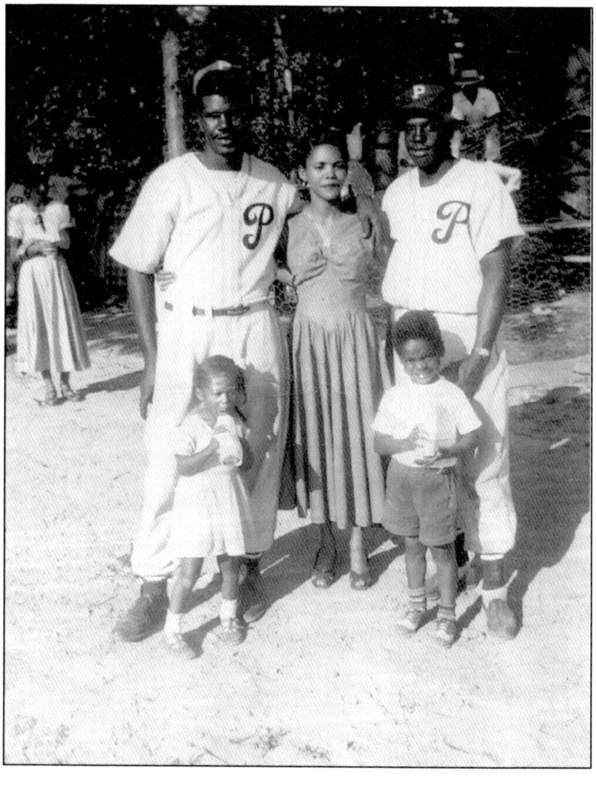

Purcellville's African American Nationals baseball team often played on the baseball field at the Emancipation Grounds. This 1930 photograph shows one of the Bull Run Mountain games. Pictured from left to right are (first row) Helen Campbell and Barry Middleton; (second row) James "Speed" Campbell (the Nationals' pitcher and third baseman), Grace Allen, and Charles Smith (outfielder). (Courtesy of Reginald Simms.)

Of those who started the Loudoun Golf and Country Club in 1927, "fewer than five had ever seen a golf ball," J. Terry Hirst, an early club member, once shared with historian Eugene Scheel. Purcellville's newspaper, the *Blue Ridge Herald*, predicted that the club would be a success, noting that it was within easy driving distance on recently paved roads of "four of Loudoun's wealthiest communities—Middleburg, Leesburg, the Blue Ridge Mountain colony and Waterford." The first pool in the county, built by Clark Simpson in 1936, was the most popular summer destination for its members. This photograph shows Gertie Ball and lifeguard Hawpe Adams relaxing by the club's pool. Adams became one of Purcellville's most popular government officials. Even after he moved in with his wife, Ethel Littlejohn Adams, in her family's home in Leesburg, he won as mayor with write-in votes—despite the fact that he was not even running. He was Purcellville's mayor from 1942 to 1949. (Courtesy of Jane Hirst Bogle.)

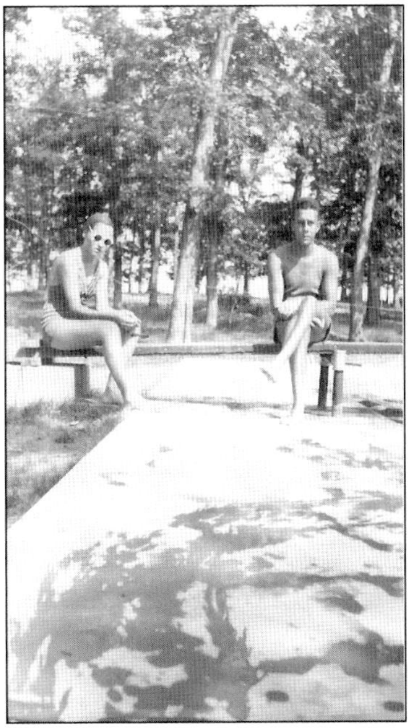

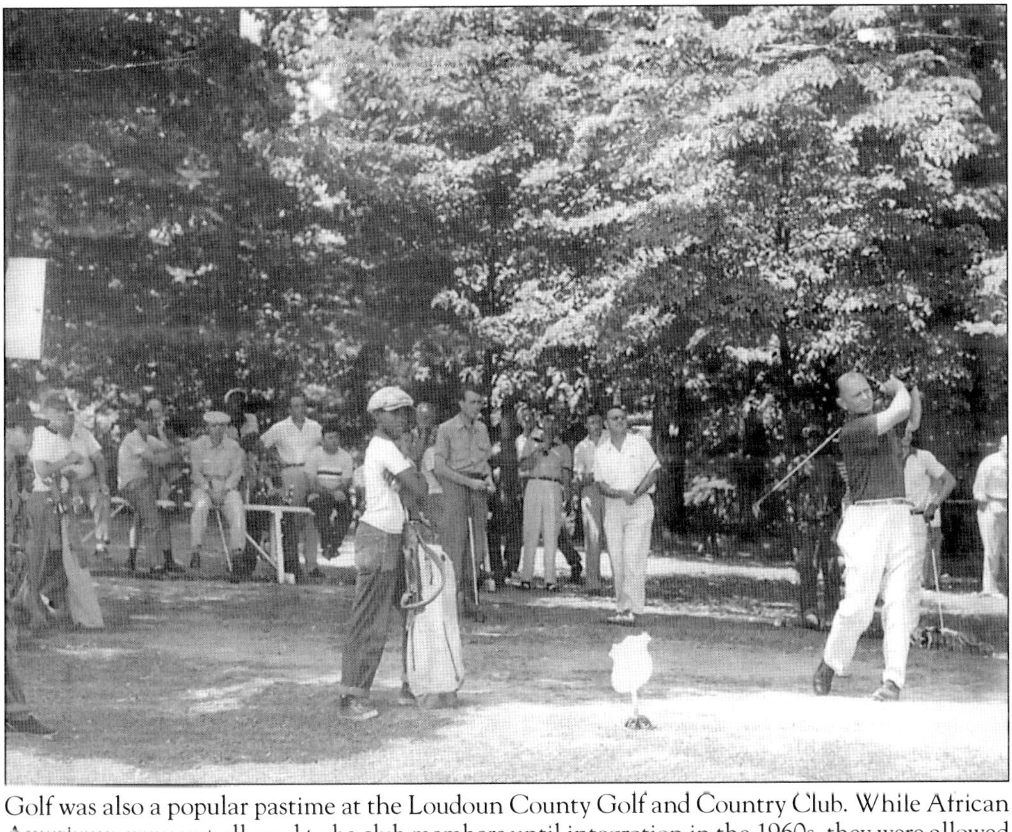

Golf was also a popular pastime at the Loudoun County Golf and Country Club. While African Americans were not allowed to be club members until integration in the 1960s, they were allowed to work at the club. Taken in the 1950s, this photograph shows Carroll Hirst and caddie Randolph Campbell Jr., during one of the club's championships. (Courtesy of Paul McCray.)

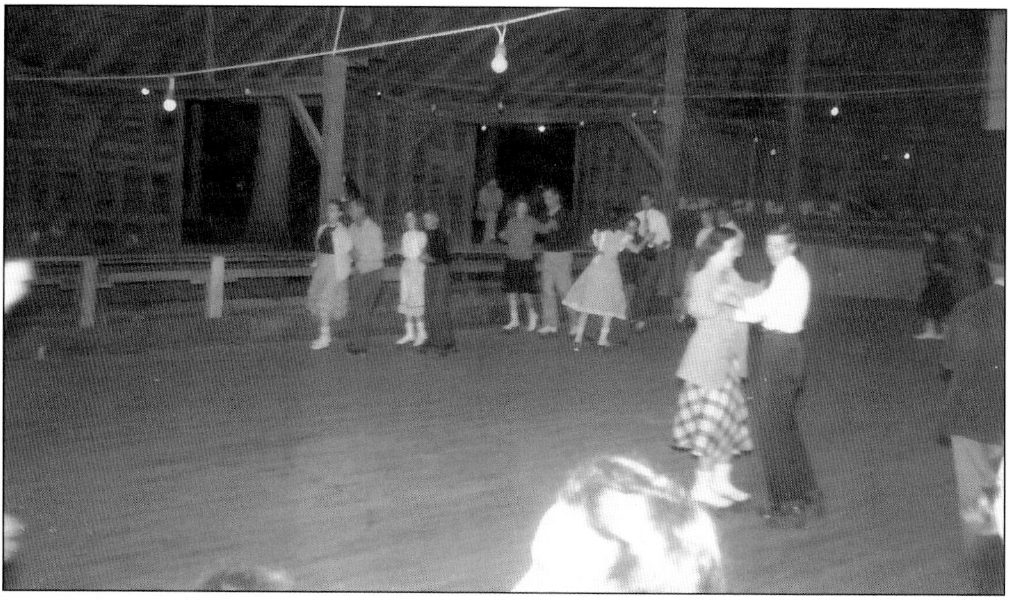

In 1947, the Purcellville Fire Department bought the bush tabernacle auditorium with the grounds, subletting it to William Tabb, who opened a roller rink at the newly named Firemen's Community Center. Tradition asserts that Patsy Cline sang at the center prior to her rise to stardom. The roller-skating rink continues to be one of the most popular destinations for recreation, especially on Friday nights, when it opens as a "teen center." (Courtesy of Thomas Balch Library.)

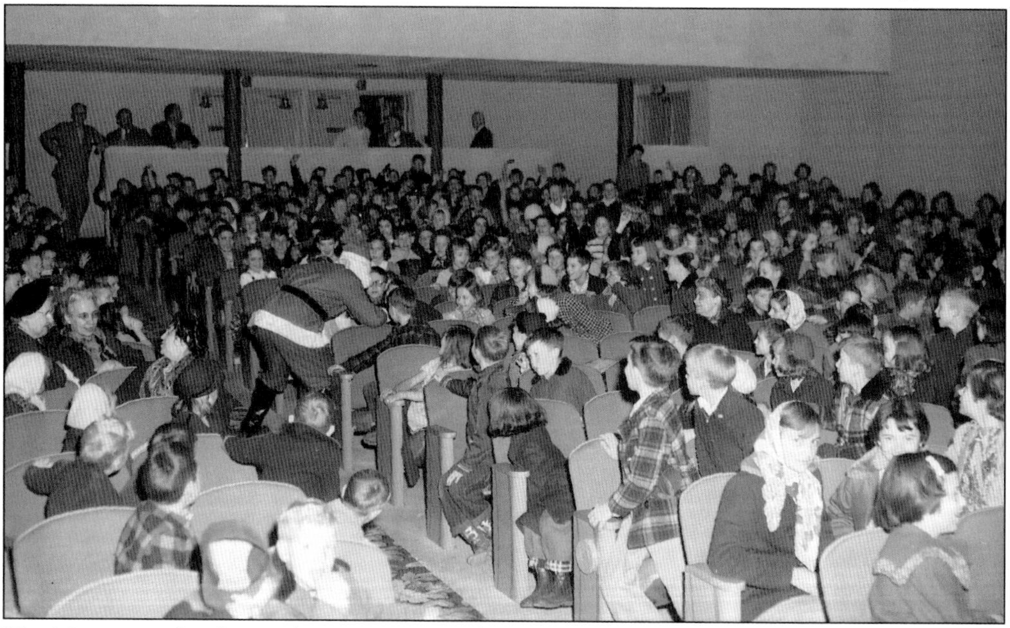

The Moorcones family ran the town's movie theater on the east end of Main Street. In this 1950 photograph, Santa Claus is visiting the children before the movie begins. Moorcones Theater opened on Dec. 25, 1949, and closed in 1976 because—according to the Oct. 14, 1976, *Tri City Herald*—owner Mary Moorcones didn't approve of the foul language in the film *The Bad News Bears*, starring Tatum O'Neal and Walter Mathau. The theater is still standing and is now divided into several businesses. (Courtesy of Thomas Balch Library.)

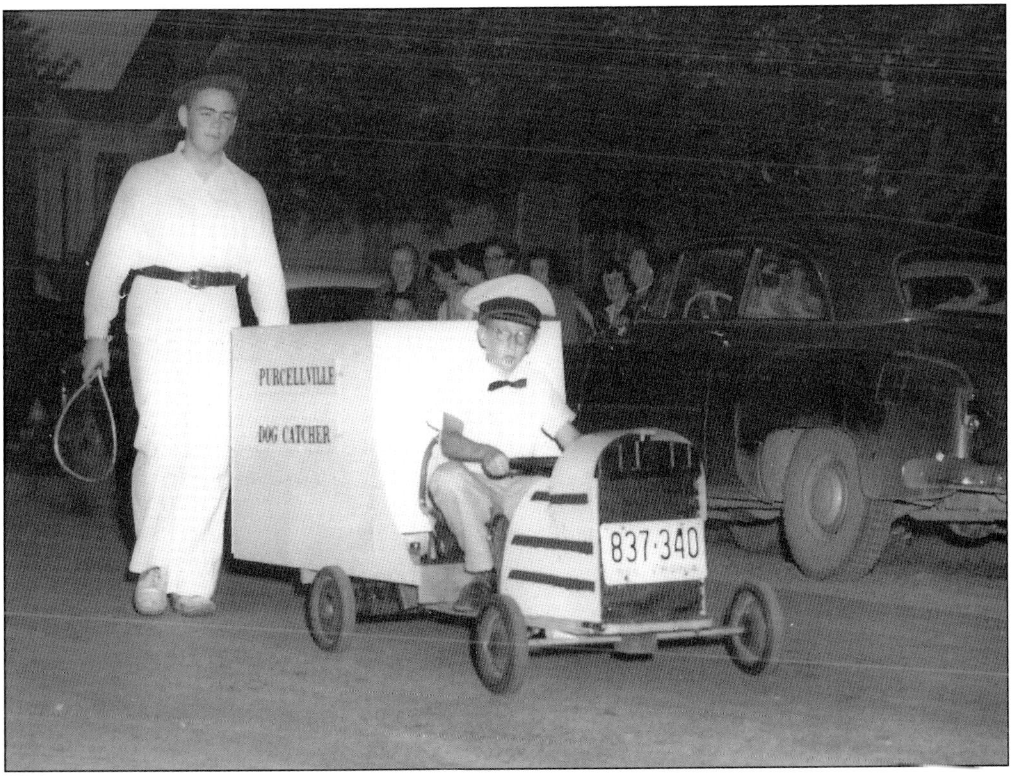

Taken in the early 1960s, this photograph shows Curl Piggott, costumed as a dogcatcher, participating in the Purcellville Halloween parade down Main Street. (Courtesy of Curl Piggott.)

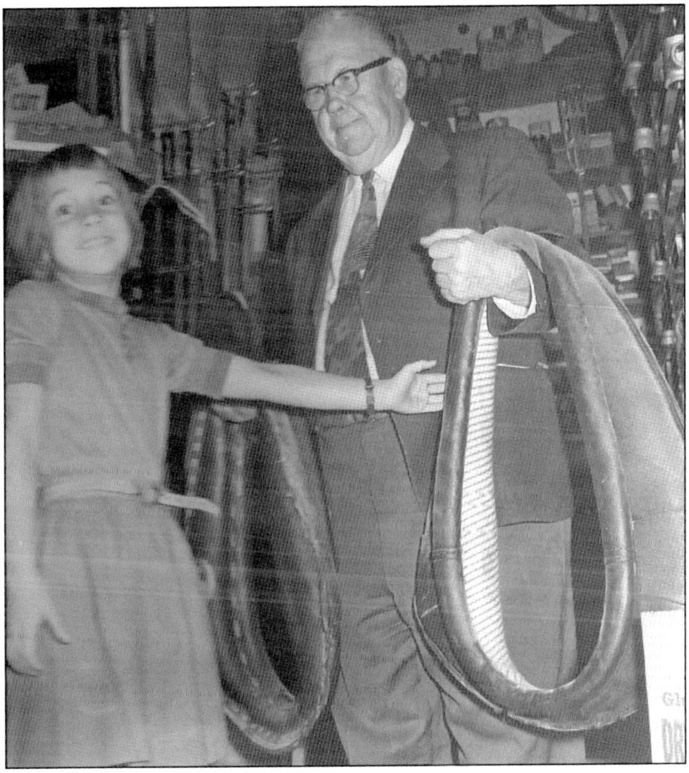

This 1961 photograph shows Beverly Bowman Chiasson and J.V. Nichols at Nichols Hardware, showing off the new shipment of horse collars. Townspeople remember how, when the horse collars stopped selling, Nichols would cut mirrors to fit inside the frame of the collar. There are many of these mirror hanging in Purcellville homes today. On December 28, 1961, this photograph appeared on the front page of the *Loudoun Times-Mirror*. (Courtesy of Beverly Bowman Chiasson.)

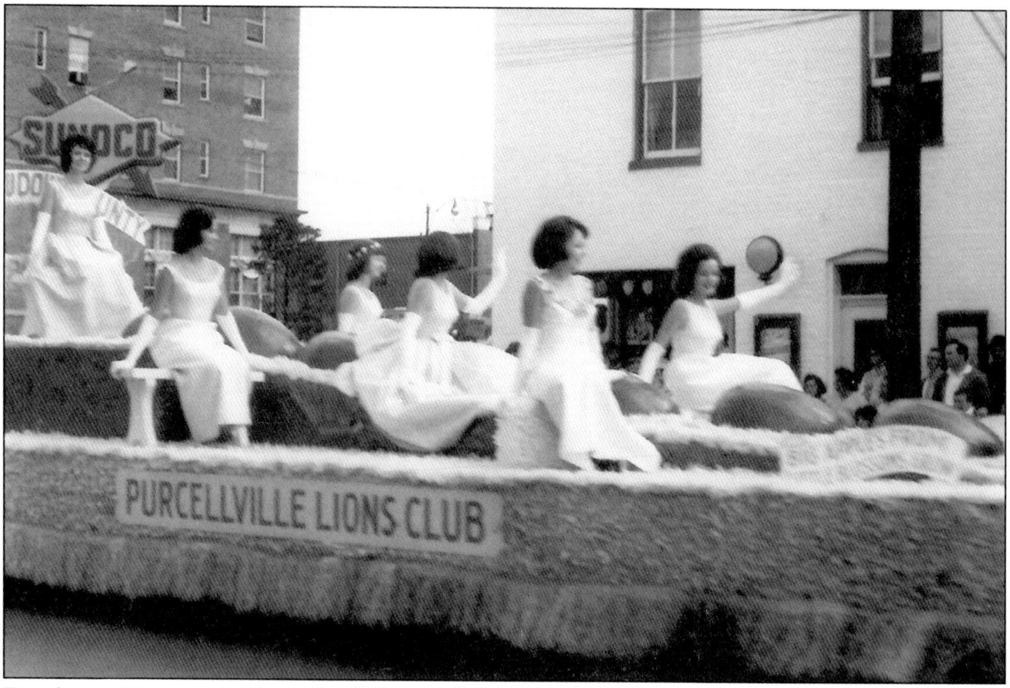

For almost 30 years, the Purcellville Lions Club hosted and organized the Miss Loudoun County Pageant, but it ended the program in 2001. This 1965 photograph shows Miss Loudoun County and her court waving to the crowd during Winchester's Apple Blossom Parade. (Courtesy of Jim and Betty Wiley.)

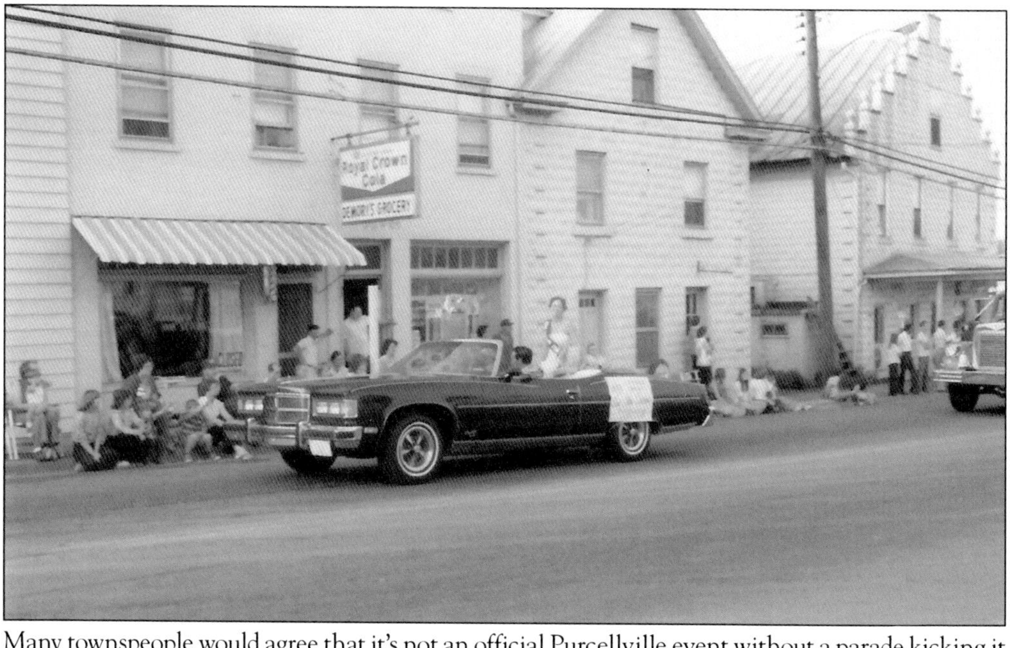

Many townspeople would agree that it's not an official Purcellville event without a parade kicking it off. On Independence Day 1978, Miss Loudoun County heads west on Main Street. Today, most of the town parades move east and downhill on Main Street. (Courtesy of Jim and Betty Wiley.)

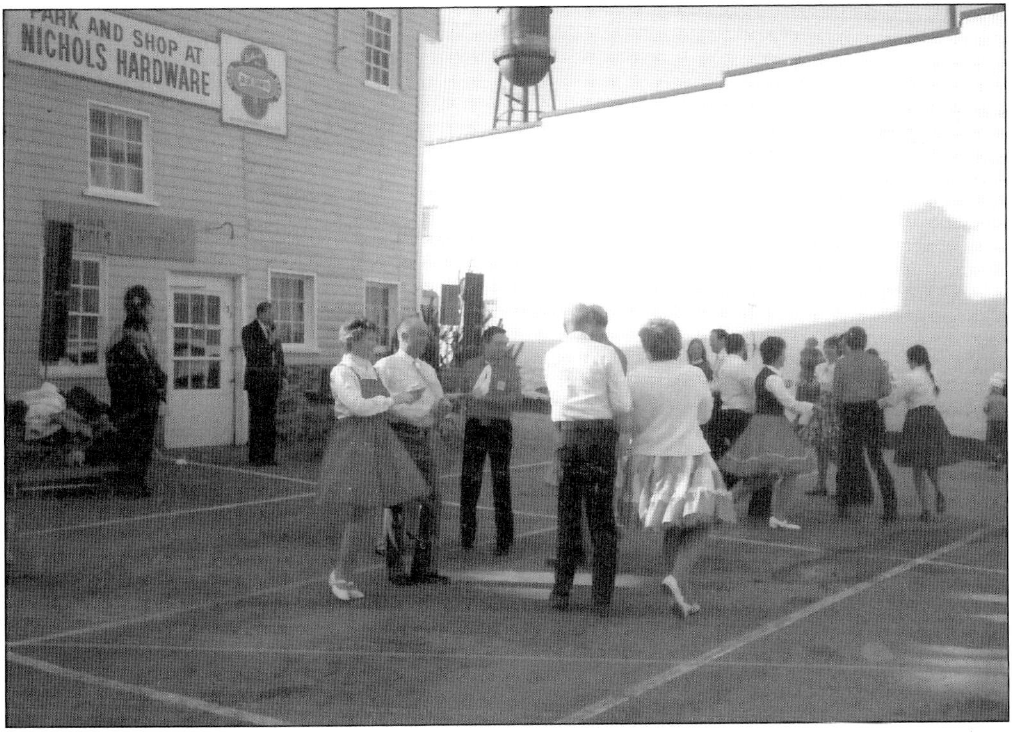

While celebrating "Christmas in the Valley" in 1985, the Beaux and Belles demonstrate their square dance moves in the Nichols Hardware parking lot. The Beaux and Belles were a countywide square dancing group. Purcellville continues to celebrate the holiday by lighting the Christmas tree at the teardrop in front of Bethany Methodist Church, evening trolley rides, a morning parade on Main Street, and "Breakfast with Santa" at the Purcellville Train Station. (Courtesy of Jim and Betty Wiley.)

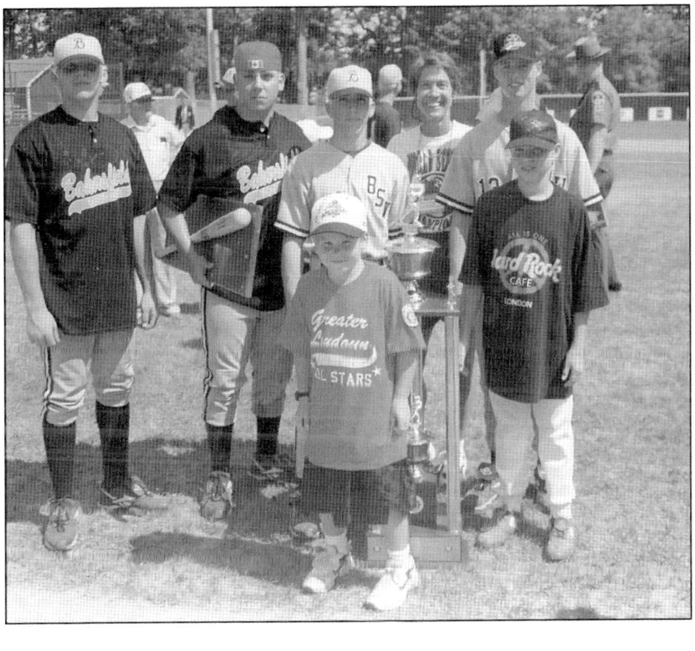

Since 1998, Purcellville has proudly hosted the prestigious Babe Ruth World Series at its Firemen's Field stadium. Baseball teams from all over the country compete during this weeklong event. Families throughout town host the ballplayers. This 1998 photograph shows the winning team from Bakersfield, California, and the MacDonald-Chiasson family, who were their family hosts for the week. (Courtesy of Beverly Bowman Chiasson.)

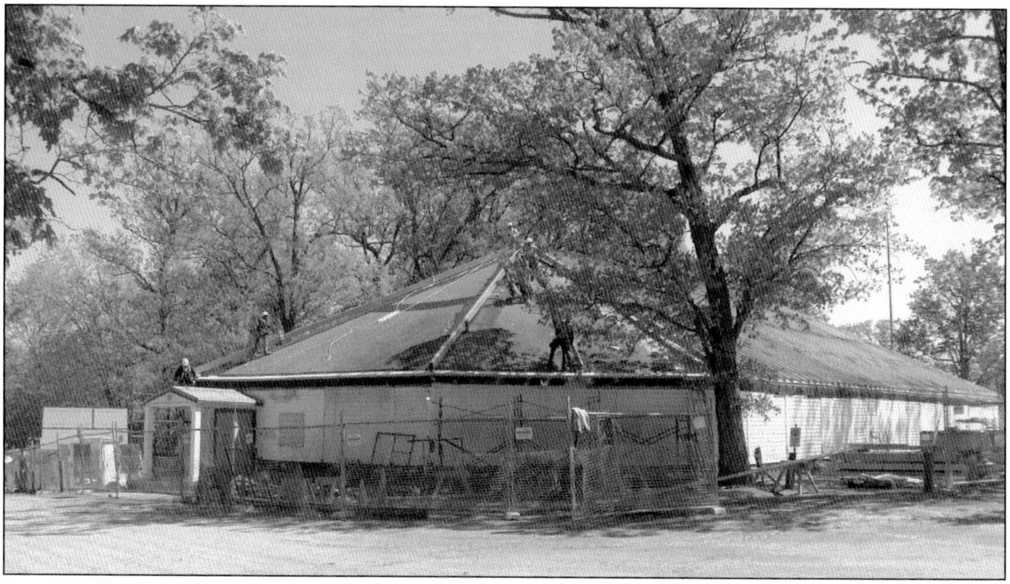

Purcellville's firemen owned the Bush Tabernacle auditorium, the grounds, and the stadium for decades. The Town of Purcellville purchased the properties in 2008, and immediately began extensive renovations, eventually making it a community center. Local athletic leagues now lease the stadium and ball fields, and the tabernacle auditorium is leased for a roller-skating rink and community events. (Courtesy of Purcellville Preservation Association.)

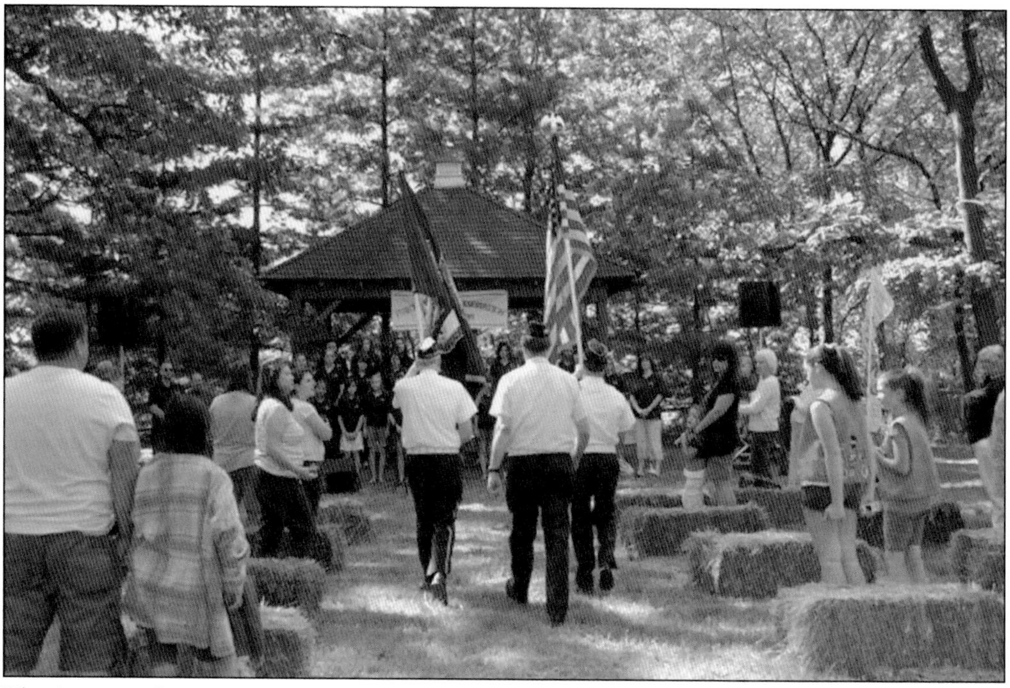

The American Legion Post 293 ceremoniously leads the guard, starting the Purcellville Preservation Association's Heritage Day in 2010. The annual event, which is held at Fireman's Field, attracts hundreds of guests and celebrates Purcellville's history. (Courtesy of Cathy Darby.)

Seven

URBAN SPRAWL

The basic formula for life in Purcellville changed only a little from the days of settlement in the late 1700s to the early 1900s. Most Loudouners were farmers and lived on ancestral lands, with their houses dating back generations. Life swirled around the rural community for a very long time. A few automobiles chugged along the rutted roads of Purcellville and neighboring towns, but horses were still the main mode of transportation. Horses were indispensable in pulling farm implements or hauling grain to the mill or local markets. The population in Purcellville remained static for most of the 20th century. Over the last century, many changes occurred, but they left the bucolic life intact. Tractors diminished the role of the horse, and the mass production of automobiles and trucks eventually changed everything. Purcellville saw major growth coming. By 1988, Purcellville had its first bypass. People were moving to this small town for the country life, the openness, and safety, because it lay a good distance from the bustling pace of Washington. Purcellville's traditional dependence on agriculture diminished as more residents became employed outside of the community. One of Purcellville's challenges is to accept the changes without losing its historical identity.

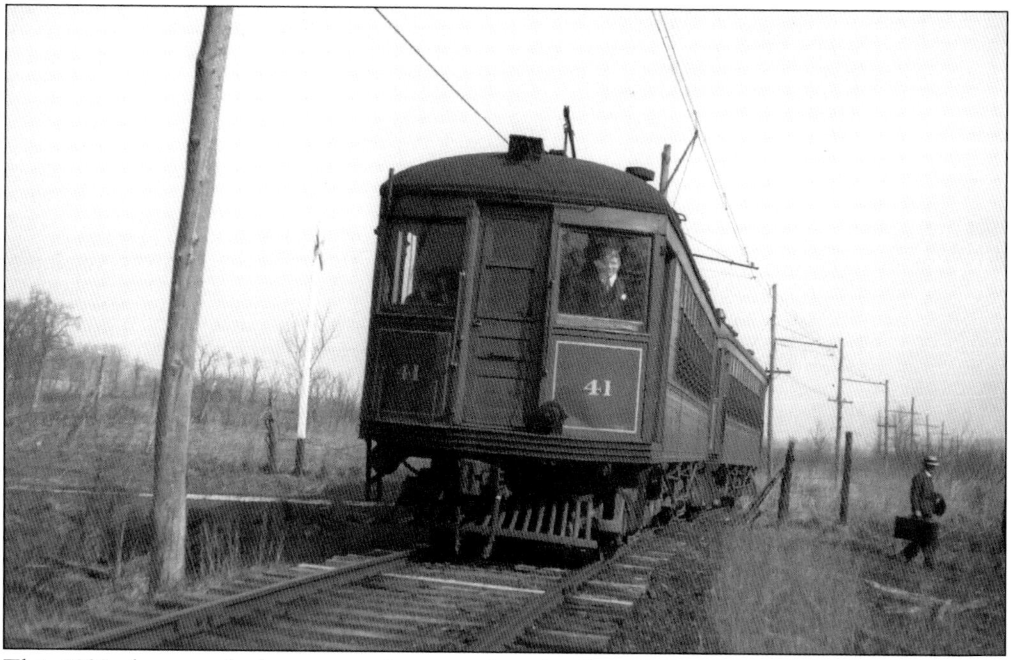

This 1939 photograph shows one of western Loudoun's earliest commuters, Frank McComb, heading home. The railroad had an accommodating nature as a rural system, and it used to stop at a random crossroad to let a single traveler off. (Courtesy of Northern Virginia Regional Park Authority.)

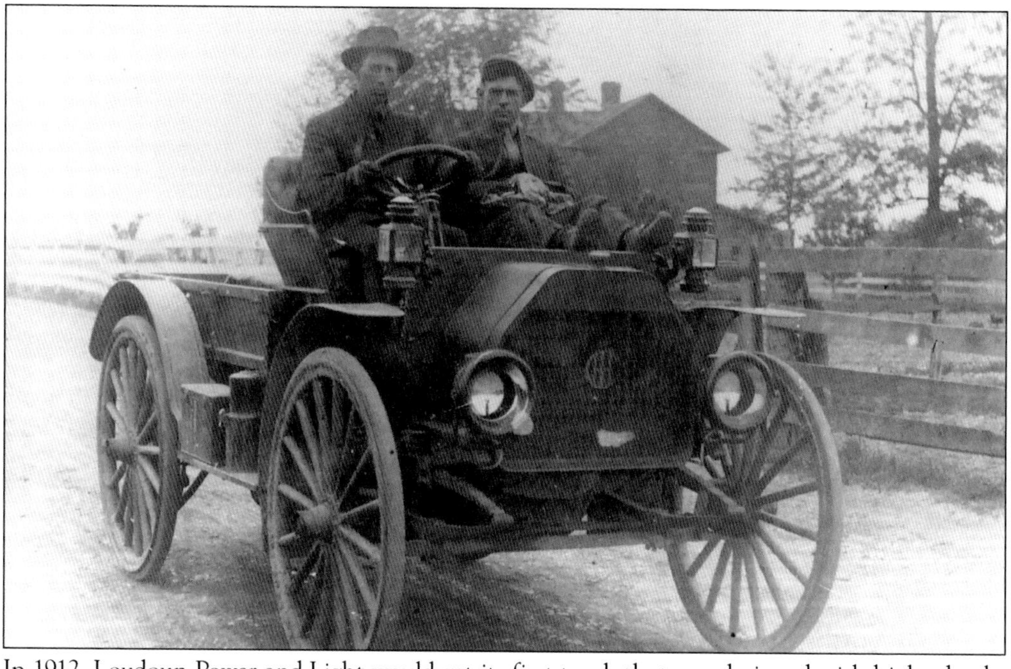

In 1912, Loudoun Power and Light would get its first truck that was designed with high wheels, which were practical for driving on the muddy, rutted roads. Behind the wheel is Chief Engineer King and "Shortie" Hough, who were making their way through town on an unpaved Main Street. (Courtesy of Robert Lyon.)

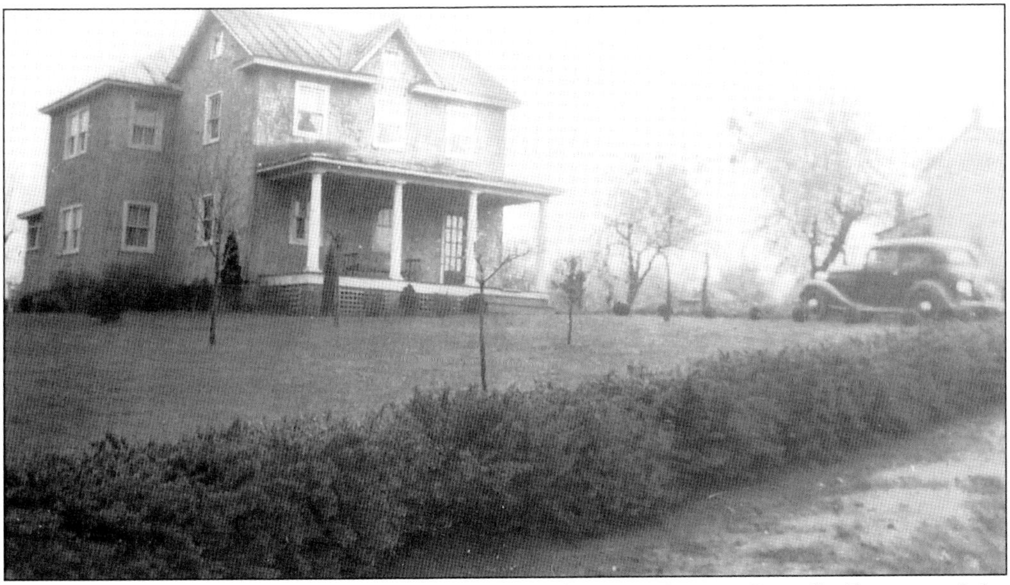

In 1928, with the paving of Virginia State Route 7 from Leesburg to Purcellville, most of the town would choose the automobile for transportation, including local barber George E. Lee, who lived on G Street and commuted the short distance to his barber shop in Round Hill. (Courtesy of Purcellville Preservation Association.)

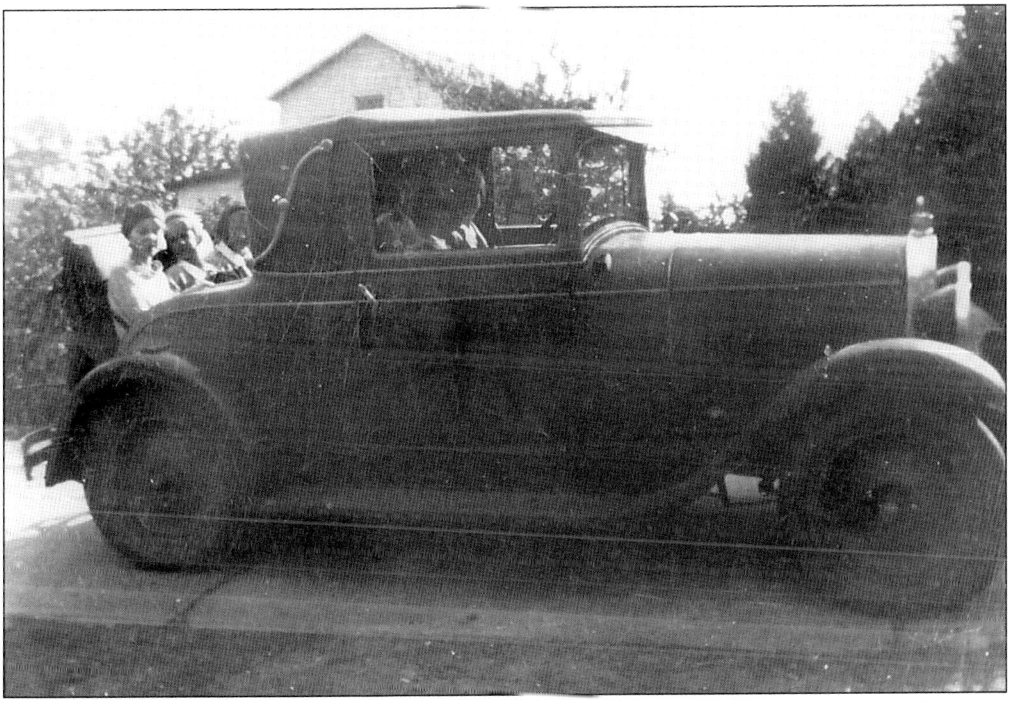

In this 1932 photograph, neighbors and friends climbed into the Lyon family's new Chevrolet Coupe complete with a "rumble seat," an upholstered exterior seat that opened out from the rear deck of a pre–World War II automobile. It became largely obsolete in the mid-1930s, when cars became too fast and streamlined. (Courtesy of Robert Lyon.)

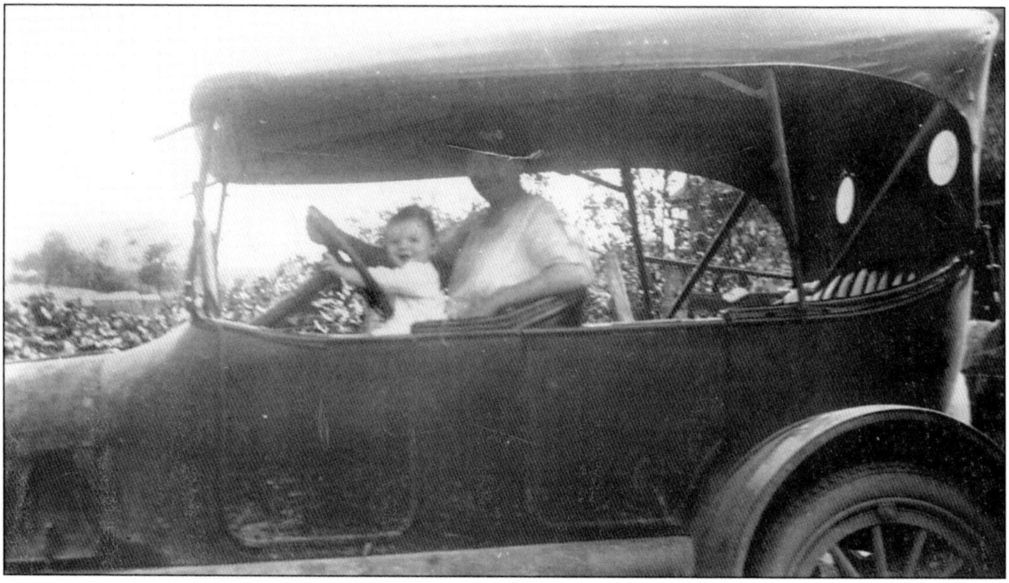

In this 1935 photograph, Addie and Sid Purcell try out their new automobile. Townspeople became self-reliant and were starting to choose not to wait for an often dirty, uncomfortable, and unreliable train. (Courtesy of Thomas Balch Library.)

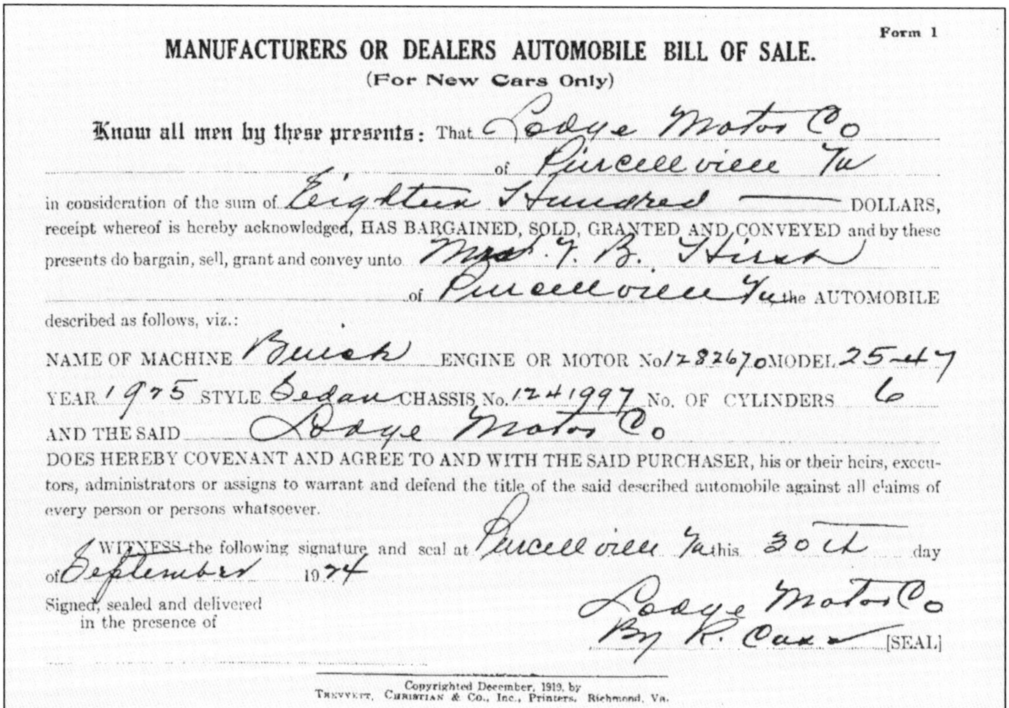

Form 1

MANUFACTURERS OR DEALERS AUTOMOBILE BILL OF SALE.

(For New Cars Only)

Know all men by these presents: That Lodge Motor Co of Purcellville Va in consideration of the sum of Eighteen Hundred DOLLARS, receipt whereof is hereby acknowledged, HAS BARGAINED, SOLD, GRANTED AND CONVEYED and by these presents do bargain, sell, grant and convey unto Mrs. F. B. Hirst of Purcellville Va the AUTOMOBILE described as follows, viz.:

NAME OF MACHINE Buick ENGINE OR MOTOR No. 1282670 MODEL 25-47

YEAR 1925 STYLE Sedan CHASSIS No. 1241997 No. OF CYLINDERS 6

AND THE SAID Lodge Motor Co

DOES HEREBY COVENANT AND AGREE TO AND WITH THE SAID PURCHASER, his or their heirs, executors, administrators or assigns to warrant and defend the title of the said described automobile against all claims of every person or persons whatsoever.

~~WITNESS~~ the following signature and seal at Purcellville Va this 30th day of September 1924

Signed, sealed and delivered in the presence of

Lodge Motor Co
By R. Cox [SEAL]

Copyrighted December, 1919, by
Trevvett, Christian & Co., Inc., Printers, Richmond, Va.

In 1924, Joe Lodge's Buick Motor Company sold Mrs. Hirst a new machine for a grand total of $1,800. Passenger service to Washington ended in 1951, and the W&OD continued to glide into Purcellville until 1968. (Courtesy of Jane Hirst Bogle.)

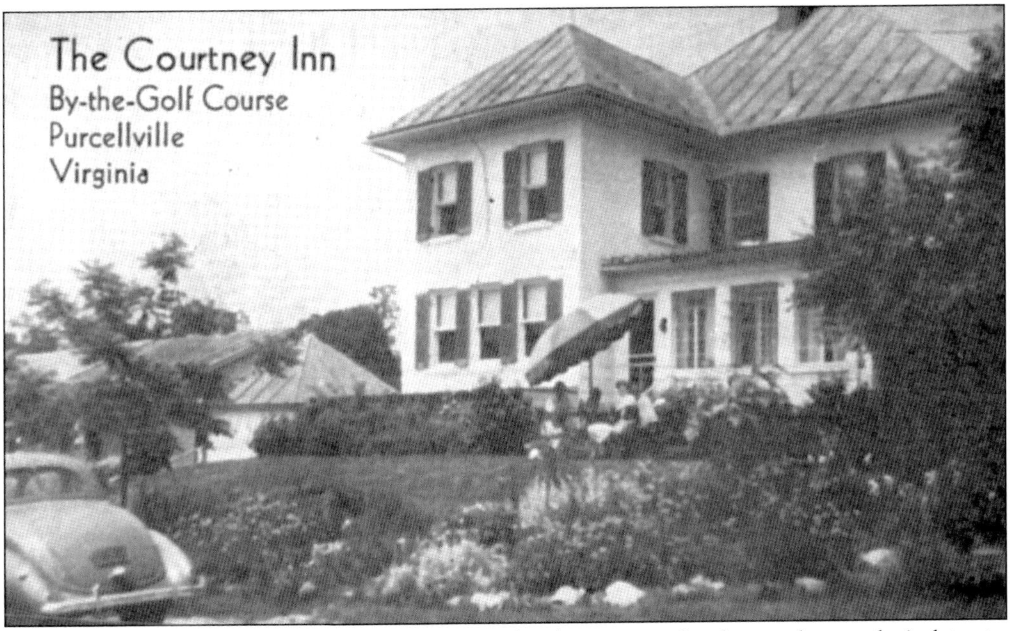

During the 1950s, the Courtney Inn was a popular destination for those taking a day's drive in the country from the city. Former guests remember the cozy pub downstairs and the dining room upstairs. (Courtesy of Thomas Priscilla.)

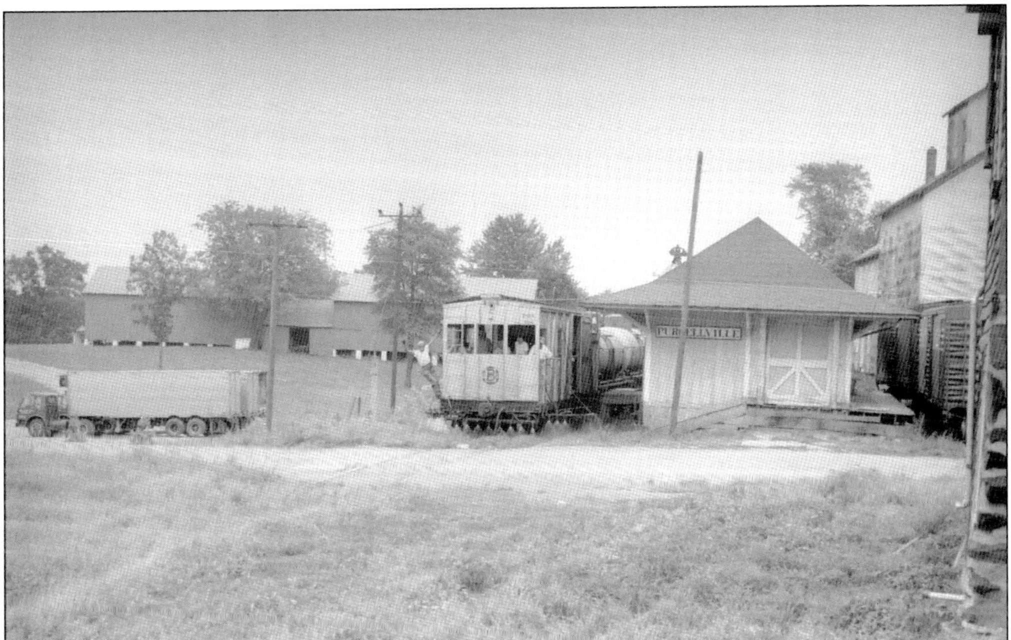

Trucks greatly influenced the demise of train service in Purcellville. This photograph, taken during the 1960s, captures the competitors in action near the train station, where goods were loaded and unloaded. (Courtesy of Paul McCray.)

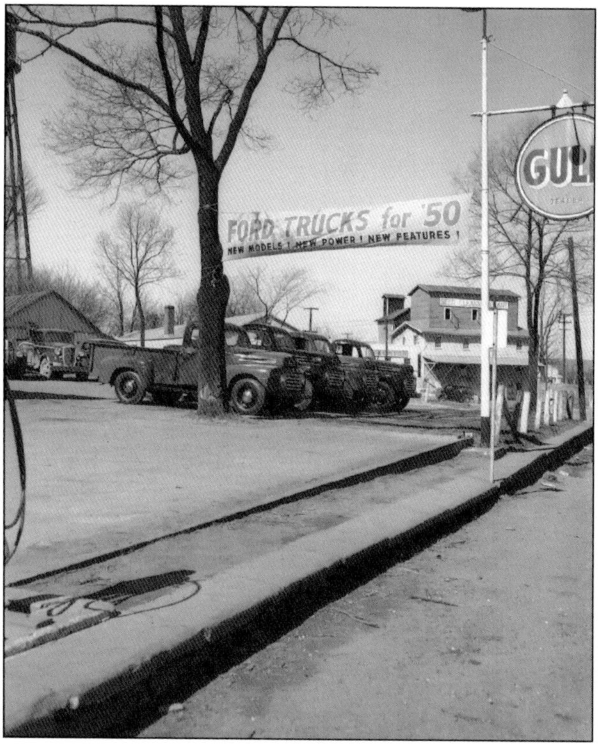

New car sales centers started opening around town. Taken in the 1950s, this photograph shows the Purcellville Motor Company with the Dillon Building, which was built in 1874, in the background. The building used to be the site of Baker's Carriage in 1886, which was later managed by Stuart Steele in 1892. (Courtesy of Thomas Balch Library.)

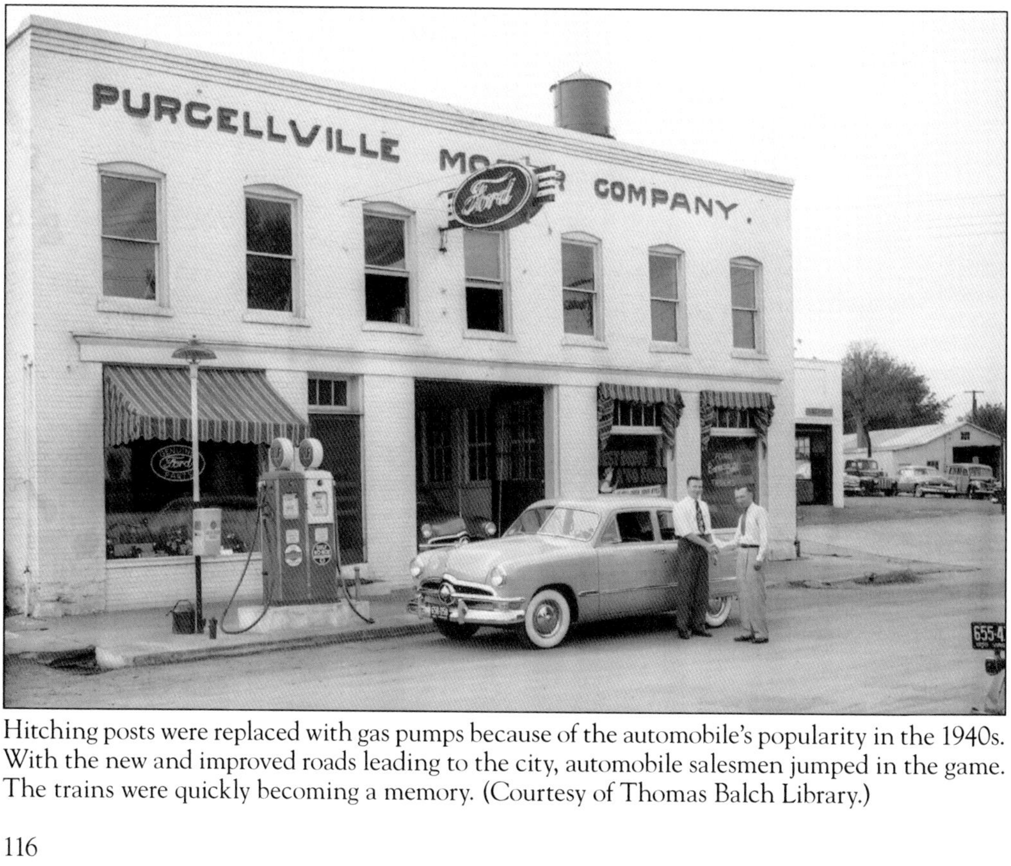

Hitching posts were replaced with gas pumps because of the automobile's popularity in the 1940s. With the new and improved roads leading to the city, automobile salesmen jumped in the game. The trains were quickly becoming a memory. (Courtesy of Thomas Balch Library.)

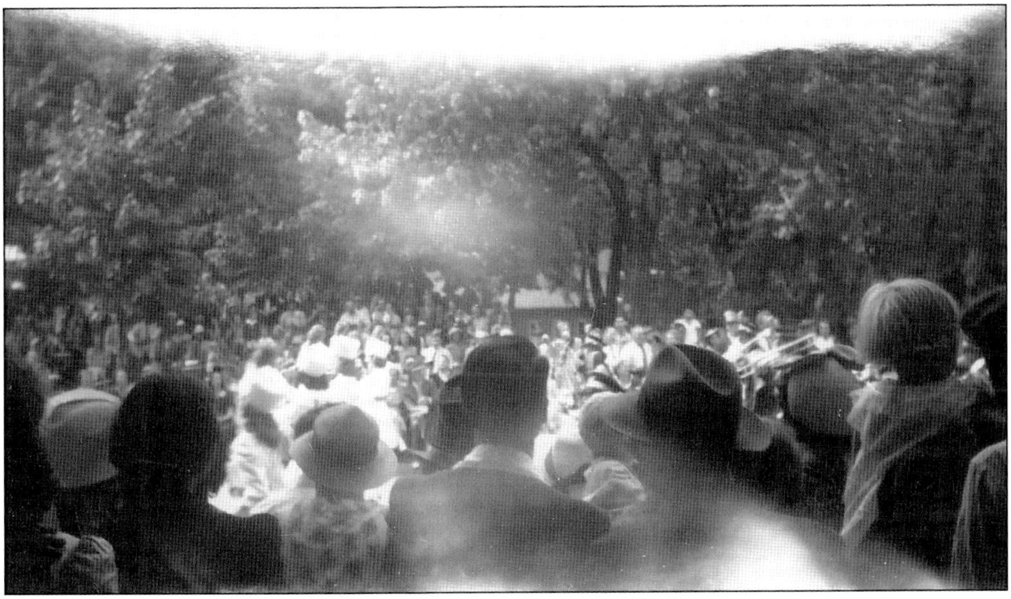

This 1940 photograph shows families gathering in Purcellville for a school performance at Fireman's Field. Friends would meet at the local stores, attend the same church, help each other during harvest, go to the same school, and take care of one another. Townspeople remember a social life taking place close to home. (Courtesy of Geraldine Potts James.)

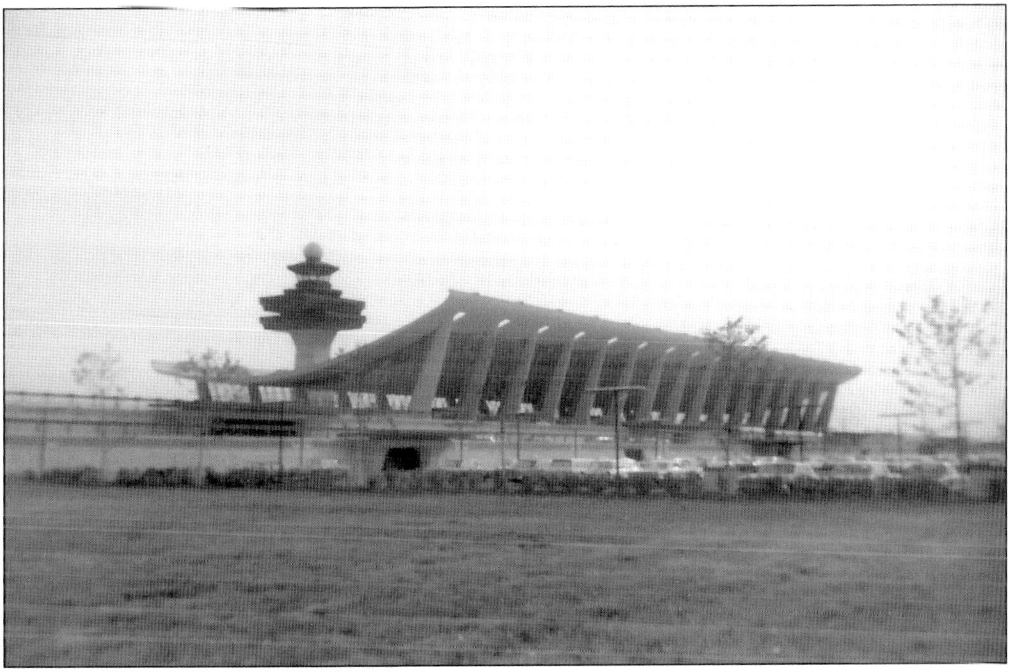

The automobile and the airplane changed Loudoun County significantly. Dulles International Airport opened in 1962. New residents were lured to Loudoun, and in 1995, a new six-lane highway linked Dulles to Loudoun County. The median household income in Loudoun County for 2005 was $98,483, the highest in the nation. Loudoun was the fastest growing county in the nation in 2006. (Courtesy of Brad Kilgour.)

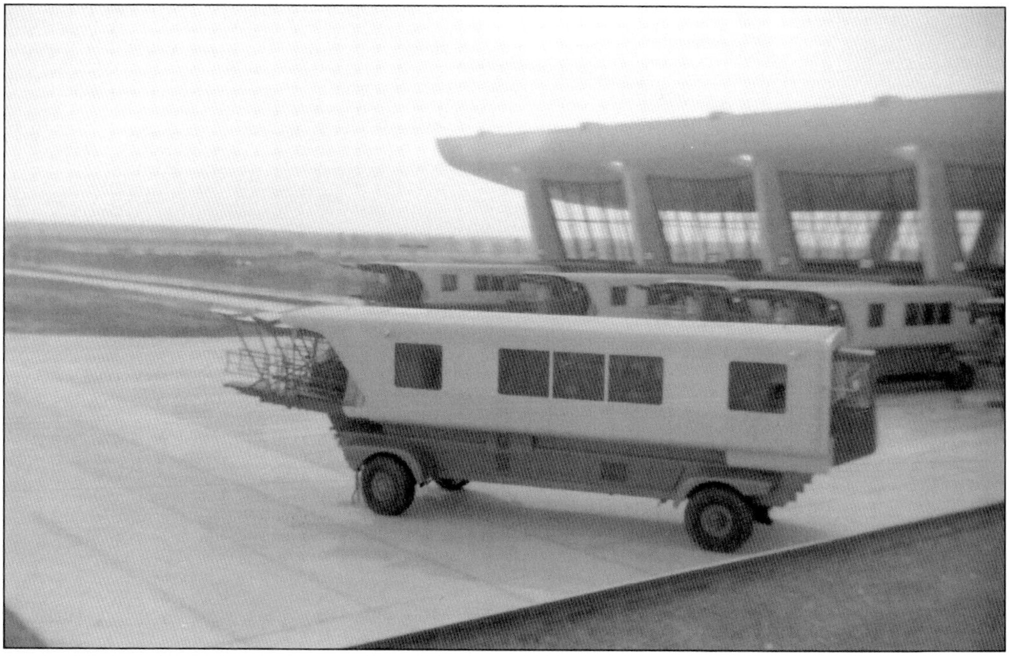

Commercial and residential development boomed in Loudoun County. Commercial developers realized that the new airport would draw businesses that sought global access, and residential developers knew that housing would be in demand by the new employees. In 1968, a county commemorative license plate reflected the pride in the new international airport with the slogan "Loudoun County: Gateway to the World." (Courtesy of Brad Kilgour.)

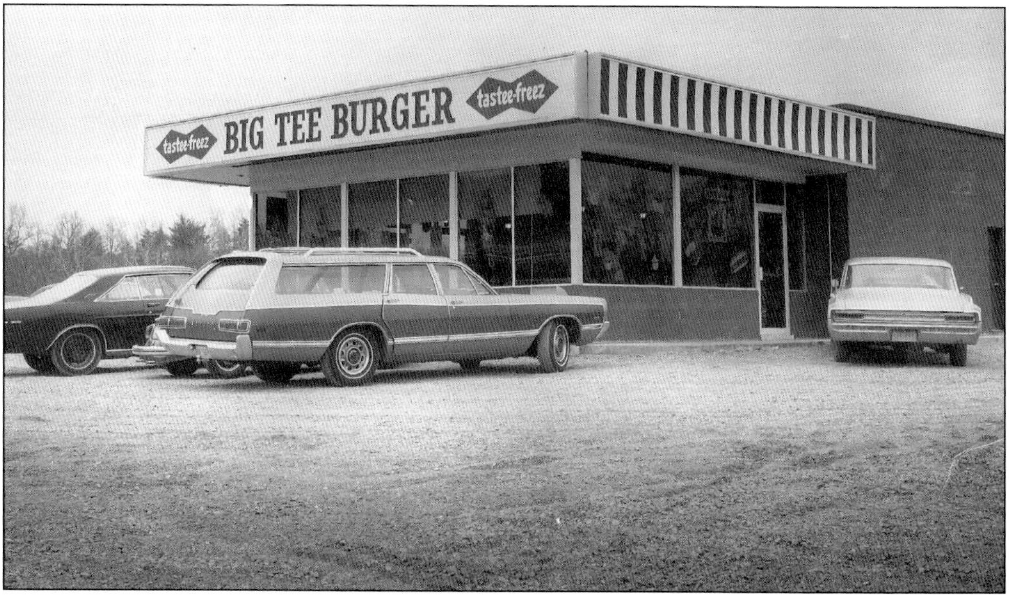

Townspeople recall the days of "cruising Main Street" in the 1970s, when the Tastee Freeze was on the west side of town and the Huddle was on the east. The Huddle was owned by Washington Redskins defensive lineman Bill Brundige, who helped the team to the Super Bowl in 1972. The Huddle would be packed on Monday nights with famous Redskins players who watched the games with Brundige. (Courtesy of Lawrence White.)

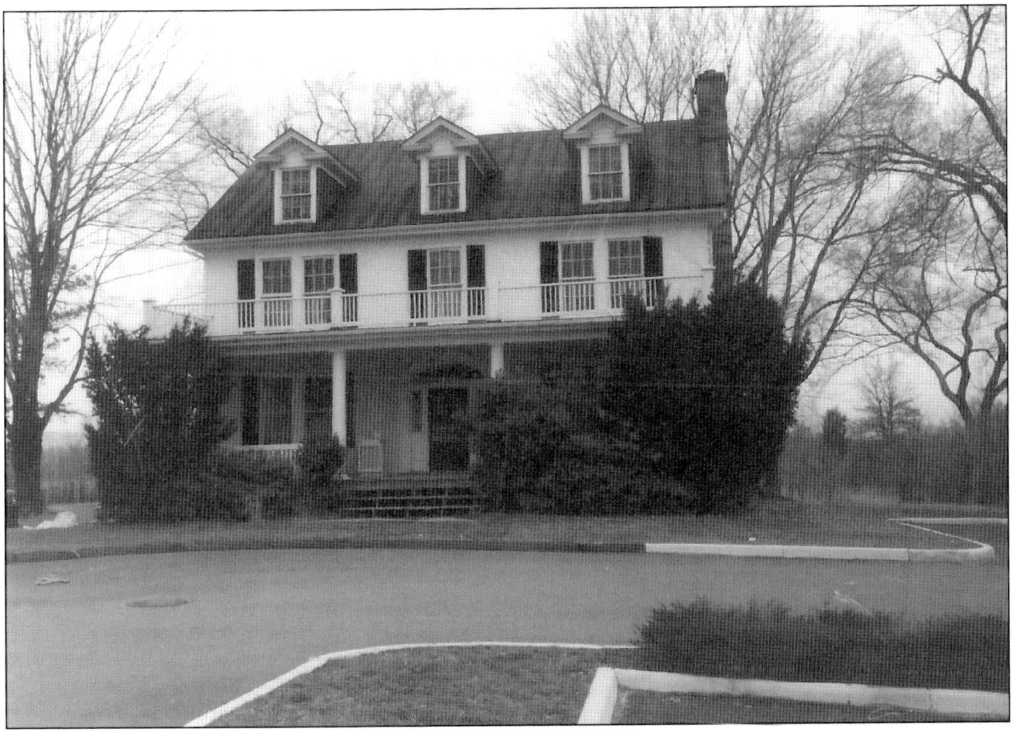

By 1970, most of Purcellville's commercial development happened on the east side of town due, in part, to the building of Loudoun Valley High School in 1962. This 1984 photograph shows the historical home of the Gregg family, which oddly remained in the middle during the construction of Blue Ridge Shopping Center. (Courtesy of Thomas Balch Library.)

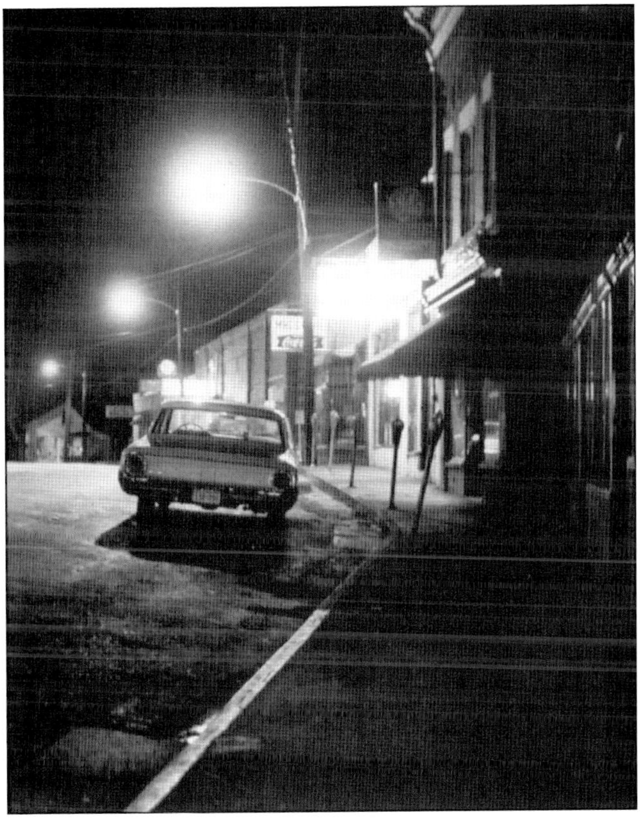

By 1973, most of Purcellville's residents had given up on any kind of major shopping on Twenty-First Street. There were a few businesses that were still popular, such as the White Palace Restaurant, Mac's Market, and Nichols Hardware. However, many headed to shopping areas that were bigger and had more options. (Courtesy of Loudoun Valley High School.)

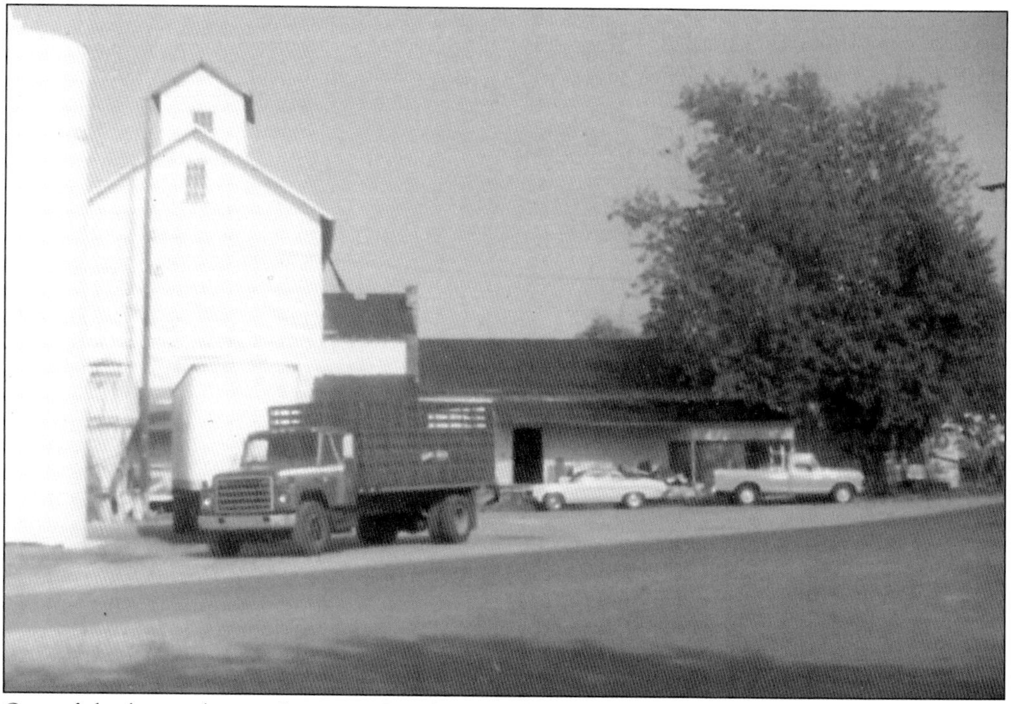

One of the last pick-ups of grain at Loudoun Valley Milling would occur a few years after this photograph, which was taken in 1975. Bruce Brownell, with the help of architect Beck Dickerson and financial partner Bob Lewis, bought up most of the land and buildings, while renovating them to their current luster. (Courtesy of Northern Virginia Regional Park Authority.)

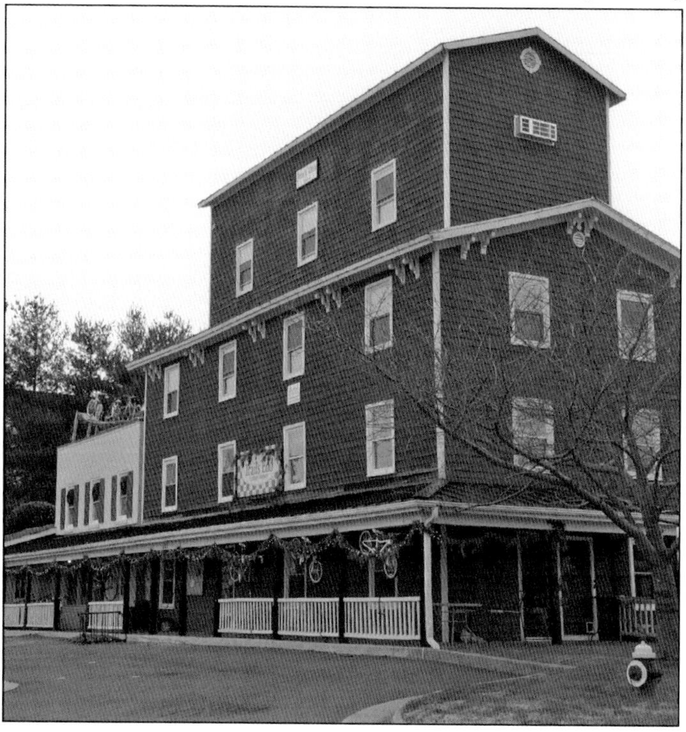

In an effort to recharge the energy of the historical downtown area, Bruce Brownell started with the renovation of the train station in the late 1990s for the Purcellville Preservation Association, using ISTEA funding. The renovation of the Dillon Building, the transformation of the mill into a restaurant, and the construction of the town gazebo were his crowning contributions to what was once known as Depot Street. Several years later, the association all but donated the building to the town for community activities and as a museum. (Courtesy of Cathy Darby.)

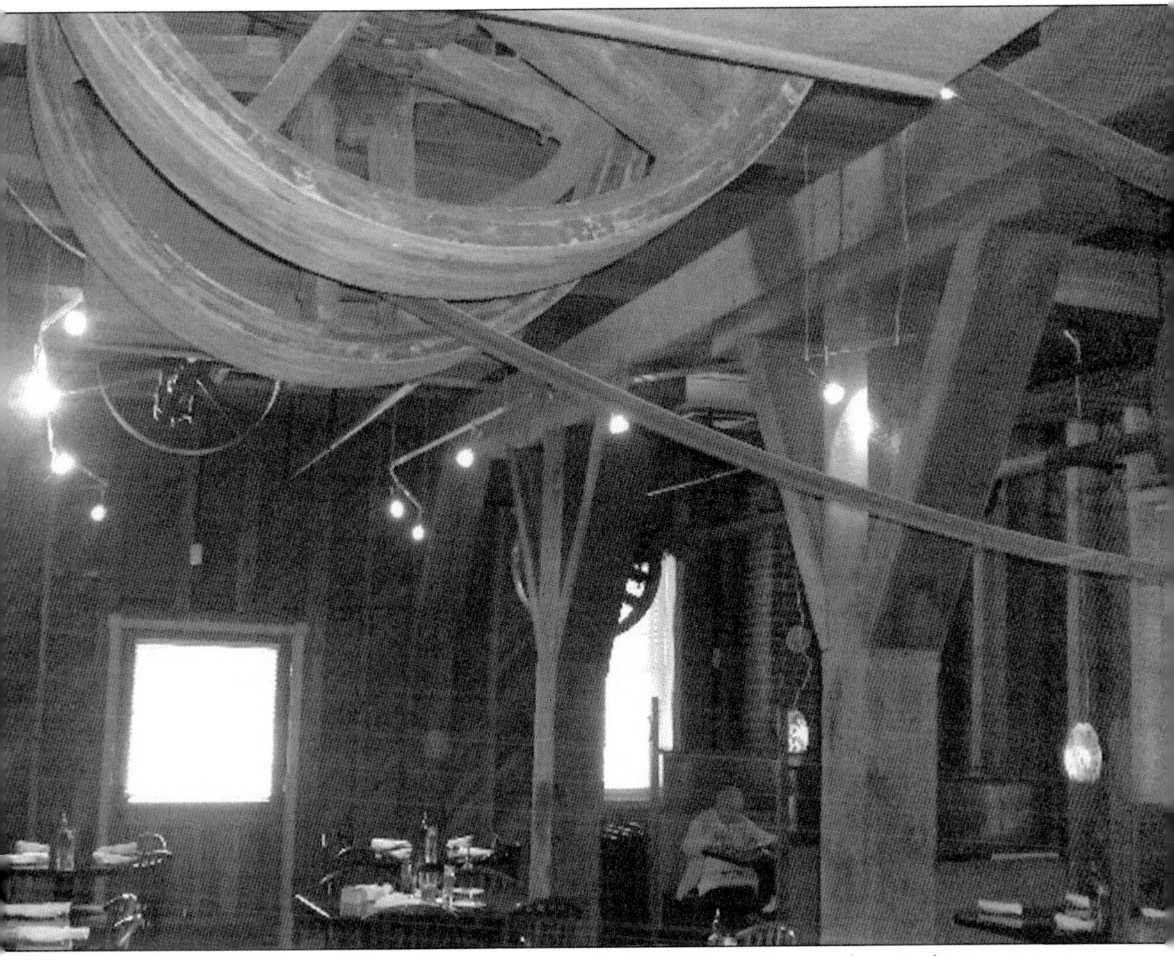

Bruce Brownell renovated the mill as a restaurant in 2003. His goal was to keep its history intact, including the special features of its authentic equipment. Employee Eston Thomas remembers, "When first starting the job, we opened the old electrical panel box and found a mummified cat with a rat still in its mouth, either placed there long ago as a joke or an unlucky victim of electrocution while searching for a meal." Magnolia's Restaurant opened its doors in 2004. This 2010 photograph shows the ceiling inside the mill with diners below. (Courtesy of Purcellville Preservation Association.)

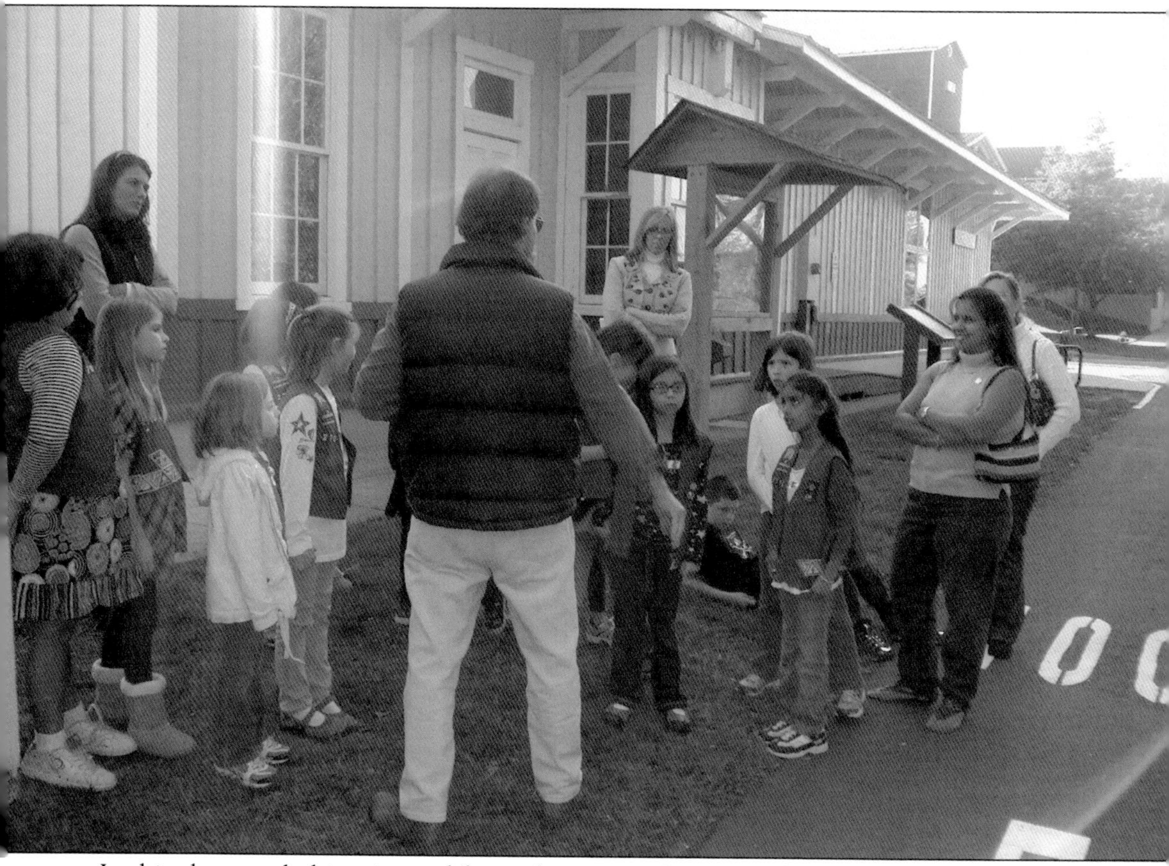

In this photograph, historian and former history teacher at Loudoun Valley High School Rich Gillespie shares information on trains during a walking tour with a Brownie troop from Kenneth Culbert Elementary School as part of the ongoing effort to educate the community on how Purcellville came to be. (Courtesy of Purcellville Preservation Association.)

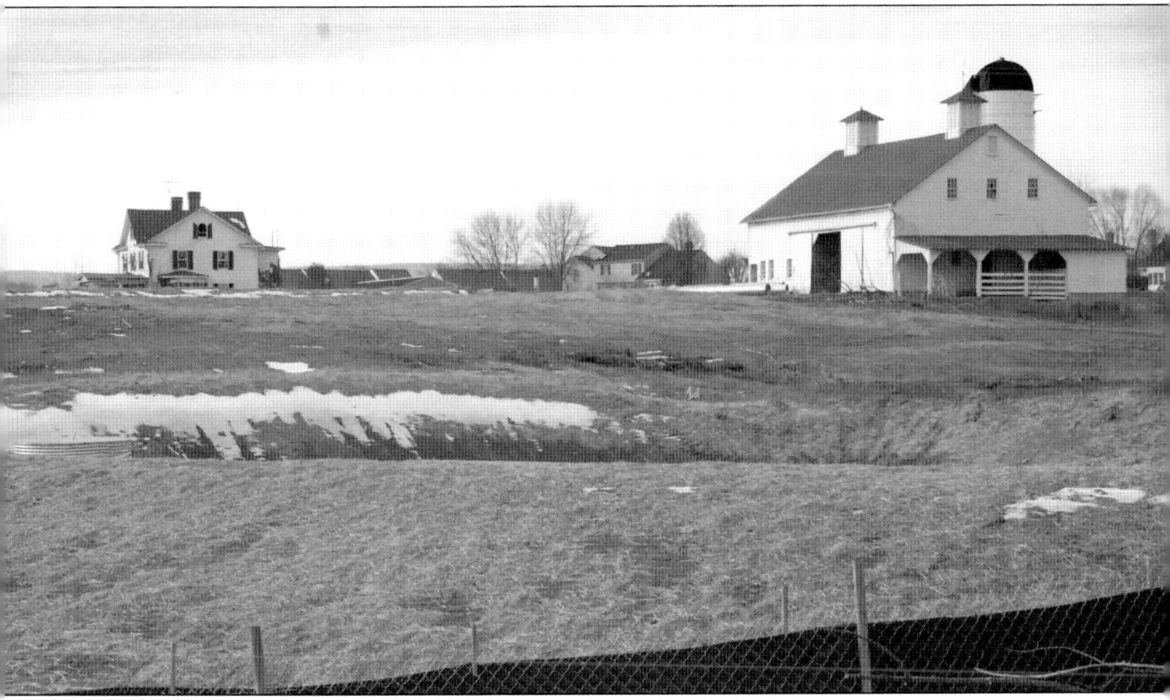

The increase of commercial growth to the east continues with the construction of Purcellville's new "Gateway" in 2011. Since 1917, the Cole family owned Shadowlawn Farm, which was one of the town's leading dairy farms. In 2003, the family sold the property to make way for new development. (Courtesy of Jack Darby.)

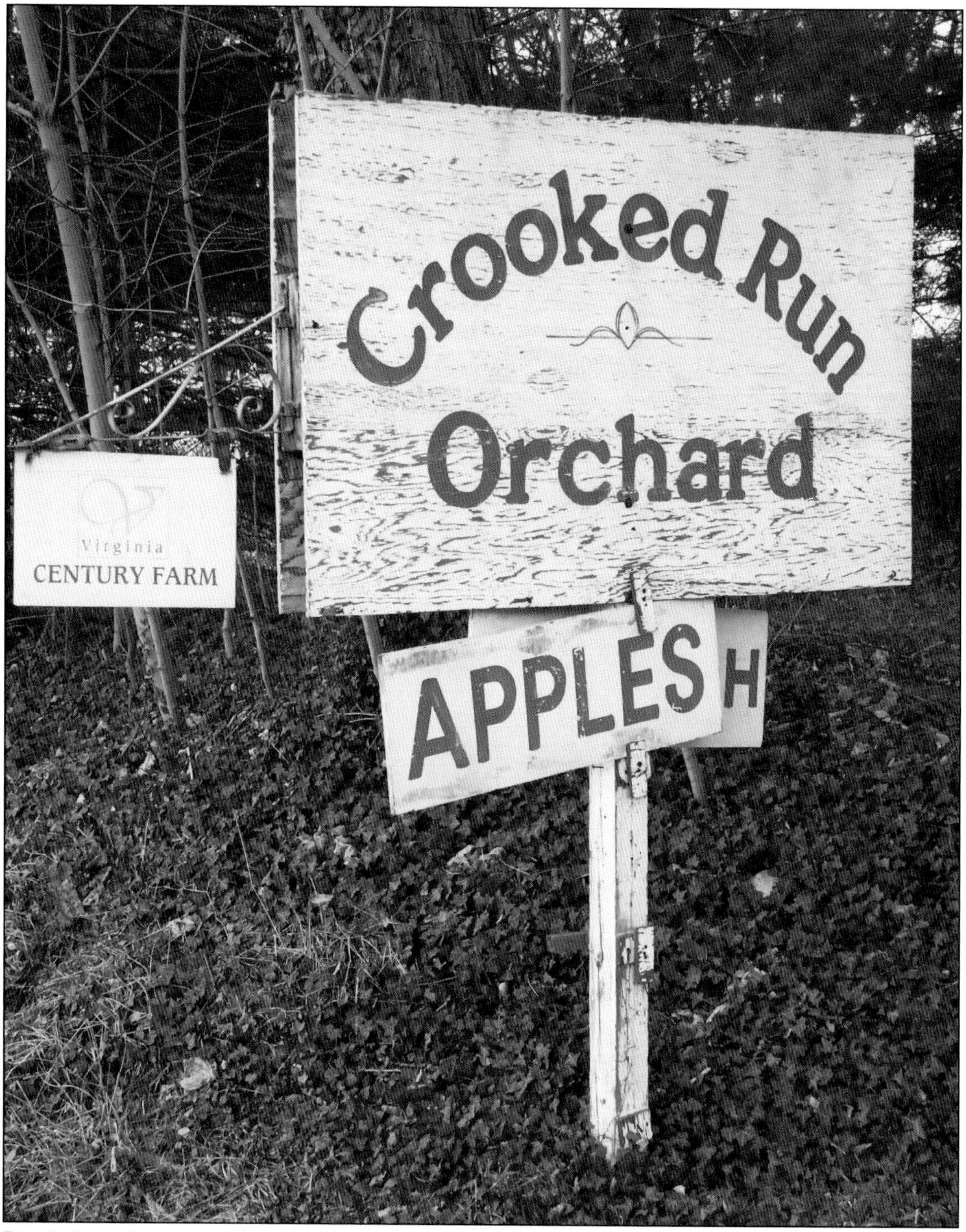

By 1960, 28.6 percent of employed Loudoun residents commuted to work outside the county. By 1970, the number had reached 40.6 percent. The increase of commuters was accompanied by a decrease in the number of farms. Today, Crooked Run Farms, owned by the Brown family since 1908, is one of Purcellville's few surviving operating farms. (Courtesy of Cathy Darby.)

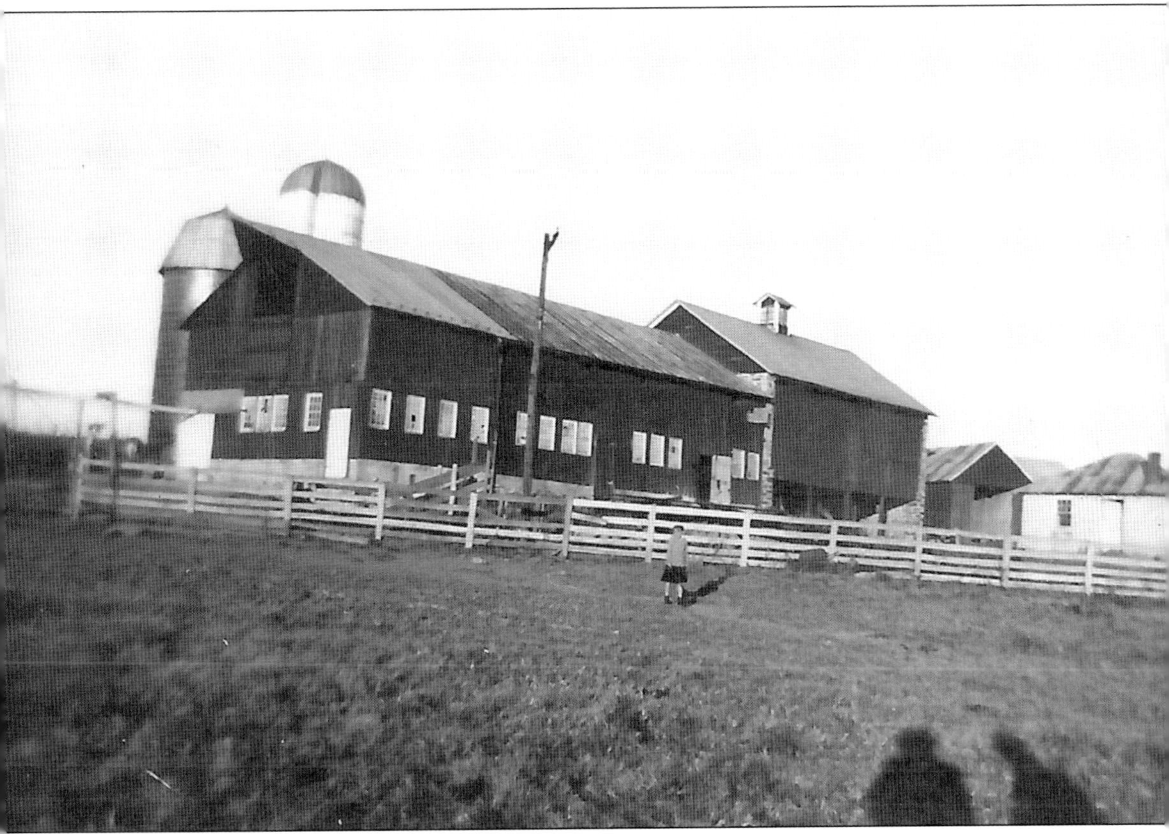

In 1946, Hirst Farm was a thriving dairy farm south of town. In 2008, its land was subdivided, and it is now a neighborhood of 260 homes. Farmland continues to be at risk of being replaced by housing or commercial developments. However, many farms continue to thrive, redeveloping into wineries, bed-and-breakfast inns, or organic farms. (Courtesy of Jane Hirst Bogle.)

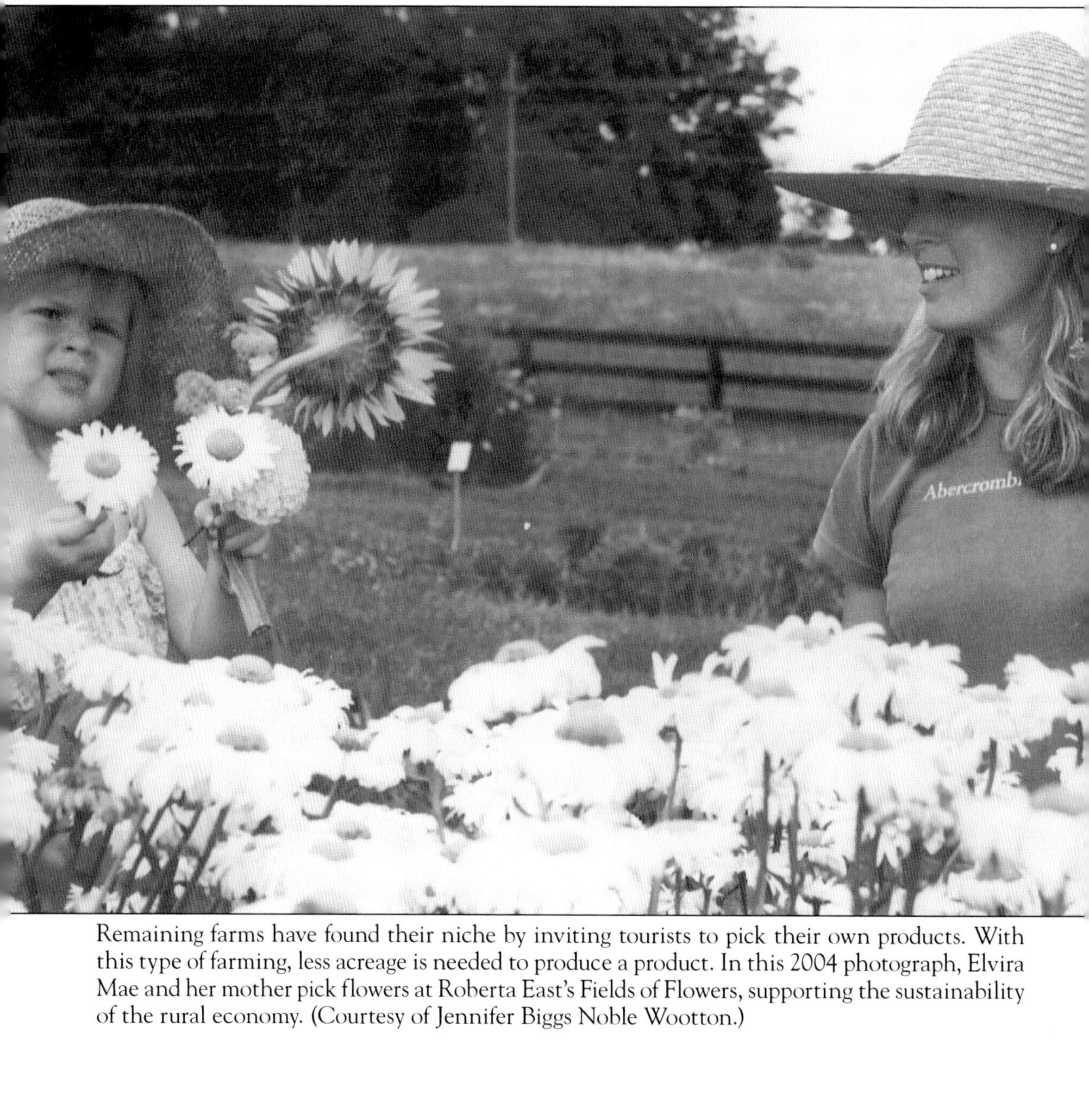

Remaining farms have found their niche by inviting tourists to pick their own products. With this type of farming, less acreage is needed to produce a product. In this 2004 photograph, Elvira Mae and her mother pick flowers at Roberta East's Fields of Flowers, supporting the sustainability of the rural economy. (Courtesy of Jennifer Biggs Noble Wootton.)

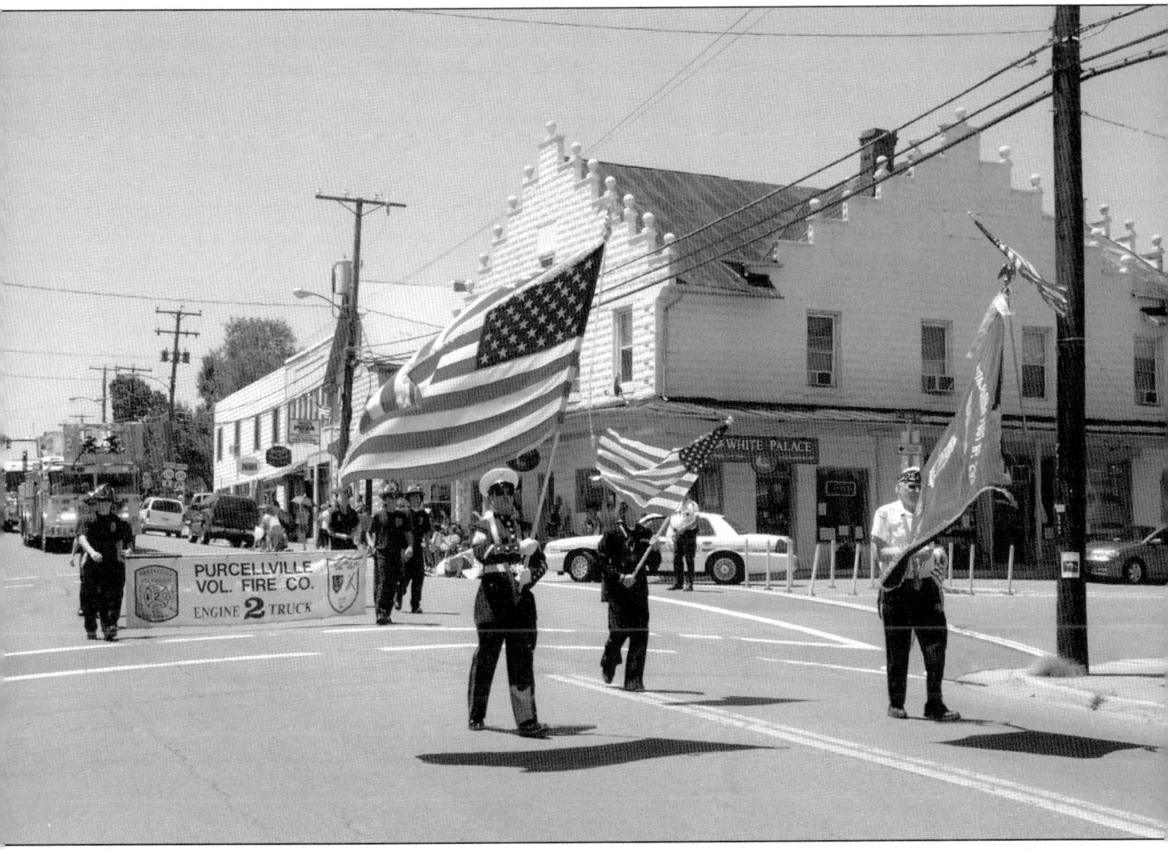

Despite the many changes, Purcellville has grown into a respectable place with its 7,727 residents in 2010. Purcellville retains its small-town feel. Parades continue down Main Street during the holidays. Gentlemen still hold doors for ladies in town, and the waitress at the local restaurant calls you "hon." Farm tractors still chug along Main Street during harvest, and children can leave their lemonade stand unattended while they go play. Many residents can still be found sitting for a spell in the sun on the benches along Main Street ready to share their stories and their love of their hometown. (Courtesy of Cathy Darby.)

Consistent with our mission to preserve history on a local level, this book was printed in South Carolina on American-made paper and manufactured entirely in the United States. Products carrying the accredited Forest Stewardship Council (FSC) label are printed on 100 percent FSC-certified paper.

MADE IN THE USA